12/97

THE GROLIER LIBRARY
OF
SCIENCE BIOGRAPHIES

VOLUME 8

Partington–Salisbury

Grolier Educational
Sherman Turnpike, Danbury, Connecticut 06816

REF
509.2
GRO

Published 1997 by
Grolier Educational
Danbury Connecticut 06816

Copyright © 1996 by Market House Books Ltd.
Published for the School and Library market exclusively
by Grolier Educational, 1997

Compiled and Typeset by Market House Books Ltd, Aylesbury, UK.

General Editors
    John Daintith BSc, PhD
    Derek Gjertsen BA

Market House Editors
    Elizabeth Martin MA
    Anne Stibbs BA
    Fran Alexander BA
    Jonathan Law BA
    Peter Lewis BA, DPhil
    Mark Salad

Picture Research
    Linda Wells

Contributors
    Eve Daintith BSc
    Rosalind Dunning BA
    Garry Hammond BSc
    Robert Hine BSc, MSc
    Valerie Illingworth BSc, MPhil
    Sarah Mitchell BA
    Susan O'Neill BSc
    W. J. Palmer MSc
    Roger F. Picken BSc, PhD
    Carol Russell BSc
    W. J. Sherratt BSc, MSc, PhD
    Jackie Smith BA
    B. D. Sorsby BSc, PhD
    Elizabeth Tootill BSc, MSc
    P. Welch DPhil
    Anthony Wootton

All rights in this book are reserved. No part of this book may be used or reproduced in any manner whatsoever or transmitted in any form, or by any means, electronic or mechanical, including photocopying, recording, or any information storage and retrieval system, without written permission from the copyright owner except in the case of brief quotations embodied in critical articles and reviews. For information, address the publisher:
Grolier Educational, Danbury, Connecticut, 06816

Published by arrangement with
The Institute of Physics Publishing
Bristol BS1 6NX
UK

ISBN   Volume 8   0-7172-7634-1
           Ten-Volume Set   0-7172-7626-0
Library of Congress Catalog Number: 96-31474
Cataloging Information to be obtained directly from Grolier Educational.
First Edition
Printed in the United States of America

CONTENTS

The following copyrighted photographs appear in this volume:

AEA Technology, Harwell Laboratory, Oxford: RUTHERFORD, E.F.B.R.N.
AIP Emilio Segrè Visual Archives: PAULI, W.; ROSSI, B.B.; ROWLAND, H.A.
AIP Emilio Segrè Visual Archives E. Scott Barr Collection: PRINGSHEIM, E.; RANKINE, W.J.M.
AIP Emilio Segrè Visual Archives W.F. Meggers Collection: RYDBERG, J.R.
AIP Meggers Gallery of Nobel Laureates: PAUL, W.; PERL, M.L.; PROKHOROV, A.M.; RUSKA, E.A.F.
by permission of the President and Council of the Royal Society: PETIT, J.L.; QUETELET, L.; RA-MANUJAN, S.I.; RAMSDEN, J.
California Institute of Technology: ROBERTS, J.D.
CERN/Science Photo Library: RUBBIA, C.; SALAM, A.
courtesy of the Royal Society of Chemistry Library and Information Centre: PELIGOT, E.M.; PERKIN, W.H.J.; PICTET, A.; POGGENDORFF, J.C.; POULTON, E.B.; PROUST, J.L.; PROUT, W.; RAOULT, F.M.; REGNAULT, H.V.; REICH, F.; RICHTER, H.T.; RIGHI, A.; ROBERTSON, J.M.; ROBERTSON, R.; ROOZEBOOM, H.W.B.; ROUELLE, G.F.; RUBNER, M.; RUSSELL, E.J.; RUTHERFORD, D.
Godfrey Argent: PENROSE, R.; PETERS, R.A.; PHILLIPS, D.C.; PIPPARD, A.B.; PIRIE, N.W.; POLANYI, M.; PONTECORVO, G.; PROUDMAN, J.; RANDALL, J.T.; RICHARDSON, L.F.; RUSHTON, W.A.H.; RUSSELL, F.S.
Harvard University News Office/courtesy AIP Emilio Segrè Visual Archives: RAMSEY, N.F.
Hulton Getty: PENNEY, W.G.B.P.; PERRAULT, C.; PFEIFFER, R.F.J.; PICCARD, A.; PINCUS, G.G.; PLAY-FAIR, L.B.; POISSON, S.D.; POND, J.; POPPER, K.R.; PORTER, R.R.; PRELOG, V.; PRESTWICH, J.; PRIGOGINE, I.; PRITCHARD, C.; PROCTOR, R.A.; PTOLEMY (OR CLAUDIUS PTOLEMAEUS); RAINWATER, L.; REAUMUR, R.A.F.; REDI, F.; REICHSTEIN, T.; RICHARDS, D.W.; RICHET, C.R.; RIDEAL, E.K.; ROGET, P.M.; ROKITANSKY, K.; ROSCOE, H.E.; ROSSE, W.P.E.; ROUX, P.E.; RUBIK, E.; RUNCORN, S.K.; RUSSELL, B.A.W.E.R.; RYLE, M.; SADRON, C.L.; SAKHAROV, A.D.; SALISBURY, E.J.
Jean-Loup Charmet/Science Photo Library:
Los Alamos Photo Laboratory/courtesy AIP Emilio Segrè Visual Archives: REINES, F.
Museum of Fine Arts, Liepzig/Photo AKG London: PETTENKOFER, M.J.
National Library of Medicine/Science Photo Library: RHAZES; RICKETTS, H.T.
Novosti/Science Photo Library: PAVLOV, I.P.; POPOV, A.S.
Peter Menzel/Science Photo Library: RICHTER, B.
Philip Bermingham Photography: RUBIN, V.C.
Photo AKG London: PFEFFER, W.F.P.; RATZEL, F.; REGIOMONTANUS
Roger Ressmeyer, Starlight/Science Photo Library: PAULING, L.C.
Science Photo Library: PASCAL, B.; PASTEUR, L.; PEARSON, K.; PEIERLS, R.E.; PELLETIER, P.J.; PENZIAS, A.A.; PEREY, M.C.; PERKIN, W.H.; PERRIN, J.B.; PERUTZ, M.F.; PIAZZI, G.; PLANCK, M.K.E.L.; PLATO; PLAYFAIR, J.; PLINY THE ELDER; POINCARE, J.; POPE, W.J.; POWELL, C.F.; PRIESTLEY, J.; PURCELL, E.M.; PURKINJE, J.E.; PYTHAGORAS; RABI, I.I.; RAMAN, C.V.; RAMSAY, W.; RAY, J.; RAYLEIGH, J.W.S.B.; REED, W.; REMSEN, I.; REYNOLDS, O.; RIEMANN, G.F.; ROBINSON, R.; ROSS, R.; RUMFORD, B.T.C.; RUSH, B.; RUSSELL, H.N.; SABINE, E.; SABINE, W.C.W.; SACHS, J.
Sinclair Stammers/Science Photo Library: PORTER, B.G.
source the Royal Society: SAHA, M.N.
Steve Smith: SAGAN, C.E.
© The Nobel Foundation: PEDERSEN, C.; POLANYI, J.C.; PREGL, F.; RAMÓN Y CAJAL, S.; RICHARDSON, O.W.; RICHARDS, T.W.; ROBBINS, F.C.; ROBERTS, R.; RODBELL, M.; ROHRER, H.; ROUS, F.P.; ROWLAND, F.S.; RUŽIČKA, L.; SABATIER, P.; SAKMANN, B.
Will & Deni McIntyre/Science Photo Library: SABIN, A.B.

Every endeavor has been made to obtain permission to use copyright material.
The publishers would appreciate errors or omissions being brought to their attention.

PREFACE

ABOUT THE GROLIER LIBRARY OF SCIENCE BIOGRAPHIES

The 19th-century poet and essayist Oliver Wendell Holmes wrote:

> Science is a first-rate piece of furniture for a man's upper chamber, if he has common sense on the ground floor.
>
> *The Poet at the Breakfast-Table* (1872)

While it has been fashionable in this century to assume that science is capable of solving all human problems, we should, perhaps, pause to reflect on Holmes's comment. Scientific knowledge can only be of value to the human race if it is made use of wisely by the men and women who have control of our lives.

If this is true, all thinking people need a solid piece of scientific furniture in their upper chambers. For this reason the editors and publishers of this series of books have set out to say as much about science itself as about the scientists who have created it.

All the entries contain basic biographical data – place and date of birth, posts held, etc. – but do not give exhaustive personal details about the subject's family, prizes, honorary degrees, etc. Most of the space has been devoted to their main scientific achievements and the nature and importance of these achievements. This has not always been easy; in particular, it has not always been possible to explain in relatively simple terms work in the higher reaches of abstract mathematics or modern theoretical physics.

Perhaps the most difficult problem was compiling the entry list. We have attempted to include people who have produced major advances in theory or have made influential or well-known discoveries. A particular difficulty has been the selection of contemporary scientists, in view of the fact that of all scientists who have ever lived, the vast majority are still alive. In this we have been guided by lists of prizes and awards made by scientific societies. We realize that there are dangers in this – the method would not, for instance, catch an unknown physicist working out a revolutionary new system of mechanics in the seclusion of the Bern patent office. It does, however, have the advantage that it is based on the judgments of other scientists. We have to a great extent concentrated on what might be called the "traditional" pure sciences – physics, chemistry, biology, astronomy, and the earth sciences. We also give a more limited coverage of medicine and mathematics and have included a selection of people who have made important contributions to engineering and technology. A few of the entries cover workers in such fields as anthropology and psychology, and a small number of philosophers are represented.

A version of this book was published in 1993 by the Institute of Physics, to whom we are grateful for permission to reuse the material in this set. Apart from adding a number of new biographies to the Institute of Physics text, we have enhanced the work with some 1,500 photographs and a large number of quotations by or about the scientists themselves. We have also added a simple pronunciation guide (the key to which will be found on the back of this page) to provide readers with a way of knowing how to pronounce the more difficult and unfamiliar names.

Each volume in this set has a large biographical section. The scientists are arranged in strict alphabetical order according to surname. The entry for a scientist is given under the name by which he or she is most commonly known. Thus the American astrophysicist James Van Allen is generally known as Van Allen (not Allen) and is entered under V. The German chemist Justus von Liebig is commonly referred to as Liebig and is entered under L. In addition, each volume contains a section on "Sources and Further Reading" for important entries, a glossary of useful definitions of technical words, and an index of the whole set. The index lists all the scientists who have entries, indicating the volume number and the page on which the entry will be found. In addition scientists are grouped together in the index by country (naturalized nationality if it is not their country of origin) and by scientific discipline. Volume 10 contains a chronological list of scientific discoveries and publications arranged under year and subject. It is intended to be used for tracing the development of a subject or for relating advances in one branch of science to those in another branch. Additional information can be obtained by referring to the biographical section of the book.

JD
DG 1996

PRONUNCIATION GUIDE

A guide to pronunciation is given for foreign names and names of foreign origin; it appears in brackets after the first mention of the name in the main text of the article. Names of two or more syllables are broken up into small units, each of one syllable, separated by hyphens. The stressed syllable in a word of two or more syllables is shown in **bold** type.

We have used a simple pronunciation system based on the phonetic respelling of names, which avoids the use of unfamiliar symbols. The sounds represented are as follows (the phonetic respelling is given in brackets after the example word, if this is not pronounced as it is spelled):

a *as in* bat
ah *as in* palm (pahm)
air *as in* dare (dair), pear (pair)
ar *as in* tar
aw *as in* jaw, ball (bawl)
ay *as in* gray, ale (ayl)
ch *as in* chin
e *as in* red
ee *as in* see, me (mee)
eer *as in* ear (eer)
er *as in* fern, layer
f *as in* fat, phase (fayz)
g *as in* gag
i *as in* pit
I *as in* mile (mIl), by (bI)
j *as in* jaw, age (ayj), gem (jem)
k *as in* keep, cactus (**kak**-tus), quite (kwIt)
ks *as in* ox (oks)
ng *as in* hang, rank (rangk)
o *as in* pot

oh *as in* home (hohm), post (pohst)
oi *as in* boil, toy (toi)
oo *as in* food, fluke (flook)
or *as in* organ, quarter (**kwor**-ter)
ow *as in* powder, loud (lowd)
s *as in* skin, cell (sel)
sh *as in* shall
th *as in* bath
th as in feather (**feth**-er)
ts *as in* quartz (kworts)
u *as in* buck (buk), blood (blud), one (wun)
u(r) *as in* urn (but without sounding the "r")
uu *as in* book (buuk)
v *as in* van, of (ov)
y *as in* yet, menu (**men**-yoo), onion (**un**-yon)
z *as in* zoo, lose (looz)
zh *as in* treasure (**tre**-zher)

The consonants b, d, h, l, m, n, p, r, t, and w have their normal sounds and are not listed in the table.

In our pronunciation guide a consonant is occasionally doubled to avoid confusing the syllable with a familiar word, for example, -iss rather than -is (which is normally pronounced -iz); -off rather than -of (which is normally pronounced -ov).

Pa

Partington, James Riddick

(1886–1965)

BRITISH CHEMIST

Born in Bolton, northwestern England, Partington was educated at Manchester University and in Berlin, where he worked under Walther Nernst. After working during World War I at the Ministry of Munitions, he was appointed, in 1919, to the chair of chemistry at Queen Mary College, London, where he remained until his retirement in 1951.

Partington is remembered chiefly as a historian of chemistry and he was also a prolific writer, compiling over 20 substantial volumes in his lifetime. He produced a number of textbooks of which his five-volume *Advanced Treatise on Physical Chemistry* (1949–54) is perhaps the best known. It is however but one of many, written on all the main branches of chemistry, at all levels, from the introductory to the advanced.

Partington published his first major work on the history of chemistry in 1935, *Origins and Development of Chemistry*. This was followed by *A Short History of Chemistry* (1937), which heralded his vast four-volume *History of Chemistry* (1961), of which one volume remained unfinished on his death. These works have proved invaluable to students and historians of chemistry.

Pascal, Blaise

(1623–1662)

FRENCH MATHEMATICIAN,
PHYSICIST, AND RELIGIOUS
PHILOSOPHER

> Contradiction is not a sign of falsity, nor the
> lack of contradiction a sign of truth.
> —*Pensées* (1670; Thoughts)

> The more intelligence one has the more people one finds original. Commonplace
> people see no difference between men.
>
> —As above

Pascal (pas-**kal**) was the son of a respected mathematician and a local administrator in Clermont-Ferrand, France. Early in life Pascal displayed evidence that he was an infant prodigy and apparently discovered Euclid's first 23 theorems for himself at the age of 11. While only 17 he published an essay on mathematics that René Descartes refused to acknowledge as being the work of a youth. Pascal produced (1642–44) a calculating device to aid his father in his local administration; this was in effect the first digital calculator.

Pascal conducted important work in experimental physics, in particular in the study of atmospheric pressure. He tested the theories of Evangelista Torricelli (who discovered the principle of the barometer) by using mercury barometers to measure air pressure in Paris and, with the

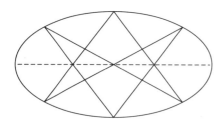 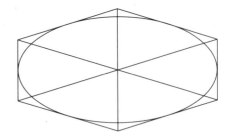

PASCAL'S THEOREM   The opposite sides of a hexagon inscribed in a conic intersect in three points on a line. The dual theorem, that the opposite vertices of a hexagon circumscribed about a conic may be connected by three lines that meet in a point, is Brianchon's theorem.

help of his brother-in-law, on the summit of the Puy de Dôme (1646). He found that the height of the column of mercury did indeed fall with increasing altitude. From these studies Pascal invented the hydraulic press and the syringe and formulated his law that pressure applied to a confined liquid is transmitted through the liquid in all directions regardless of the area to which the pressure is applied. He published his work on vacuums in 1647.

Pascal corresponded with a contemporary mathematician, Pierre de Fermat, and together they founded the mathematical theory of probability. Pascal had been converted to Jansenism in 1646 and religion became increasingly dominant in his life, culminating in the religious revelation he experienced on the night of 23 November 1654. Following this he entered the Jansenist retreat at Port-Royal (1655) and devoted himself to religious studies from then on.

Pasteur, Louis

(1822–1895)

FRENCH CHEMIST AND MICROBIOLOGIST

> In the field of observation, chance only favors those minds which have been prepared.
> —*Encyclopaedia Britannica*, Vol XX, 11th edition (1911)

> [I have an] invincible belief that Science and Peace will triumph over Ignorance and War, that nations will unite, not to destroy, but to build, and that the future will belong to those who have done most for suffering humanity.
> —Address given at the Sorbonne, Paris, 27 December 1892

Pasteur (pa-**ster**), the son of a tanner, was born at Dôle in France and studied chemistry at the Ecole Normale Supérieure in Paris where he obtained his doctorate for crystallographic studies in 1847. His first appointments were as professor of chemistry firstly at Strasbourg (1849) and then at Lille (1854). In 1857 Pasteur returned to Paris as director of scientific studies at the Ecole Normale but moved to the Sorbonne in 1867 as professor of chemistry. He returned once more to the Ecole Normale in 1874 to direct the physiological chemistry laboratory but spent his last years, from 1888 to 1895, as director of the specially created Pasteur Institute.

Although not a physician, Pasteur was undoubtedly the most important medical scientist working in the 19th century. His work possessed an originality, depth, and precision that was apparent even in his early work, which led to the discovery of molecular asymmetry. Tartaric and racemic acid were known to have the same formula, but their crystalline salts possessed different optical properties in solution: tartrate rotates a ray of polarized light to the right, and was accordingly described as dextrorotatory or d-tartrate, while the racemic salts were optically inactive. How, it was asked, could the same compound have such contrasting properties?

Pasteur, in 1848, examined d-tartrate crystals under a magnifying glass and noticed that they all possessed an identical asymmetry, which he assumed to be sufficient to twist a ray of light to the right. The racemate however, while also asymmetrical, appeared to contain crystals divided equally between the d-tartrate form and its mirror image. Pasteur painstakingly separated the crystals into two piles and found that, in solution, one pile behaved exactly as d-tartrate while the other rotated polarized light to the left. Racemic acid was therefore, he concluded, an equal mixture of d-tartrate and its mirror image, the levorotatory l-tartrate, each of which was optically active on its own but together neutralized each other.

Such facts would later have profound consequences for structural chemistry and Pasteur, in 1860, suggested that the effect was a result of the internal arrangement of atoms. Thus he asked "Are the atoms of the dextro acid arranged on a right-hand helix, or positioned at the corners of an irregular tetrahedron, or have they some other asymmetric grouping? We cannot answer these questions. But there is no doubt that an asymmetric arrangement exists that has a nonsuperposable image. It is not less certain that the atoms of the levo acid have exactly the inverse asymmetric arrangement." The idea of an asymmetric tetrahedral carbon atom was put forward in 1874 by Jacobus van't Hoff and Joseph Le Bel. In 1857 Pasteur also noted that a mold accidentally growing on a tartrate solution selected just one of the two racemic forms, the d-form. More generally, he realized that only living organisms could distinguish between such asymmetric forms and even went so far as to argue that this ability marks the only sharply defined difference between the chemistry of dead and living matter.

By 1856 Pasteur had also begun to work on fermentation, beginning with the fermentation of milk into lactic acid. He reported the presence of microorganisms, which continued to bud and multiply; if excluded, fermentation failed to occur but they could be transferred from one ferment to produce another in uncontaminated milk. Further, such organisms were quite specific, as the yeast used to produce beer was incapable of producing lactic acid from milk. With these and many other observations and experiments behind him Pasteur was ready to dispute the chemical theory of Justus von Liebig. He declared that all true fermentations are caused by the presence and multiplication of organisms, and are not, as Liebig insisted, purely chemical phenomena. With his germ theory of fermentation Pasteur anticipated much of his later work.

He next turned to the origin of such "organisms" and "ferments" and investigated spontaneous generation. In 1862 Pasteur published his famous paper, *Mémoire sur les corpuscles organisés qui existent dans l'atmosphère* (Note on Organized Corpuscles that Exist in the Atmosphere), which finally brought to an end centuries of earlier debate. Pasteur demonstrated that if sterilized fermentable fluid was placed in a swan-neck flask (a flask with a long curved thin neck that allows air to enter but prevents dust and microorganisms entering) then the fluid remained clear. However if the neck of the flask was broken off, allowing dust to enter, contamination soon resulted.

In 1865 Pasteur was asked to investigate a new disease devastating the silkworms of southern France. Despite his protest that "I have never even seen a silkworm," despite considerable confusion caused by the presence of two quite independent infections, and despite a stroke in 1868, which partially paralyzed his left side, Pasteur still managed to provide a comprehensive analysis of the disease and its prevention.

It was not until 1877 that Pasteur finally turned to human disease and pioneered effective methods of treatment against virulent infections such as anthrax. The breakthrough came in 1880 as a result of an oversight by his assistant, who had inadvertently left a batch of chicken cholera bacilli standing in the laboratory over a long hot summer. On injection into some healthy chickens the culture produced only mild and transient signs of disease. Pasteur then instructed his assistant to prepare a fresh batch of the bacillus and once more inject it into the chickens. They survived unscathed, whereas chickens fresh from the market succumbed rapidly to a similar injection. Pasteur had accidentally discovered an attenuated vaccine for chicken cholera. By May 1882 he had succeeded in deliberately producing a comparable vaccine against anthrax and was ready to test it publicly at Pouilly-le-Fort. Here his success was total with all 24 unvaccinated sheep dying of anthrax while those receiving his vaccine survived.

Events even more dramatic followed in 1885 when Pasteur used a rabies vaccine recently developed by him on a badly bitten nine-year-old boy, Joseph Meister. Against the advice of such colleagues as Emile Roux he began the course of 14 injections using virus attenuated in the spine of rabbits. Meister survived. He committed suicide 55 years later in 1940 when, as a caretaker at the Pasteur Institute, he preferred to die rather than open the tomb of Pasteur to the invading Nazi forces.

Thus nearly a century after Edward Jenner, Pasteur had introduced only the second vaccine effective against a serious human disease. Others would rapidly follow him so that by the turn of the century several would be in use. Shortly after his triumph Pasteur suffered a second stroke in 1887, one which affected his speech. Although he lived another seven years his long creative period was at an end.

Paul, Wolfgang

(1913–1993)

GERMAN PHYSICIST

Paul (powl), who was born at Lorenzkirch in Germany, was educated at the universities of Kiel and Berlin, where he obtained his PhD in 1939. After World War II, he taught physics at Göttingen until 1952, when he was appointed professor of physics at the University of Bonn.

During the 1950s he developed the so-called *Paul trap* as a means of confining and studying electrons. The device consists of three electrodes – two end caps and an encircling ring. The ring is connected to an oscillating potential. The direction of the electric field alternates; for half the time the electron is pushed from the caps to the ring and for the other half it is pulled from the ring and pushed towards the caps.

For his work in this field Paul shared the 1989 Nobel Prize for physics with Hans Dehmelt and Norman Ramsey.

Pauli, Wolfgang

(1900–1958)

AUSTRIAN–SWISS PHYSICIST

> I don't mind your thinking slowly: I mind your publishing faster than you think.
> —Quoted by A. L. Mackay in *A Dictionary of Scientific Quotations* (1991)

> What God hath put asunder, no man shall ever join.
> —On Einstein's attempts at a unified field theory. Quoted by J. P. S. Uberoi in *Culture and Science*

Born in the Austrian capital of Vienna, Pauli (**pow**-lee or **paw**-lee) was the son of a professor of physical chemistry at the university there and the godson of Ernst Mach. He was educated at the University of Munich, where he obtained his PhD in 1922. After further study in Copenhagen with Niels Bohr and at Göttingen with Max Born, Pauli taught at Heidelberg before accepting the professorship of physics at the Federal Institute of Technology, Zurich. Apart from the war years, which he spent working in America at the Institute of Advanced Studies, Princeton, he remained there until his early death in 1958.

Pauli was a physicist much respected by his colleagues for his deep insight into the newly emerging quantum theory. His initial reputation was made in relativity theory with his publication in 1921 of his *Relativitätstheorie* (Theory of Relativity). His name is mainly linked with two substantial achievements. The first, formulated in 1924, is known as the *Pauli exclusion principle*. It follows from this that as an electron can spin in only two ways each quantum orbit can hold no more than two electrons. Once both vacancies are full further electrons can fit only into other orbits. With this principle the distribution of orbital electrons at last became clear, that is, they could be explained and predicted in purely quantum terms.

The early model of the atom by Niels Bohr had been extended by Arnold Sommerfeld in 1915. In the Bohr–Sommerfeld atom, each electron orbiting the nucleus had three quantum numbers: n, l, and m. Pauli introduced a fourth quantum number (s), which could have values of $+1/2$ or $-1/2$ and corresponded to possible values of the "spin" of the electron. Pauli's exclusion principle stated that no two electrons in an atom could have the same four quantum numbers (n, l, m, and s). The concept of electron spin was verified in 1926 by Samuel Goudsmit and George Uhlenbek. The exclusion principle explained many aspects of atomic behavior, including the spectral effects discovered by Pieter Zeeman. It has also been applied to other particles. It was for his introduction of the exclusion principle that Pauli was awarded the 1945 Nobel Prize for physics.

Pauli's second great insight was in resolving a problem in beta decay – a type of radioactivity in which electrons are emitted by the atomic nucleus. It was found that the energies of the electrons covered a continuous range up to a maximum value. The difficulty was in reconciling this with the law of conservation of energy; specifically, what happened to the "missing" energy when the electrons had lower energies than the maximum? In 1930, in a letter to Lise Meitner, Pauli suggested that an emitted electron was accompanied by a neutral particle that carried the excess energy. Enrico Fermi suggested the name "neutrino" for this particle, which was first observed in 1953 by Frederick Reines.

Pauling, Linus Carl

(1901–1994)

AMERICAN CHEMIST

Science is the search for truth, that is, the effort to understand the world: it involves the rejection of bias, of dogma, of revelation, but not of morality.

Pauling, a pharmacist's son, was born at Portland, Oregon, and graduated in chemical engineering from Oregon State Agricultural College in 1922. Having gained his PhD in physical chemistry from the California Institute of Technology in 1925, he spent two years in Europe working under such famed scientists as Arnold Sommerfeld, Niels Bohr, Erwin Schrödinger, and William Henry Bragg. He was appointed associated professor of chemistry at Cal Tech in 1927 and full professor in 1931.

Pauling worked on a variety of problems in chemistry and biology. His original work in chemistry was on chemical bonding and molecular structure. He applied physical methods, such as x-ray diffraction, electron diffraction, and magnetic effects, to determining the structure of molecules. He also made significant contributions to applying quantum mechanics to the bonding in chemical compounds. In this field he introduced the idea of hybrid atomic orbitals to account for the shapes of molecules. Another of his innovations was the idea of resonance hybrid – a molecule having a structure intermediate between two different conventional structures. Pauling also worked on the partial ionic character of chemical bonds, using the concept of negativity. Pauling's ideas on chemical bonding were collected in his influential book *The Nature of the Chemical Bond and the Structure of Molecules and Crystals* (1939).

From about 1934 he began to work on more complex biochemical compounds. He studied the properties of hemoglobin using magnetic measurements. This work led to extensive studies of the nature and structure of proteins. With Robert B. Corey, he showed that the amino-acid chain in certain proteins can have a helical structure.

He also made a number of original contributions on other biological topics. In 1940, with Max Delbrück, he introduced a theory of antibody–antigen reactions that depended on molecular shapes. In the 1940s he also studied the genetic disease sickle cell anemia. In 1960 he published a theory of anesthesia and memory. He is noted for his originality and intuition in tackling complex problems and his deep understanding of chemistry. In his book *The Double Helix*, describing the race to determine the structure of DNA, James Watson describes the concern caused by the knowledge that Pauling was working on the same problem.

Pauling was awarded the 1954 Nobel Prize for chemistry. By this time, he had been campaigning for some years against the development of nuclear weapons. He had earlier refused to join the Manhattan project, but had overcome his pacifist principles sufficiently to work on conventional weapons: "Hitler had to be stopped," he noted. By the early 1950s, campaigns against nuclear weapons were being interpreted as "un-American" and Pauling's passport was withdrawn making it impossible to travel to Stockholm for the Nobel ceremonies; his passport was returned at the last moment. Pauling continued with his campaign, publishing a book, *No More War* (1958), and organizing a petition of scientists against nuclear testing. He was awarded the Nobel Peace Prize in 1962.

Pauling later began to campaign on another issue, namely the therapeutic value of high doses of vitamin C. In 1971, in his *Vitamin C and the Common Cold*, Pauling claimed that large vitamin C doses, over 10 grams a day, would also reduce the risk of heart disease. Pauling himself took 18 grams of vitamin C daily, a figure 300 times the recommended dose, for the last 27 years of his life. To pursue the matter further Pauling set up in 1973 the Pauling Institute of Science and Medicine in Palo Alto, California.

Pavlov, Ivan Petrovich

(1849–1936)

RUSSIAN PHYSIOLOGIST

> Remember that science demands from a man all his life. If you had two lives that would not be enough for you. Be passionate in your work and in your searching.
> —*Bequest to Academic Youth* (1936)

Born at Ryazan in Russia, Pavlov (**pa**-vlof) studied medicine and general science at the University of St. Petersburg and the Military Medical Academy. He subsequently carried out research in Breslau (now Wrocław, in Poland) and Leipzig (1883–86). Returning to St. Petersburg, he became professor of physiology at the Medical Academy and director of the physiology department of the Institute of Experimental Medicine. Pavlov's early research lay in the physiology of mammalian digestion, showing, for example, that the secretion of digestive juices in the stomach is prompted by the sight of food and nerve stimulation via the brain. For this work Pavlov received the Nobel Prize for physiology or medicine (1904). He then went on to study the way that dogs and other animals may be induced to salivate and show signs of anticipation of food by actions, such as the ringing of a bell or even a powerful electric shock, that they have learned to associate with the appearance of food. Pavlov's work on conditional or acquired reflexes, which he believed to be associated with different areas of the brain cortex, has led to a new psychologically oriented school of physiology and has stimulated ideas as to the probability of many aspects of human behavior being a result of "conditioning."

Pavlov openly criticized communism and the Soviet government. In 1922 he requested and was refused permission to move his laboratory abroad. Following the expulsion of priests' sons from the Medical Academy, Pavlov, himself the son of a priest, resigned from the chair of physiology in protest. Despite such actions his work continued to be supported by state funds and Pavlovian psychology remained popular in the Soviet Union.

Payen, Anselme

(1795–1871)

FRENCH CHEMIST

> I never rely on him [Payen] where accuracy is concerned. But when it is a matter of writing pamphlet-fodder for the general public, then he is in his element.
> —Jöns Jacob Berzelius, letter to Friedrich Wöhler, 12 January 1847

Payen (pa-**yahn**), the son of a Parisian industrialist, was educated at the Ecole Polytechnique. At the age of 20 he was put in charge of a borax-refining plant, and in 1835 became professor of chemistry at the Ecole Centrale des Arts et Manufactures.

Payen's achievements were mainly concerned with improving old industrial processes and introducing new ones. He showed how borax, used widely in the glass, ceramics, and soldering industries, and as an antiseptic, could be produced from boric acid. This eliminated French dependence on the Dutch East India monopoly of borax. He then turned to the sugar-beet industry (1820) and in 1822 introduced a decolorization process for beet sugar using charcoal. He also introduced into the sugar industry the enzyme diastase for converting starch into sugar (1833). This was also the first enzyme to be obtained in concentrated form. From his subsequent researches on wood and its components he discovered cellulose.

Peano, Giuseppe

(1858–1932)

ITALIAN MATHEMATICIAN AND LOGICIAN

> The purpose of mathematical logic is to analyze the ideas and reasoning that especially figure in the mathematical sciences.
> —Letter to Felix Klein, 19 September 1894

Peano (pay-**ah**-noh), who was born at Spinetta near Cuneo, in Italy, studied at the University of Turin and was an assistant there from 1880. He became extraordinary professor of infinitesimal calculus in 1890 and was full professor from 1895 until his death. He was also professor of the military academy in Turin from 1886 to 1901.

Peano began his mathematical career as an analyst and, like Richard Dedekind before him, his interest in philosophical and logical matters was awakened by the lack of rigor in some presentations of the subject. Peano was particularly keen to avoid all illegitimate reliance on intuition in analysis. His discovery in 1890 of a curve that was continuous but filled space went against intuition. A similar discovery was Karl Weierstrass's famous function that was everywhere continuous but nowhere differentiable. As with Weierstrass's function, Peano's curve shows that the concept of a continuous function cannot be identified with that of a graph.

His interest in rigorous and logical presentation of mathematics led Peano naturally to an interest in the mathematical development of logic. In this field he was one of the great pioneers along with Georg Boole, Gottlob Frege, and Bertrand Russell. Peano's achievement was twofold. First he devised, in his *Notations de logique mathématique* (1894; Notations in Mathematical Logic), a clear and efficient notation for mathematical logic which, as modified by Bertrand Russell, is still widely used. Secondly, he showed how arithmetic can be derived from a purely logical basis. To do this he formulated, in his *Nova methodo exposita* (1889; New Explanation of Method), nine axioms, four dealing with equality, and the remaining five, listed below, characterizing the numbers series:

1 is a number

The successor of any number is a number

No two numbers have the same successor

1 is not the successor of any number

Any property that belongs to 1 and the successor of any number that also
    has that property, belongs to all numbers (mathematical induction).

Peano's axioms had been proposed, in a more complicated form, by Dedekind a year earlier.

Peano also did notable work in geometry and on the error terms in numerical calculation. Among his extramathematical interests he was a keen propagandist for a proposed international language, Interlingua, which he had developed from Volapük.

Pearson, Karl

(1857–1936)

BRITISH BIOMETRICIAN

> The right to live does not connote the right of each man to reproduce his kind...As we lessen the stringency of natural selection, and more and more of the weaklings and the unfit survive, we must increase the standard, mental and physical, of parentage.
> —*Darwinism, Medical Progress and Parentage* (1912)

Pearson, the son of a London lawyer, studied mathematics at Cambridge University. He then joined University College, London, initially (from 1884) as professor of applied mathematics and mechanics and from 1911 until his retirement in 1933 as Galton Professor of Eugenics.

Pearson's career was spent largely on applying statistics to biology. His interest in this derived ultimately from Francis Galton and was much reinforced by the work of his colleague Walter Weldon. In 1893 Weldon had argued that variation, heredity, and selection are matters of arithmetic; Pearson started in the 1890s to develop the appropriate "arithmetic" or statistics as it came to be called. Between 1893 and 1906 Pearson published over a hundred papers on statistics in which such now familiar concepts as the standard deviation and the chi-square test for statistical significance were introduced. Later work was published in *Biometrika*, the journal founded by Pearson, Galton, and Weldon in 1901 and edited by Pearson until his death. This he ran with an unashamed partisanship, rejecting outright or correcting without invitation papers expressing views Pearson considered "controversial." It is for this reason that Ronald Fisher, the most creative British statistician of the century, decided after receiving the treatment from Pearson in 1920 to publish elsewhere.

Pearson and Weldon became involved in an important controversy with William Bateson on the nature of evolution and its possible measurement. The biometricians emphasized the importance of continuous variation as the basic material of natural selection and proposed that it be analyzed statistically. Bateson and his supporters, whose views were reinforced by the rediscovery of the works of Gregor Mendel in 1900, attached more importance to discontinuous variation and argued that breeding studies are the best way to illuminate the mechanism of evolution.

The validity of Mendelism eventually became generally accepted. At the same time, however, the immense value of biometrical techniques in analyzing continuously variable characters like height, which are controlled by many genes, was also recognized. Following Weldon's death in 1906 Pearson spent less time trying to prove the biometricians' case and devoted himself instead to developing statistics as an exact science. He prepared and published many volumes of mathematical tables for statisticians. He also devoted much of his time to the study of eugenics, using Galton's data to issue various volumes of the *Studies in National Deterioration* (1906–24). In 1925 he founded and edited until his death the *Annals of Eugenics*.

To many, Pearson is best known as the author of *Grammar of Science* (1892), a widely read positivist work on the philosophy of science in which he argued, like his earlier teacher Ernst Mach, that science does not explain but rather summarizes our experience in a convenient language.

Pecquet, Jean

(1622–1674)

FRENCH ANATOMIST

Born at Dieppe in France, Pecquet (pe-**kay**) was educated in Paris and Montpellier, gaining his medical qualifications at the latter in 1652. He then entered the service of Nicolas Fouquet, Louis XIV's superintendent of finance, and followed him into the Bastille in 1661 with his fall from power. In later life Pecquet was reported to have fallen a victim to the seductive fallacy that brandy could cure all disease.

In 1651 he published the first description of the thoracic duct. The lymphatic system had been discovered by Gaspare Aselli in 1622 when he first observed the "white vessels" or lacteals of the intestines. It was assumed that they would go to and terminate at the liver. Pecquet was able to show that no such vessels went to the liver. Instead, he went on to trace their path into the "receptaculum chyli," later known as the thoracic duct, which eventually led to and drained into the subclavian vein in the shoulder. The significance of this lay in its rejection of the view of Galen that food or "chyle" from the intestines is transported to the liver to be turned into blood. This lent support to the work of William Harvey on the circulation of the blood.

Pedersen, Charles

(1904–1989)

AMERICAN CHEMIST

The son of Norwegian parents, Pedersen was born in Pusan, Korea, and moved with his family to America in the 1920s. He became a naturalized American citizen in 1953. Pedersen was educated at the Massachusetts Institute of Technology and, for most of his career up to his retirement in 1969, he worked as a research chemist for DuPont.

While working on synthetic rubber, Pedersen noted that one of his materials had been contaminated. He investigated the impurity and found that it had a ring structure of 12 carbon and 6 oxygen atoms, with a pair of carbon atoms between each oxygen. Such structures are known as cyclic polyethers. Normally, organic solvents such as ether and benzene will not dissolve sodium hydroxide. Yet Pedersen found that caustic soda did dissolve in his new compound, with the sodium ions binding loosely to the oxygen atoms of the ether. To accomplish this the polyether formed a nonplanar ring with a crownlike structure, with the sodium ions sitting neatly in the center. For this reason, Pedersen named what turned out to be a new class of compounds "crown ethers." Although he made his first observations in 1964, DuPont delayed publication until 1967.

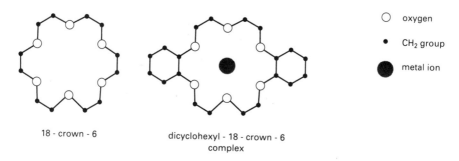

○ oxygen

● CH$_2$ group

⬤ metal ion

18 - crown - 6

dicyclohexyl - 18 - crown - 6 complex

CROWN ETHERS   *Structures of simple crown ethers and their complexes.*

The implications of Pedersen's work were varied and important. If one crown ether could coordinate sodium ions, it was likely that others of different ring size would be able to bind to other metal ions. Crown ethers could therefore be used as a simple means of gathering specific ions from aqueous solutions.

Other chemists were also quick to see the implications of Pedersen's work and it was with two of these, Jean Lehn and Donald Cram, that he shared the 1987 Nobel Prize for chemistry.

Peebles, James

(1935–   )

CANADIAN ASTRONOMER

Born at Winnipeg in Canada, Peebles was educated at the University of Manitoba and at Princeton, where he took his PhD in 1962. He has remained at Princeton ever since, becoming Einstein Professor of Science in 1984.

Peebles has made a number of contributions to modern cosmology. In 1965, in collaboration with Robert Dicke, he made the important prediction that a background radiation should be detectable as a remnant of the big bang. He also calculated that the amount of helium present in the universe as a consequence of the big bang should be about 25–30%, a figure that agrees with current observations.

In 1979, again in collaboration with Dicke, Peebles drew the attention of cosmologists to the so-called "flatness problem" and asked how the standard model of the big-bang theory could deal with it. Cosmologists ask if the universe is "open" or "closed." If it is open it will continue to expand forever; if closed, the expansion will cease at some future point and it will begin to contract. To answer the question the value of omega (Ω) must be found.

Omega (Ω) is the ratio of the average density of mass in the universe to the critical mass density. This latter factor is the mass density needed just to halt the universe's expansion. If Ω is less than 1 the universe is open, and if Ω is greater than 1 the universe is closed. If Ω is equal to 1 the universe will be flat, that is, the universe will continue to expand, although at a decreasing rate.

The actual measured value of Ω is close to 1. A bit more matter in the universe and it would have collapsed long ago; a little less matter, and it would have expanded too quickly for galaxies to form. But if Ω is close to 1 now, it must have been close to 1 soon after the big bang. If it had differed significantly, Ω would either be approaching infinity and the universe would have the density of a black hole, or equal to 0 and the universe would be indistinguishable from a vacuum.

The question thus becomes why so early in the history of the universe was Ω so close to 1? Instead of merely laying this down as an arbitrary initial condition, there should be some way to see why, given the big bang, Ω should have this value. As Peebles's problem seemed to have no solution in the standard model of the big bang, it has been left to astronomers such as Guth to propose alternative foundations based on an inflationary model.

Peebles is also the author of two important books, *Physical Cosmology* (Princeton, 1971) and *The Large Scale Structure of the Universe* (Princeton, 1980), which have between them done much to define the subject of cosmology for a generation of astronomers.

Peierls, Sir Rudolph Ernst

(1907–1995)

GERMAN–BRITISH
THEORETICAL PHYSICIST

The son of a businessman, Peierls (perlz) was educated in his native city of Berlin, at Munich, and at Leipzig where he completed his PhD in 1929. He spent the next three years as research assistant to Wolfgang Pauli at the Federal Institute of Technology, Zurich. After short periods at Rome, Copenhagen, and Cambridge, and fearing to return to Germany, Peierls sought a post in England. He worked first at Manchester and in 1937 was appointed professor of physics at Birmingham University. Peierls became a naturalized British citizen in 1940.

In 1939 nuclear fission had been discovered by Otto Frisch and Lise Meitner. Immediately the question arose as to whether the process could be harnessed to build a new and powerful bomb. Frisch had arrived in Birmingham soon after announcing his discovery and discussed the matter with Peierls. In 1940 they began to calculate just how much uranium–235 would be needed to sustain a chain reaction. To their astonishment their calculations revealed that an amount as small as one pound would be enough to set off an explosion equivalent to thousands of tons of high explosives.

Peierls was terrified that similar calculations had been made in Germany; consequently Peierls and Frisch quickly prepared a report that eventually reached the appropriate government committee under G. P. Thomson. The committee was just about to disband having convinced itself that there was no immediate prospect for nuclear weapons. Minds were quickly changed and it was recommended that a front organization, Tube Alloys, be set up to start work on the extraction of uranium–235 by means of gaseous diffusion. After some initial confusion because of his German background Peierls was recruited by Tube Alloys and was sent to America to continue his work at Los Alamos.

At the end of the war Peierls returned to his chair at Birmingham. In 1963 he moved to Oxford to become Wykeham Professor of Physics, a position he held until his retirement in 1974. His autobiography, *Bird of Passage*, was published in 1985.

Peligot, Eugene Melchior

(1811–1890)

FRENCH CHEMIST

Peligot (pe-lee-**goh**), a Parisian by birth, studied under Jean Dumas at the Ecole Polytechnique and became professor of chemistry at the Conservatoire des Arts et Métiers in his native city.

He worked with Dumas on the theory of radicals, but his most practical discovery was made in 1838, with Bouchardat, when they demonstrated that the sweet substance found in the urine of diabetics was glucose. This prepared the way for Hermann von Fehling to develop his test for the presence and quantity of sugar in 1848.

In 1834 Peligot obtained acetone by heating calcium acetate. As acetone is a product of the distillation of wood this was, following Friedrich Wöhler's work, another example of the synthesis of an organic compound from inorganic materials. He also attempted to explain what happens in the lead chamber in the manufacture of sulfuric acid. He realized that the catalyst nitric oxide forms nitrogen dioxide and then the nitrogen dioxide reacts with the sulfur dioxide present so that nitric oxide is formed again. In 1841 Peligot succeeded in isolating uranium from its oxide.

Pelletier, Pierre Joseph

(1788–1842)

FRENCH CHEMIST

Pelletier (pel-e-**tyay**) was born the son of a pharmacist in Paris, France. He both studied and taught at the Ecole de Pharmacie until his retirement in 1842. His major work was the investigation of drugs, which he began in 1809. By pioneering the use of mild solvents he successfully isolated numerous important biologically active plant products: working with Bienaimé Caventou he discovered caffeine, strychnine, colchicine, quinine, and veratrine. Their greatest triumph, however, came in 1817, when they discovered chlorophyll – the green pigment in plants that traps light energy necessary for photosynthesis.

Peltier, Jean Charles Athanase

(1785–1845)

FRENCH PHYSICIST

Born in the Somme department of France, Peltier (pel-**tyay**) was a watchmaker who gave up his profession at the age of 30 to devote himself to experimental physics. In 1821 T. J. Seebeck had shown that if heat is applied to the junction of a loop of two different conductors a current will be generated. In 1834 Peltier demonstrated the converse effect (the *Peltier effect*). He found that when a current is passed through a circuit of two different conductors a thermal effect will be found at the junctions. There is a rise or fall in temperature at the junction depending on the direction of current flow.

Penck, Albrecht

(1858–1945)

GERMAN GEOGRAPHER AND GEOLOGIST

> He used to be liked as much as admired but during the war [World War I] some of his statements have lessened the esteem formerly felt for him.
> —On Penck's outspoken nationalism. William Morris Davis,
> *Geographical Review* (1920)

Penck (pengk) studied at the university in his native city of Leipzig in Germany. After teaching briefly at the University of Munich, he was appointed professor of physical geography at the University of Vienna in 1885. He moved in 1906 to the chair of geography at Berlin, where he remained until his retirement in 1926.

Penck is remembered chiefly for his collaboration with his assistant Eduard Brückner on the three-volume *Die Alpen im Eiszeitalter* (1901–09; The Alps in the Ice Age). Working in the Bavarian Alps and studying the succession of gravel terraces occurring at different heights above the present river-valley floors, they were able to reconstruct the sequence of past ice ages. They recognized four, which they called Günz, Mindel, Riss, and Würm after the river valleys where they were first identified. For over half a century this scheme provided the framework for the discussion of the European Pleistocene, which they underestimated as lasting for 650,000 years.

Penck produced a fundamental work on geomorphology, a term he is also believed to have introduced, *Morphologie der Erdoberfläche* (1894; Morphology of the Earth's Surface), in which he identified six topographic forms – the plain, scarp, valley, mountain, hollow, and cavern – and discussed their origins.

After World War I he turned more to political geography.

Penney, William George, Baron

(1909–1991)

BRITISH MATHEMATICAL PHYSICIST

The son of a sergeant-major in the British army, Penney was born in the British crown colony of Gibraltar. He was educated at Imperial College, London, at the University of Wisconsin, and at Cambridge, where he obtained his PhD in 1935. In the following year he was appointed to a lectureship in mathematics at Imperial College.

With the outbreak of World War II, Penney was recruited by the Admiralty to work on blast waves. In 1944 he was sent to Los Alamos to apply his knowledge to the development of the atomic bomb. He witnessed the Nagasaki bomb and was also present at Bikini in 1946 when the Americans first tested their hydrogen bomb. On this latter occasion Penney was able to calculate the bomb's blast power using his own simple equipment.

Penney remained in government service after the war. When the British government decided to build a nuclear bomb Penney became responsible for its design and production, first at the Ministry of Supply (1946–52) and then at the Atomic Weapons Research Establishment, Harwell (1952–59). The bomb used plutonium made in the Windscale reactor. The task was made harder by the passage in the United States in 1946 of legislation forbidding the release of any information on the design of nuclear weapons. Everything, therefore, had to be dredged from memory or discovered anew. By 1952 Penney was ready to test the first British bomb at Montebello, a small island off the northwest coast of Australia. He went on to direct the production of the first British hydrogen bomb, successfully exploded at Christmas Island in 1957.

The success of the British nuclear program led in 1958 to a bilateral treaty with the United States sanctioning the exchange of information on nuclear weapons. Penney played a significant role in these negotiations; as he also did in the talks that led to the 1963 nuclear test-ban treaty.

In 1959 Penney left Harwell for the UK Atomic Energy Authority (UKAEA) where he served as chairman from 1964 to 1967, when he returned to Imperial College as rector, a post he held until his retirement in 1973. He was raised to the British peerage in 1967, becoming Baron Penney of East Hendred.

Penrose, Sir Roger

(1931–)

BRITISH MATHEMATICIAN AND THEORETICAL PHYSICIST

Penrose, the son of the geneticist Lionel Penrose, was born at Colchester in the eastern English county of Essex. He graduated from University College, London, and obtained his PhD in 1957 from Cambridge University. After holding various lecturing and research posts in London, Cambridge, and in America at Princeton, Syracuse, and Texas, Penrose was appointed professor of applied mathematics at Birkbeck College, London, in 1966. In 1973 he was elected Rouse Ball Professor of Mathematics at Oxford.

Penrose has done much to elucidate the fundamental properties of black holes. These result from the total gravitational collapse of large stars that shrink to such a small volume that not even a light signal can escape from them. There is thus a boundary around a black hole inside which all information about the black hole is trapped; this is known as its "event horizon." With Stephen Hawking, Penrose proved a theorem of Einstein's general relativity asserting that at the center of a black hole there must evolve a "space–time singularity" of zero volume and infinite density where the present laws of physics break down. He went on to propose his hypothesis of "cosmic censorship," that such singularities cannot be "naked"; they must possess an event horizon. The effect of this would be to conceal and isolate the singularity with its indifference to the laws of physics.

Despite this Penrose went on in 1969 to describe a mechanism for the extraction of energy from a Kerr black hole, an uncharged rotating body first described by Roy Kerr in 1963. Such bodies are surrounded by an ergosphere within which it is impossible for an object to be at rest. If, Penrose demonstrated, a body fell into this area it would split into two particles; one would fall into the hole and the other would escape with more mass-energy than the initial particle. In this way rotational energy of the black hole is transferred to the particle outside the hole.

From the mid-1960s Penrose has been working on the development of a new cosmology based on a complex geometry. Penrose began with "twistors" – massless objects with both linear and angular momentum in twistor space. From these he attempted to reconstruct the main outlines of modern physics. The matter is pursued not only by Penrose but through a number of "twistor groups" who communicate through a *Twistor Newsletter*. The fullest account of twistor theory is to be found in *Spinors and Space-Time* (2 vols., 1984–86) by Penrose and W. Windler.

In 1974 Penrose introduced a novel tiling of the affine plane (*Penrose tiling*). Periodic tilings in which a unit figure is endlessly repeated can be constructed from triangles, squares, and hexagons – figures with three-, four-, or six-fold symmetry. The plane cannot be tiled by pentagons, which have a five-fold symmetry; three pentagons fitted together always leave a crack, known to crystallographers as a "frustration." It was also known that crystal structures could have two-, three-, four-, or six-fold rotational symmetries only. No crystal, that is, could have a five-fold rotational symmetry.

Penrose's method of tiling the plane involved constructing two rhombuses by dividing the diagonal of a regular parallelogram by a golden section. These could be combined according to simple rules so as to cover the plane, even though there was no simple repeated unit cell. The rhombuses can be assembled in such a way as to have an almost five-fold symmetry. As such they were seen as an interesting oddity, usually discussed in columns devoted to recreational mathematics. However, things changed

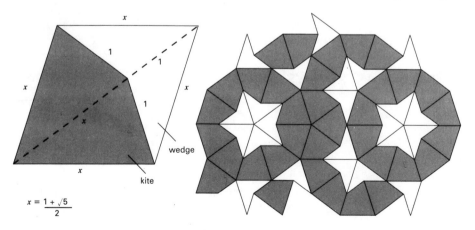

PENROSE TILING

dramatically in 1984 when Dany Schectman of the National Bureau of Standards and his colleagues found that a rapidly cooled sample of an aluminum–manganese alloy formed crystals that displayed a five-fold symmetry. "Quasicrystals," as they soon became known, developed rapidly into a major new research field and the subject of hundreds of papers.

In addition to continuing his work on twistor theory Penrose also published a widely read book, *The Emperor's New Mind* (1989). The book is an attack on aspects of artificial intelligence. In it he argues that there are aspects of mathematics that cannot be tied to a set of rules. We cannot allow "one universally formal system...equivalent to all the mathematicians' algorithms for judging mathematical truth." Such a system would violate Gödel's theorem. Nor can we accept that algorithms used are so complicated and obscure that their validity can never be known. We do not in fact ascertain mathematical truth solely through the use of algorithms. "We must see the truth of a mathematical argument to be convinced of its validity," Penrose has insisted. Consequently when we *see* the validity of a theorem, in *seeing* it "we reveal the very nonalgorithmic nature of the 'seeing' process itself."

He further developed his arguments in *Shadows of the Mind* (1994), in which he also answered many of the objections raised against the earlier work. Penrose has also published (in collaboration with Stephen Hawking) *The Nature of Space and Time* (1996), in which they develop their own cosmological viewpoints. Thus while Penrose presents his own "twistor view" of the universe, Hawking concentrates on problems connected with "quantum cosmology."

Penzias, Arno Allan

(1933–   )

AMERICAN ASTROPHYSICIST

Penzias (**pent**-see-as), who was born in Munich, Germany, earned his BS at City College, New York, in 1954 after fleeing with his parents as a refugee from the Nazis. He gained his PhD from Columbia University in 1962. In 1961 he joined Bell Laboratories at Holmdel, New Jersey, and

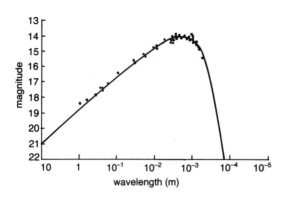

COSMIC BACKGROUND RADIATION   *The distribution of background microwave radiation as found by Penzias and Wilson.*

was made director of their radio research laboratory in 1976. From 1979 he has been executive director of research in the communications division.

Penzias and his co-worker Robert W. Wilson are credited with one of the most important discoveries of modern astrophysics, the cosmic microwave background radiation. This is considered to be the remnant radiation produced in the "big bang" in which the universe was created some billions of years ago. As the universe has expanded, the radiation has lost energy: it has effectively "cooled." Its existence was originally predicted by George Gamow and Ralph Alpher in 1948, who calculated that the radiation should now be characteristic of a perfectly emitting body (a black body) at a temperature of about 5 kelvin (−268°C). This radiation should lie in the microwave region of the spectrum. Similar calculations were later made by Robert Dicke and P. J. E. Peebles.

The discovery of the remnant radiation was made while Penzias and Wilson were working at the Bell Laboratories. They were using a 20-foot (6-m) directional radio antenna, designed for communication with satellites, and found what appeared to be excessive radio noise in their instrument. They decided to investigate further thinking that it could be due to radio waves from our own Galaxy. In May 1964 they found that there was a background of microwave radiation that came from all directions uniformly and was not accountable simply as instrumental noise. They calculated its effective temperature as about 3.5 kelvin (−269.65°C). An explanation was proposed by Dicke at nearby Princeton University that this was the predicted remnant radiation of the creation of the universe. Subsequent experiments confirmed that it was isotropic and apparently unchanging (on human timescales).

For their discovery Penzias and Wilson were awarded the 1978 Nobel Prize for physics, which they jointly shared with Pyotr L. Kapitza, who received the award for his (unrelated) developments in low-temperature physics. Penzias and Wilson have continued to collaborate on research into intergalactic hydrogen, galactic radiation, and interstellar abundances of the isotopes. In particular their work has led to the discovery of a large number of interstellar molecules and rare isotopic species.

Perey, Marguerite Catherine

(1909–1975)

FRENCH NUCLEAR CHEMIST

Perey (pe-**ray**), the daughter of an industrialist, was born at Ville-momble in France and educated at the Faculté des Sciences de Paris. She began her career in 1929 as an assistant in the Radium Institute in Paris under Marie Curie. In 1940 she moved to the University of Strasbourg, becoming professor of nuclear chemistry in 1949 and director of the Center for Nuclear Research in 1958.

By the 1930s chemists had discovered all the elements of the periodic table below uranium except for those with atomic numbers 43, 61, 85, and 87. Many claims had been made for the discovery of element 87 with it being variously and prematurely named russium, moldavium, and virginium. In 1939 Perey found in the radioactive decay of actinium–227 the emission of alpha-particles as well as the expected beta-particles. As an alpha-particle is basically a helium nucleus with an atomic mass of 4 this implied that Perey had discovered a nuclide of mass number 223. Further investigation showed it to be one of the missing elements, with an atomic number of 87. She originally called it actinium K but in 1945 named it francium (for France).

Perkin, Sir William Henry

(1838–1907)

BRITISH CHEMIST

> Before you began work there was little, almost nothing, known of this subject [Faraday rotation], certainly nothing of practical use to the chemist. You created a new branch of science.
> —W. Bruehl, letter to Perkin (1906)

Perkin was born in London, the youngest son of a builder. His interest in chemistry was aroused early by some experiments shown to him by a young friend and he was fortunate to attend the City of London School, which was one of the few London schools where science was taught. Perkin's teacher there, Thomas Hall, was a pupil of Johann Hofmann at the Royal College of Chemistry and Hall pleaded with Perkin's father to allow his son to study chemistry and not to force him into a career in architecture. Hall was successful and Perkin entered the college in 1853.

In 1855 he was made Hofmann's assistant and the following year was given the task of synthesizing quinine (despite much effort, this difficult task was not achieved until 1944, by Robert Burns Woodward and William von Eggers Doering). Perkin started from the coal-tar derivative allyltoluidine, which has a formula very similar to that of quinine. He thought the conversion could be achieved by removing two hydrogen atoms and adding two of oxygen. Although no quinine was formed by this reaction, it did produce a reddish-brown precipitate. Perkin decided to treat a more simple base in the same manner and tried aniline and potassium dichromate. This time a black precipitate was produced. Addition of alcohol to this precipitate yielded a rich purple color. Perkin soon realized that this coloring matter had the properties of a dye and resisted the action of light very well. He sent some specimens of dyed silk to a dyeing firm in Perth, Scotland, which expressed great interest provided that the cost of the cloth would not be raised unduly. With this behind him Perkin took out the appropriate patents, borrowed his father's life savings, and in 1857 built a dye factory at Greenford Green, near Harrow, for mass production of the first synthetic dye – mauveine.

Initially there were difficulties. Since aniline was not readily available, it had to be produced at the factory from benzene. There was also the conservatism of the dye industry to overcome.

The significance of Perkin's discovery lay in its being the first *synthetic* dye; before this all dyes were derived from such organic sources as insects, plants, and mollusks. Purple had traditionally come from a Mediterranean shellfish and could be produced only at great cost, so that it was used only by royalty. Apart from the difficulty of supply there was also the problem of the quality of the dyes: vegetable and animal dyes were not particularly fast and tended to fade in the light. The market was ripe for anyone who could provide a dye in bulk that was cheap, fast, and did not fade. Perkin quickly made his fortune and stimulated a rush to find other synthetics. Carl Graebe and C. T. Liebermann soon synthesized alizarin, the coloring ingredient of madder. Magenta and Bismarck brown were among the other new colors that were soon to flood the market.

In 1874 Perkin sold his factory and retired, a wealthy man, at the age of 35, devoting the rest of his life to research in pure science. He became particularly interested in Faraday rotation and produced over 40 papers on this topic.

Perkin was knighted in 1906. His son and namesake was also a chemist.

Perkin, William Henry, Jr.

(1860–1929)

BRITISH CHEMIST

Perkin, who was born at Sudbury near London, was the elder son of the famous chemist who discovered the aniline dyes, also called William Henry Perkin. As a child he assisted his father in his private laboratory. He was educated at the City of London School and then in 1877 followed his father to the Royal College of Chemistry. He then went to Germany where he studied at the universities of Würzburg and Munich. On his return to England he worked at Manchester before being appointed professor of chemistry at Heriot-Watt College, Edinburgh, in 1887. In 1892 he returned to Manchester as professor of organic chemistry and in 1912 he became Waynflete Professor of Chemistry at Oxford.

Perkin was a very practical chemist who, in a long career, achieved many syntheses and analyses. His first success came in his student days in Munich. It had been argued by Victor Meyer in 1876 that no ring with fewer than six carbon atoms could exist. Perkin succeeded in 1884 in preparing rings with four carbon atoms.

Of the many molecules he synthesized are the terpenes, limonene (1904), the oxygenated terpineol (1904), and camphoric acid (1903). He worked on many alkaloids, including strychnine, and on natural coloring compounds like brazilin. Perkin also worked with William Pope, showing that optical activity can be found in compounds in which the carbon atoms are not necessarily asymmetrical.

He produced three chemical works in collaboration with Frederic Kipping and also did much to stimulate the growth of chemistry at Oxford by campaigning for the new laboratories that were opened there in 1922.

Perl, Martin Lewis

(1927–)

AMERICAN PHYSICIST

Born in New York, Perl first graduated in chemistry in 1948 at the Brooklyn Polytechnic Institute. After working in industry as a chemical engineer for General Electric, Perl became interested in nuclear physics. Consequently he returned to college and in 1955 he was awarded his PhD from Columbia, New York. He immediately moved to the University of Michigan, where he remained until he took up his present position of professor of physics at Stanford University, California, in 1963.

In 1972 physicists were aware of four leptons: the electron, the muon, and their corresponding neutrinos. Further, leptons, unlike hadrons such as the proton, are genuinely pointlike elementary particles, which interact by the weak force. In 1972 Stanford opened its new accelerator, SPEAR

(Stanford Positron–Electron Asymmetry Ring). While no new lepton had been found since the discovery of the muon in 1936, Perl decided to use the SPEAR facilities to see whether the lepton family could be extended.

Theoretical reasons led him to believe that any new lepton would have a charge of plus or minus 1, have a mass greater than a billion electron-volts (1 GeV), decay in less than a billionth of a second, and respond only to the weak and electromagnetic forces. Like any other particle the new lepton would have to be identified by detecting its characteristic decay products. The particle had been tentatively named the "tau particle" from the initial letter of the Greek word for third, "triton." Perl argued that the tau would decay into either a muon or an electron, plus a neutrino and an antineutrino. In 1974 a sample of 10,000 events yielded twenty four of the predicted kind. Despite some initial skepticism the existence of a heavy lepton with a mass greater than the proton was quickly confirmed.

Perl's discovery had an important theoretical implication. The four previously known leptons were linked with the four known quarks. The discovery of a new lepton suggested the symmetry could only be maintained by the existence of a new quark. The prediction was confirmed in 1977 when Leon Lederman discovered the upsilon particle. For his discovery of the tau particle Perl shared the 1995 Nobel Prize for physics with Frederick Reines.

Perrault, Claude

(1613–1688)

FRENCH ANATOMIST, ENGINEER, AND ARCHITECT

Perrault (pe-**roh**), the son of an advocate, came from a most distinguished Parisian family. Of his two brothers Charles and Pierre, the first was the author in 1697 of one of the most famous of all collections of fairy tales, while the latter was a hydrologist of note. Claude himself was educated at the University of Paris and after graduating in 1639 opened a private practice.

As a founder member of the French Academy of Sciences in 1666 he became a figure of some consequence in French science. He appears to have been put in control of a group of anatomists charged with the dissection of the more exotic species as they died in the Royal Menagerie. His *Descriptions anatomiques de divers animaux* (1682; Anatomical Descriptions of Various Animals) covered the dissection of some 25 mammalian species alone and thus constitutes one of the earliest works on comparative anatomy grounded in reality.

Perrault also published a comprehensive work on physics and was a celebrated architect, taking part in the design of the Louvre. At the age of 75 Perrault is supposed to have died from an infection contracted while dissecting a camel.

Perrin, Jean Baptiste

(1870–1942)

FRENCH PHYSICIST

Accustomed as we are, by laboratory work, to clear predictions, we see clearly what the more ignorant still have not realized; and I put into this category of ignorant certain men who are cultivated, but are completely unaware of science and its enormous potential, and who...think that the future will always have to be like the past and conclude that there will always be wars, poverty, and slavery.
—*Science and Hope* (1948)

Perrin (pe-**ran**) was born in Lille, France, the son of an army officer. He was educated at the Ecole Normale, where he received his doctorate in 1897. He was appointed to the Sorbonne where he was made professor of physical chemistry in 1910. He remained there until 1941, when he went to America to escape the Nazis.

Perrin's early work was in the developing field of cathode rays and x-rays. In 1895 he established the important result that cathode rays are deflected by a magnetic field and thus carry a negative charge. He began to calculate the ratio of charge to mass for these particles but was anticipated by J. J. Thomson. In 1901 he produced a work on physical chemistry, *Les Principes* (Principles).

His most important work however was on Brownian motion and the molecular hypothesis. In 1828 Robert Brown had reported that pollen granules immersed in water moved continuously and erratically. However, it was left to Albert Einstein to provide some quantitative explanations for the motion, in 1905. Assuming that the pollen was being moved by water molecules, he showed that the average distance traveled by a particle increased with the square of the elapsed time. Making the necessary corrections for temperature, size of particles, and nature of the liquid involved, Einstein made precise predictions about how far a particle should travel in a given time. In 1908 Perrin finally confirmed Einstein's predictions experimentally. His work was made possible by the development of the ultramicroscope by Richard Zsigmondy and Henry Siedentopf in 1903. He worked out from his experimental results and Einstein's formula the size of the water molecule and a precise value for Avogadro's number.

The fundamental importance of this work was that it established atomism as something more than a useful hypothesis. It was mainly as a result of Perrin's work that the most eminent skeptic, Wilhelm Ostwald, at last relented. Perrin was awarded the Nobel Prize for physics in 1926 for his work on Brownian motion and sedimentation.

In 1913 he published *Les Atomes* (Atoms), which collected together not only his own work on molecules but new material from radiochemistry, black-body radiation, and many other fields, to demonstrate the reality of molecules. It was an enormously influential work, going through four editions in its first year and being translated into many languages.

Perutz, Max Ferdinand

(1914–   )

AUSTRIAN–BRITISH BIOCHEMIST

> True science thrives best in glass houses, where everyone can look in. When the windows are blacked out, as in war, the weeds take over; when secrecy muffles criticism, charlatans and cranks flourish.
> —*Is Science Necessary?* (1989)

While studying chemistry at the university in his native Vienna, Perutz (pe-**roots**) became interested in x-ray diffraction techniques; after graduation he went to England to work on the x-ray diffraction of proteins with William L. Bragg at the Cavendish Laboratory, Cambridge. A meeting in Prague with the biochemist Felix Haurowitz in 1937 turned his attention to the blood protein hemoglobin and he received his PhD in 1940 for work in this field. Soon after, he was arrested as an alien and interned, first on the Isle of Man and then in Canada with Hermann Bondi and Klaus Fuchs. He was released and allowed to return to Britain in 1941. In the following year he joined the staff of Lord Mountbatten, examining various applications of science for the war effort.

After the war Perutz organized the setting up, in 1946, of the molecular biology laboratory in Cambridge, where he was soon joined by John Kendrew. After seven years' hard work Perutz was still far from his objective of working out the three-dimensional structure of hemoglobin, a molecule containing some 12,000 atoms. Then in 1953 he applied the heavy atom or isomorphous replacement technique to his work whereby heavy metal atoms, e.g., mercury or gold, are incorporated into the molecule under study. This alters the diffraction patterns, making it easier to compute the positions of atoms in the molecule. By 1959 he had shown hemoglobin to be composed of four chains, together making a tetrahedral structure, with four heme groups near the molecule's surface.

For this achievement Perutz received the 1962 Nobel Prize in chemistry, sharing it with Kendrew, who had worked out the structure of the muscle protein, myoglobin, using similar methods. In later work Perutz demonstrated that in oxygenated hemoglobin the four subunits are rearranged. This explained the change in structure noted by Haurowitz in 1938. Perutz also investigated the various mutated forms of hemoglobin characteristic of inherited blood diseases.

While indulging his hobby of mountaineering, Perutz made some notable contributions to the understanding of glaciers, particularly by his demonstration that the rate of flow is faster at the glacier surface than at the base.

Perutz continued as head of the Medical Research Council molecular biology unit at Cambridge until his retirement in 1979. He published a brief account of his early life and his views on science in his *Is Science Necessary?* (1989).

Peters, Sir Rudolph Albert

(1889–1982)

BRITISH BIOCHEMIST

Peters, the son of a London doctor, was educated at Cambridge University and St. Bartholomew's Hospital, London. After teaching briefly in Cambridge, he accepted the Whitley Chair of Biochemistry at Oxford, which he held from 1923 until his retirement in 1954.

Between 1928 and 1935 Peters and his Oxford colleagues succeeded in showing for the first time the precise activity of a vitamin in the body. Working with vitamin B_1, or thiamine – the antiberiberi factor first described by Christiaan Eijkman – they fed pigeons on a diet of polished rice. This was free of thiamine and produced a number of debilitating symptoms in most of the birds. As one of these symptoms was convulsions, Peters suspected that the thiamine deficiency could involve the central nervous system. He consequently began a search of the pigeon's brain for what he termed a "biochemical lesion."

The first hint of the role of thiamine was provided by the failure of minced pigeon brain to take up as much oxygen as the brain of a normally fed bird. The lesion was promptly reversed by the addition of thiamine. Further work showed an accumulation of lactic acid in the pigeon brain. As this is one of the intermediate products in the metabolism of carbohydrates into carbon dioxide and water it seemed clear that thiamine must be an essential ingredient in this metabolic pathway.

Peters's work therefore provided the first proof of the action of any vitamin upon an enzyme system *in vitro*.

Petit, Alexis-Thérèse

(1791–1820)

FRENCH PHYSICIST

Petit (pe-**tee**), who was born at Vesoul in France, entered the Ecole Polytechnique in 1807. He spent a period teaching physics in Paris, and received a doctorate in 1811. He was one of the professors of physics at the Ecole Polytechnique. Petit did some research with his brother-in-law D. F. J. Arago on the variation of refractive index with temperature. However, he is known solely for his work with Pierre Dulong in which they established the law (*Dulong and Petit's law*) that the specific heat of a solid multiplied by the atomic weight is (approximately) a constant for different solids.

Petit, Jean Louis

(1674–1750)

FRENCH SURGEON

Petit was the leading French surgeon of the first half of the 18th century. Born in Paris, he served as first director of the Royal Academy of Surgery, founded in 1731.

His major surgical innovation was that of the screw tourniquet in 1718. In the 16th century Ambrose Paré had introduced the ligature into surgery. It had found little use in such major surgery as the amputation of a limb because of the difficulty involved in arresting the blood flow in order to permit the tying of up to 50 ligatures. Surgeons therefore continued with their customary mode of controlling bleeding, namely cauterization.

Petit's innovation thus allowed surgeons at last to utilize the earlier work of Paré. Petit was also the first to open the mastoid process for the evacuation of pus.

Petri, Julius Richard

(1852–1921)

GERMAN BACTERIOLOGIST

Petri (**pay**-tree or **pet**-ree), who was born at Barmen in Germany, worked initially as an assistant to Robert Koch before his later appointment to a curatorship of the Hygiene Museum in Berlin. In 1887 Petri introduced a modification into the craft of the bacteriologist, which has persisted virtually unchanged to the present day. Koch's practice was to spread his bacterial sample on a glass slide, which was then placed under a bell jar to avoid contamination. The covered dishes introduced by Petri were less bulky, easier to handle, and could also be conveniently stacked. They consequently gained rapid acceptance throughout the laboratories of the world.

Pettenkofer, Max Joseph von

(1818–1901)

GERMAN CHEMIST AND PHYSICIAN

> Impurity cleaves longest and most tenaciously to the soil, which suffers no change of place, like air and water.
> —*The Relations of the Air to the Clothes We Wear, the House We Live In, and the Soil We Dwell On* (1872)

Born at Lichtenheim in Germany, Pettenkofer (**pet**-en-koh-fer) qualified as a physician in 1843. He became professor of medical chemistry at Munich in 1847 and later was appointed to the first chair of hygiene. In 1882 he published one of the earliest textbooks on hygiene, *Handbuch der Hygiene* (Handbook of Hygiene). Although he was one of the earliest campaigners for better sanitation and hygiene in general, he was one of the most bitter and articulate opponents of the germ theory of disease, which, through the work of Louis Pasteur and Robert Koch, was becoming widely accepted. Pettenkofer supported the miasma theory of disease, which supposed that infection was caused and spread by toxic vapors that tended to concentrate in special areas. The job of the hygienist was to eliminate such concentrations.

In 1883 Koch claimed to have discovered the causative agent of cholera. In 1892 Pettenkofer attempted to disprove Koch's theory by drinking a glass of water swarming with cholera vibrios. Fortunately he survived this dramatic experiment, which supported his belief in the miasma theory until his death.

Earlier he had collaborated with Carl Voit in constructing a calorimeter big enough for a human being, which they used in attempting to calculate the basic metabolic rate of man.

Pfeffer, Wilhelm Friedrich Philipp

(1845–1920)

GERMAN BOTANIST

Born the son of a pharmacist in Grebenstein, Germany, Pfeffer (**pfeffer**) gained his PhD in botany and chemistry from the University of Göttingen in 1865. He continued pharmaceutical studies at Marburg until, realizing his increasing preference for botany, he left in 1867 for Berlin where he studied the germination of *Selaginella*. He continued this research at Würzburg under Julius Sachs who encouraged him to pursue a career in plant physiology. He was professor of botany at Basel, Tubingen, and Leipzig universities.

Pfeffer did much work on irritability in plants, but he is best remembered for his improvement of the semipermeable membrane and its application in the measurement of osmotic pressure. He demonstrated that osmotic pressure is correlated with the concentration of the solution within the membrane and with temperature.

Pfeiffer, Richard Friedrich Johannes

(1858–1945)

GERMAN BACTERIOLOGIST

Born at Zduny in Poland, Pfeiffer (**pfI**-fer) trained as a military surgeon in Berlin, serving in the German army until 1889. He then worked with Robert Koch at the Institute of Hygiene before being appointed (1899) professor of hygiene at the University of Königsberg. In 1909 Pfeiffer moved to a similar post at the University of Breslau, where he remained until his retirement in 1926.

In 1892 Pfeiffer discovered the bacillus *Haemophilus influenzae* (known as *Pfeiffer's bacillus*), which he found in the throats of patients in the influenza epidemic of 1889–92 and declared to be responsible for the disease. Influenza was later shown (in 1933) by the British pathologist Christopher Andrewes and his colleagues to be a viral infection, with Pfeiffer's bacillus responsible for many of the complications.

Pfeiffer's most important discovery, however, was that of bacteriolysis in 1894. He had injected cholera germs into a guinea pig already immunized against the infection. When he extracted some of the germs from the guinea pig and examined them under the microscope he observed that they first became motionless and then swelled up and burst. He went on to note that this destruction (lysis) of the bacteria would also take place in an artificial environment but could be stopped by heating to over 60°C.

Pfeiffer was in fact observing and describing for the first time a complicated immune reaction by the body to an invading germ. It was this work that stimulated Jules Bordet to look more closely at the immune system and led to his discovery of complement. It also did much to confirm Emil von Behring's theory of antibodies in 1891.

Philips, Peregrine

(about 1830)

BRITISH CHEMIST

Philips, who was born in the port of Bristol, western England, became a manufacturer of vinegar. In 1831 he took out a patent for a new way to produce sulfuric acid which, although not immediately taken up, was to account for more than half the world's production later in the 19th century. In the lead chamber process introduced by John Roebuck, sulfur was burned in a lead chamber with water and a potassium nitrate catalyst. The disadvantages of this were that it was slow, produced dilute acid, and required considerable expense in the construction of the lead chambers.

Philips proposed oxidizing the sulfur dioxide into sulfur trioxide by passing it through a tube packed with a catalyst of fine platinum wires. This gas was then dissolved in water or in sulfuric acid. There were difficulties with the process, which prevented its immediate adoption. The platinum soon became contaminated and useless, requiring costly replacement and, although the contact process could make much more concentrated acid there was at the time no real demand for very strong acid. The difficulty was initially overcome by Rudolph Messel in 1876, and today the contact process accounts for the production of over 90% of the world's sulfuric acid.

Phillips, David Chilton, Baron

(1924–   )

BRITISH BIOPHYSICIST

Phillips, who was born at Ellesmere in Shropshire, gained his doctorate from University College, Cardiff. He then moved to the National Research Laboratories in Ottawa, where he worked until his return to

Britain in 1955. He worked first at the Royal Institution before being appointed in 1966 to the chair of molecular biophysics at Oxford, a post he held until his retirement in 1990. He was raised to the British peerage in 1994.

In 1965 Phillips achieved the major success of working out the full three-dimensional structure of lysozyme, the first enzyme to be so analyzed and, following the success of John Kendrew with myoglobin and Max Perutz with hemoglobin, only the third protein to be so treated. Lysozyme was first identified by Alexander Fleming in 1922 and shown by him to be capable of dissolving certain bacterial cells. In 1966 Phillips related the structure of the molecule to its bacteriolytic power. He demonstrated that the 129-amino-acid molecule is folded so as to form a cleft that holds the substrate molecule while it is being broken in two. More precisely, he was able to show that hexasaccharides of the bacterial cell wall are split between the fourth and fifth sugar rings by the charged amino-acid residues, aspartic and glutamic acid, which align with them in the enzyme's cleft.

Phillips had thus succeeded in explaining for the first time the catalytic activity of an enzyme in stereochemical terms.

Philolaus of Croton

(about 475 BC)

GREEK PHILOSOPHER

Little of any reliability is known of Philolaus (fil-oh-**lay**-us). Apart from such stories as that Plato derived his *Timaeus* from him and that he settled in Tarentum in southern Italy, he is generally only mentioned by classical writers as the author of the Pythagorean cosmology. He proposed, for unknown reasons, that the center of the universe was occupied not by the Earth or even the Sun but by a previously unsuspected fire. The reason this had never been seen was simply that the Earth in its orbit always turned its inhabited face away from it. There was also the counter-Earth or *antichthon*, again out of our view for always being between the Earth and the "central hearth." All Aristotle, the main source of Pythagorean cosmology, could suppose was that it was introduced to make the number of heavenly bodies in orbit – the fixed stars, five planets, Earth, Moon, Sun, and antichthon – equal ten, the Pythagorean sacred number.

The Pythagorean model with its apparently arbitrary features lay well outside the mainstream of Greek cosmology. However, it did propose that the Earth moved in an orbit – the first recorded instance of such a speculation.

Philon of Byzantium

(about 100 BC)

GREEK SCIENTIST

Philon (**fī**-lon) studied the flow of liquids and gases. He designed an instrument for showing the expansion of air, which may have been one of the earliest thermometers.

Piazzi, Giuseppe

(1746–1826)

ITALIAN ASTRONOMER

> I congratulate you on your splendid discovery of this new star. I do not think that others have noticed it, and because of its smallness, it is unlikely that many astronomers will see it.
> —On the discovery of Ceres. Barnaba Oriani, letter to Piazzi, January 1801

Born at Ponte in Valtellina, Italy, Piazzi (**pyaht**-see or pee-**aht**-see) was a monk who originally taught philosophy but later in life developed an interest in astronomy. He became professor of mathematics at Palermo, Sicily, setting up an observatory there in 1787. He was a careful observer, publishing a catalog of 7,646 stars in 1814. In his work he had found that proper motion was not the rarity assumed by some but the property of most stars and he found that 61 Cygni had a very large proper motion of 5.2″. His most dramatic discovery was that of the minor planet Ceres in 1801. He named it after the goddess of agriculture, once widely worshipped in Sicily. Although Piazzi lost the planet, its position was precisely predicted by Karl Gauss after a staggering feat of calculation based on three observations of Piazzi. Three more similar bodies were quickly found. He had a dispute with William Herschel over their nature. Piazzi proposed that they shoud be called "planetoids" but Herschel's alternative suggestion of "asteroid" has proved more acceptable until quite recently.

Picard, Jean

(1620–1682)

FRENCH ASTRONOMER

Born at La Flèche in northwestern France, Picard (pee-**kar**) succeeded Pierre Gassendi as professor of astronomy at the Collège de France in 1655. He helped to found the Paris Observatory and conducted fundamental researches into the size of the Earth. Using new instruments such as William Gascoigne's micrometer he established an accurate baseline and by a series of 17 triangles between Malvoisin and Amiens calculated one degree to be 69.1 miles (111.2 km). This result proved to be extremely valuable to Newton in his calculations on the attractive force of the Moon.

Picard also determined accurately the position of Tycho Brahe's observatory at Uraniborg (this information was necessary in order to analyze and interpret Tycho's observations). He further noted, but was not able to explain, an annual periodic motion of Polaris (approximately 40″). James Bradley later explained this as the aberration of light.

Piccard, Auguste

(1884–1962)

SWISS PHYSICIST

Piccard (pee-**kar**) was born at Basel in Switzerland, where his father was a professor of chemistry at the university, and was educated at the Federal Institute of Technology, Zurich. Although he taught in America at

Chicago and Minnesota and in Switzerland at Lausanne he spent the main part of his career in Belgium where, from 1922 to 1954, he was professor of physics at the Brussels Polytechnic.

Piccard is remembered for his explorations of both the atmosphere and the ocean floor. Dissatisfied with sending up unmanned instruments, he designed a pressurized cabin to be attached to a balloon and with his brother, Jean Felix, ascended to a height of about 11 miles (18 km) in 1931. Later balloonists using his techniques extended this to 20 miles (32 km).

He was equally dissatisfied with attempts to study the ocean floor and introduced (1947) a craft he called a bathyscape, which was maneuverable and on its first test in 1948 reached a depth of nearly a mile. He then built a second craft, the *Trieste*, which descended 2½ miles (4 km) into the Mediterranean. This was later sold to the U.S. Navy and in 1960 Piccard's son Jacques, together with a naval officer, descended 7 miles (11 km) in it to the bottom of the Marianas trench in the Pacific.

Pickering, Edward Charles

(1846–1919)

AMERICAN ASTRONOMER

Born in Boston, Massachusetts, Pickering graduated from Harvard in 1865. He taught physics at the Massachusetts Institute of Technology before becoming professor of astronomy and director of the observatory at Harvard in 1876, remaining there until his death in 1919.

Pickering made innovations in spectrography. Instead of placing a small prism at the focus to capture the light of a single star, he put a large prism in front of the objective, obtaining at the same time a spectrogram of all the stars in the field sufficiently bright to affect the emulsion. This made possible the massive surveys he wanted to organize and enabled the publication in 1918 of the *Henry Draper Catalogue*, compiled by Annie Cannon, giving the spectral types of 225,300 stars. The other innovation in instruments due to him was the meridian photometer introduced in 1880. In this, images of stars near the meridian would be reflected at the same time as the image of Polaris. The brightness could then be equalized and as the brightness of Polaris was known, that of the meridian stars could easily be calculated. More than a million observations with such instruments permitted the compilation of the Harvard catalog giving the magnitude of some 50,000 stars. He was able to include stars of the southern hemisphere in this catalog, for in 1891 he had established an observatory in Arequipa, Peru, with the help of his brother William Henry Pickering.

One further improvement due to Edward Pickering was his introduction, around 1900, of the alphabetic system of spectral classes.

Pickering, William Henry

(1858–1938)

AMERICAN ASTRONOMER

Pickering, the younger brother of Edward Pickering, was also an astronomer. Born in Boston, Massachusetts, he studied at the Massachusetts Institute of Technology where he worked after graduating in 1879. In 1887 he moved to the Harvard College Observatory where his brother was director. He set up a number of observing stations for Harvard including that at Arequipa, Peru, in 1891 and Mandeville, Jamaica, in 1900. He took charge of the latter in 1911, converting it into his own private observatory following his retirement in 1924.

He also helped Percival Lowell set up his private observatory in Flagstaff, Arizona, and, also like Lowell, concerned himself with the trans-Neptunian planet. In 1919, on the basis of past records, he predicted that a new planet would be found near the constellation of Gemini but photographic surveys failed to confirm his prediction. When the planet was finally detected in 1930 by Clyde Tombaugh, Pickering made a somewhat exaggerated claim to be its discoverer.

He made extensive observations of Mars and claimed, like Lowell, that he saw signs of life on the planet by observing what he took to be oases in 1892. He went further than Lowell, however, when in 1903 he claimed to observe signs of life on the Moon. By comparing descriptions of the Moon from Giovanni Riccioli's 1651 chart onward, he thought he had detected changes that could have been due to the growth and decay of vegetation.

He was more successful in 1899 when he discovered Phoebe, the ninth satellite of Saturn. This was the first planetary satellite with retrograde motion to be detected, i.e., with orbital motion directed in an opposite sense to that of the planets. His 1905 report of a tenth satellite, which he confidently named Themis, was not substantiated.

Pictet, Ame

(1857–1937)

SWISS CHEMIST

Pictet (peek-**tay**), a banker's son from Geneva in Switzerland, became professor of chemistry there. He synthesized a number of alkaloids including nicotine (1903), confirming the formula that had been proposed in 1891. He also synthesized laudanosine and papaverine (1909).

Pictet, Raoul Pierre

(1846–1929)

SWISS CHEMIST AND PHYSICIST

Born in Geneva, Pictet was professor of physics at the university there from 1879 and at the University of Berlin from 1886. He later moved to Paris.

Pictet was first interested in the production of artificial ice and then turned his attention to the study of extremely low temperatures and the liquefaction of gases. On 22 December 1877 he was involved in one of those strange simultaneous discoveries that sometimes occur in science. He announced on that day, by telegram to the French Academy, that he had liquefied oxygen. Just two days later the French physicist Louis Cailletet made a similar announcement.

Both Pictet and Cailletet had recognized that both cooling and compression were necessary to liquefy oxygen but they had achieved this using different techniques. Pictet had used his cascade method, in which he evaporated liquid sulfur dioxide to liquefy carbon dioxide, which in turn was allowed to evaporate and to cool oxygen to below its critical temperature. The oxygen could then be liquefied by pressure. The advantage over Cailletet's method was that it produced the liquid gas in greater quantity and was easier to apply to other gases.

Pierce, John Robinson

(1910–   )

AMERICAN COMMUNICATIONS ENGINEER

Born in Des Moines, Iowa, Pierce was educated at the California Institute of Technology, graduating in 1933 and obtaining his PhD in 1936. He then worked for the Bell Telephone Laboratories, New York, from 1936 until 1971 when he became professor of engineering at the California Institute of Technology, retiring in 1980.

At the Bell Laboratories Pierce improved the design of traveling wave tubes for microwave equipment. He also invented the electrostatically focused electron-multiplier tube and the electron gun, the basis of television sets and other visual display equipment. During World War II he helped to develop the equipment used in the U.S. radar system. In 1952 he became the director of electronics research at the Bell Laboratories. His efforts, ignored at first, later helped to establish the NASA communications satellites, the first attempt being a simple radio-reflector balloon, Echo 1, which was launched in 1960.

After retiring from the Bell Laboratories Pierce became a professor of engineering at the California Institute of Technology. He has also written science fiction throughout his career using the pseudonym J. J. Coupling.

Pilbeam, David Roger

(1940–   )

BRITISH PHYSICAL ANTHROPOLOGIST

Pilbeam was born in the English coastal town of Brighton and educated at Cambridge University, where he completed his PhD in 1967. He moved to Yale in 1968 and was appointed professor of anthropology in

1974, a post he held until 1981 when he accepted a similar position at Harvard.

Anthropologists distinguish between hominids, which are human species and their extinct ancestors, and the hominoids, which comprise the superfamily containing humans and apes. Pilbeam has sought to identify the time in the Miocene (between 25 million and 5 million years ago) which saw the separation of the hominids from the hominoids. In 1932 in the Siwalik Hills in India G. E. Lewis had discovered the fossil remains of a creature he named *Ramapithecus* (Rama's ape) in rocks about 15 million years old. In 1961 Elwyn Simon, later to be a Yale colleague of Pilbeam, was struck by the small canines and the shape of the dental arch of *Ramapithecus*, seeing in them hominid characteristics.

Pilbeam began a general review of Miocene hominoid fossils. In *Ramapithecus* he thought he could see signs of bipedality. With its reduced canines, he argued, food must have been prepared in some way, implying that the hands must have been free, possibly to use tools. The creature could well have been both bipedal and terrestrial. In 1968 Pilbeam argued that about 20 million years ago there had been three species of *Dryopithecus* (tree ape) and that these had been ancestral to the chimpanzee, gorilla, and orangutan (pongids). This left the 15 million year old *Ramapithecus* as a hominid and the possibility that hominid and pongid lines could have been separated for 30 million years and more.

Pilbeam's account received wide support and appeared to become increasingly confirmed with the discovery of further fossils. Yet by the late 1960s evidence of another kind that would seriously question the position of *Ramapithecus* was beginning to appear. Biologists such as Vincent Sarich had begun to use variations in protein structure to measure evolutionary divergence. Their evidence suggested that humans and African apes had been separated for no longer than five million years. Clearly, *Ramapithecus* could not have been a Miocene hominid.

Following Sarich's revelations and further fieldwork, Pilbeam has proposed a new evolutionary sequence. In 1980 in Turkey he discovered a partial skull of *Sivapithecus*, a hominoid fossil very similar to *Ramapithecus*. It also closely resembled the sole surviving Asian great ape, the orangutan, but showed little resemblance to any of the australopithecines. Thus the 15 million year old *Ramapithecus* represents not the hominid–hominoid split, but the hominoid divergence between the African and Asian great apes.

Pilbeam has since offered the opinion that he would "never again cling so firmly to one particular evolutionary scheme," and that "fossils themselves can solve only part of the puzzle, albeit an important part."

Pincus, Gregory Goodwin

(1903–1967)

AMERICAN PHYSIOLOGIST

Born in Woodbine, New Jersey, and educated at Cornell and Harvard, Pincus was research director at the Worcester Foundation for Experimental Biology, Shrewsbury, Massachusetts. His most significant work was in reproductive physiology, notably his investigations of human birth control, which led to his developing, with Min Chueh Chang and John Rock, the now famous "pill." This form of oral contraception is based upon the use of synthetic hormones that have an inhibitory effect on the female reproductive system, preventing fertilization but still allowing sexual freedom. Pincus discovered that the steroid hormone progesterone, which is found in greater concentrations during pregnancy, is responsible for the prevention of ovulation in pregnancy. With the development, in the fifties, of synthetic hormones, similar in action to progesterone, Pincus saw the possibility of using such synthetics as oral contraceptives. The first clinical trials were conducted in 1954 and proved extremely successful.

In 1963, Pincus became the first chairman of the Oral Advisory Group of the International Planned Parenthood Federation.

Pinel, Philippe

(1745–1826)

FRENCH PHYSICIAN AND PSYCHIATRIST

Pinel (pee-**nel**), who was born at Saint-André in France, obtained his MD in 1773 from the University of Toulouse. He then worked as a translator and teacher, visiting mentally disturbed people in his spare time. The articles published as a result of these visits led to his appointment at the Hospice de Bicêtre, the Paris asylum for men, in 1793. Two years later Pinel moved to the Saltpêtrière, the hospital for the poor, aged, and insane, where he served as chief physician until his death in 1826.

Pinel is mainly remembered for his dramatic act in unchaining the insane of Paris, believing "air and liberty" to be a far more effective treatment. His general approach seems to have been to bring the patient to an awareness of his position and a recognition of his surroundings.

Pinel published a full account of his new techniques in his *Traité medico-philosophique sur l'aliénation mentale ou la manie* (1801; Medico-Philosophical Treatise on Mental Alienation or Mania). His influence led to the general adoption of a far more enlightened approach to the treatment of mental patients. In 1798 Pinel published a more conventional work, *Nosographie philosophique* (Philosophical Classification of Diseases), an attempt to classify diseases in the way Linnaeus had earlier classified animals.

Pippard, Sir Alfred Brian

(1920–   )

BRITISH PHYSICIST

> The value of a formalism lies not only in the range of problems to which it can be successfully applied, but equally in the degree to which it encourages physical intuition in guessing the solution of intractable problems.
> —*Physics Bulletin* No. 20 (1969)

Pippard, the son of a professor of engineering, was born at Leeds in the north of England and educated at the University of Cambridge. After wartime research on the development of radar, he obtained his PhD from Cambridge in 1947. He remained at the university for the rest of his career, serving as Plummer Professor of Physics from 1960 until 1971 and Cavendish Professor until 1982.

After World War II Pippard began to use microwaves to study superconductors, in particular the conduction in a thin layer at the surface of the material. He introduced the idea of "coherence" in superconductors – the way in which electrons "act together" so that an effect at one point influences electrons a certain distance away. Pippard's ideas were explained by the BCS theory of John Bardeen and his colleagues. Pippard has also worked on microwave absorption at metal surfaces as a method of investigating the conduction electrons. His book *Dynamics of Conduction Electrons* (1964) deals with metallic conductivity. His most recent work is *Magnetoresistance in Metals* (1989).

Pirie, Norman Wingate

(1907–   )

BRITISH BIOCHEMIST

My teacher, [Frederick Gowland] Hopkins, often commented on the craving for certainty that led so many physicists into mysticism or into the Church and similar organisations... Faith seems to be an occupational hazard for physicists.
—*Penguin New Biology* (1954)

Pirie, son of the painter Sir George Pirie, was educated at Cambridge University where he studied under Frederick Gowland Hopkins. He remained at Cambridge as a demonstrator in the Biochemical Laboratory from 1932 until 1940. Pirie then moved to the Agricultural Research Station at Rothamsted, where he worked first as a virus physiologist (1940–46) and then as head of the biochemistry department (1947–73).

In 1935 Wendell Stanley succeeded in growing crystals of tobacco mosaic virus (TMV), claiming them to be protein. However, when, in collaboration with Frederick Bawden, Pirie repeated Stanley's work in 1936 he came across a small amount (about 0.5%) of phosphorus in the virus. As no amino acids contain phosphorus as an ingredient, this could only mean that TMV was not a pure protein. Pirie and Bawden concluded that TMV was in fact a nucleoprotein and went on to show that the nucleic acid present was the same as that derived from yeast, namely, RNA. This finding was of fundamental importance, providing an impetus for work on molecular biology in the following decade.

Pirie, a prolific author, has written on such topics as contraception, the origin of life, and the organization of science. In later life he turned to the technical problem of extracting edible protein in large quantities from plants, and in such popular books as *Food Resources* (1969) he has given publicity to the nutritional problems of the world.

Pitzer, Kenneth Sanborn

(1914–   )

AMERICAN THEORETICAL CHEMIST

Born in Pomona, California, Pitzer was educated at the California Institute of Technology and the University of California, Berkeley, where he obtained his PhD in 1937. He immediately joined the staff at Berkeley and served there as professor of chemistry from 1945 until 1961. Pitzer then moved to Rice University, Houston, where he served both as president and professor of chemistry until his return to California in 1968. After a brief period at Stanford, he was once more appointed professor of chemistry at Berkeley.

Pitzer has worked extensively on problems of molecular structure and in particular on a conformational analysis of cyclic and polycyclic paraffins. This he linked with detailed studies of the thermodynamic properties of hydrocarbons. His work here began in the late 1930s when it became apparent that supposedly straightforward calculations of the thermodynamic properties of such a simple molecule as ethane, C_2H_6, disagreed with experimental results. Pitzer and his colleagues were able to show that the anomaly was due to an unexpected restriction of the free rotation of the methyl groups, CH_3, around the carbon–carbon bonds. This in turn was shown to be due to the hydrogen atoms of the methyl group adopting different conformations with different potential energies as they rotated around the carbon–carbon bond. Later work by Pitzer concerned more complex molecules and motions and also extended his calculations to substances in the liquid, solid, and dissolved states. He has also produced a widely read textbook, *Quantum Chemistry* (1953).

Planck, Max Karl Ernst Ludwig

(1858–1947)

GERMAN PHYSICIST

An important scientific innovation rarely makes its way by gradually winning over and converting its opponents: it rarely happens that Saul becomes Paul. What does happen is that its opponents gradually die out, and that the growing generation is familiarized with the ideas from the beginning.
—*Scientific Autobiography* (1949)

Planck (plahngk or plangk) was born at Kiel in Germany, where his father was a professor of civil law at the university. He was educated at the universities of Berlin and Munich where he obtained his doctorate in 1880. He began his teaching career at the University of Kiel, moving to Berlin in 1889 and being appointed (1892) professor of theoretical physics, a post he held until his retirement in 1928.

Although Planck's early work was in thermodynamics, in 1900 he published a paper, *Zur Theorie der Gesetzes der Energieverteilung im Normal-Spektrum* (On The Theory of the Law of Energy Distribution in the Continuous Spectrum), which ranks him with Albert Einstein as one of the two founders of 20th-century physics. It is from this paper that quantum theory originated.

A major problem in physics at the end of the 19th century lay in explaining the radiation given off by a hot body. It was known that the intensity of such radiation increased with wavelength up to a maximum value and then fell off with increasing wavelength. It was also known that the radiation was produced by vibrations of the atoms in the body. For a perfect emitter (a so-called black body, which emits and absorbs at all wavelengths) it should have been possible to use thermodynamics to give a theoretical expression for black-body radiation. Various "radiation laws" were derived. Thus Wilhelm Wien in 1896 derived a law that applied only at short wavelengths. Lord Rayleigh and James Jeans produced a law applying at long wavelengths, but predicting that the body should have a massive emission of short-wavelength energy – the so-called "ultraviolet catastrophe."

Planck's problem was initially a technical one; he was simply searching for an equation that would allow the emission of radiation of all wavelengths by a hot body to be correctly described. He hit upon the idea of correlating the entropy of the oscillator with its energy. Following his intuition he found himself able to obtain a new radiation formula, which was in close agreement with actual measurements under all conditions.

There was, however, something unusual about the Planck formula. He had found that in seeking a relationship between the energy emitted or absorbed by a body and the frequency of radiation he had to introduce a constant of proportionality, which could only take integral multiples of a certain quantity. Expressed mathematically, $E = nh\nu$, where E is the energy, h is the constant of proportionality, ν is the frequency, and $n =$ 0, 1, 2, 3, 4, etc. It follows from this that nature was being selective in the amounts of energy it would allow a body to accept and to emit, allowing only those amounts that were multiples of $h\nu$. The value of h is very small, so that radiation of energy at the macroscopic level where n is very large is likely to *seem* to be emitted continuously.

Planck's introduction of what he called the "elementary quantum of action" was a revolutionary idea – a radical break with classical physics. Soon other workers began to apply the concept that "jumps" in energy could occur. Einstein's explanation of the photoelectric effect (1905), Niels Bohr's theory of the hydrogen atom (1913), and Arthur Compton's investigations of x-ray scattering (1923) were early successes of the quantum theory. In 1918 Planck was awarded the Nobel Prize for physics. The constant h (6.626196×10^{-34} joule second) is known as the *Planck constant* – the value "$h = 6,62 \cdot 10^{-27}$ erg•sec" is engraved on his tombstone in Göttingen.

By the time of his retirement Planck had become the leading figure in German science and was therefore to play a crucial role in its relations with the Nazis. His attitude was that of prudent cooperation with the overriding aim of retaining the integrity of German science and preventing it from falling into international ridicule. Although he did not publicly protest against the harassment of Jewish scientists, considering such barbarisms a temporary madness, he did, in 1933, raise the issue with Hitler himself. He argued that the racial laws of 1933, barring Jews from government positions, would endanger the preeminence of German science. Hitler is reported to have expressed a willingness to do without science for a few years. Nor did Planck succeed in protecting the institutions of German science for in 1939 the presidency of the academy went to a party member, T. Vahlen, who lost no time in turning it virtually into an organ of the party.

Planck's later years, despite the honors that came his way, were indeed bitter ones. "My sorrow cannot be expressed in words," he lamented at one point. During World War I his elder son Karl died from wounds suffered in action, and his twin daughters, Grete and Emma, died during childbirth in 1917 and 1919, respectively. In World War II he was forced to witness the destruction of his country and of German science and its institutions. His own home, with all his possessions, was totally destroyed by allied bombing in 1944. Worst of all, his one surviving child, Erwin, was executed in 1945 for complicity in the 1944 attempt to assassinate Hitler.

Planté, Gaston

(1834–1889)

FRENCH PHYSICIST

Born at Orthez in France, Planté (plahn-**tay**) worked on electric cells and was the first to design and construct a storage battery (i.e., a cell that could be recharged with electricity). His design used lead electrodes in sulfuric acid, similar to the type used today in automobile batteries.

The *Planté battery* was invented in 1859. It was soon in use to illuminate railroad carriages and drive automobiles. Its main disadvantage was its weight. In 1888 a 666 ampere-hour battery could weigh as much as 2.8 hundredweights (127 kg).

Plaskett, John Stanley

(1865–1941)

CANADIAN ASTRONOMER

Plaskett, who was born at Woodstock, Ontario, was initially trained as a mechanic and began work as such for the physics department of the University of Toronto. He eventually graduated from there in physics and mathematics in 1899. When he moved, in 1903, to the Dominion Observatory in Ottawa it was as mechanical superintendent and not as an astronomer. He gradually moved into astronomy, however, and in 1918 became director of the newly established Dominion Astrophysical Observatory at Victoria, British Columbia, for which he had organized the design, construction, and installation of a new 72-inch (1.8-m) reflecting telescope. He retired in 1935.

Plaskett's field of research was spectroscopy, in particular the measurement of radial velocities of celestial bodies, i.e., their velocities along the line of sight, from the shift in their spectral lines. Using the 72-inch reflector and a highly sensitive spectrograph, many spectroscopic binary systems were discovered. In 1922 Plaskett identified an extremely massive star as a binary, now known as *Plaskett's star*. In 1927 Plaskett provided confirmatory evidence for the theory of galactic rotation put forward by Bertil Lindblad and Jan Oort.

By 1928 Plaskett, in collaboration with J. A. Pearce, had obtained evidence for the hypothesis formulated by Arthur Eddington in 1926 that interstellar matter was widely distributed throughout the Galaxy; their results showed that interstellar absorption lines, mainly of calcium, took part in the galactic rotation and so the interstellar matter was not confined to separate star clusters. Although this result was first announced by Otto Struve in 1929, Plaskett felt he had priority and was convinced that Struve had obtained his results from him.

Plato

(*c.* 428 BC–347 BC)

GREEK PHILOSOPHER

Mind is ever the ruler of the universe.
—*Philebus*

Little is known of Plato's early life. He apparently came from an established Athenian family active in politics. With the execution of Socrates in 399 BC he left Athens for some years and visited, among other places, Sicily in about 389 where he made contact with the Pythagoreans and much impressed Dion, the brother-in-law of Dionysius I, the tyrant of Syracuse. On his return to Athens shortly afterward he founded in about 387 the most famous of all institutions of learning, the Academy, which in one form or another remained viable until its closure by the emperor Justinian in 529 AD. On the death of Dionysius I in 367 BC

Plato returned to Sicily at the invitation of Dion to try to educate Dionysius II as the new philosopher-king, attempting once more in 361. The visits were disastrous and ended with Plato dismissing Sicily as a place where "happiness was held to consist in filling oneself full twice a day and never sleeping alone at night."

It is virtually impossible to overestimate the impact of Plato on Western thought. His views, preserved and transmitted through the distorting medium of neo-Platonists and Christian fathers alike, came to influence theology, politics, ethics, education, and aesthetics just as much as they have (and still do) metaphysics and logic. Nor were his contributions to the development of science negligible. It was Plato who posed to the astronomers of his day, such as Eudoxus, the question: "By the assumption of what uniform and orderly motions can the apparent motions of the planets be accounted for?" The request that there should be but one explanation applying to the seemingly disparate observed motions of each planet did much to shape the development of Greek astronomy and to add to it a characteristic dimension of model building lacking, for example, in Babylonian astronomy.

He also, in the *Timaeus*, under the influence of the Pythagoreans of Sicily, introduced an alternative form of atomism to that of Democritus. He began with the result of Theaetetus that there can be only five regular solids, the tetrahedron, cube, octahedron, dodecahedron, and the icosahedron, and went on to assign to each of the four elements of Empedocles a characteristic shape of one of the regular solids. The cube as the most stable is assigned to the least mobile element, earth; the pyramid is assigned to fire; the octahedron to air; and the icosahedron to water. To the remaining figure, the dodecahedron, most closely approaching the sphere, Plato associated the "spherical heaven."

The main significance of Plato's thought for science was thus to establish the vital tradition, originating with the Pythagoreans and finding ready echoes in the work of Galileo and Kepler, of the mathematical analysis of nature. It is said that an inscription over the vestibule of the Academy read: "Let no one enter here who is ignorant of Geometry."

Playfair, John

(1748–1819)

SCOTTISH MATHEMATICIAN AND GEOLOGIST

> How different would geological literature be today if men had tried to think and write like Playfair.
> —Archibald Geikie, *The Founders of Geology* (1905)

Born at Benvie in Scotland, Playfair studied at St. Andrews University before becoming minister of Liff and Benvie in 1773. He was made a professor of mathematics at Edinburgh University in 1785 and professor of natural philosophy in 1805.

Playfair was a friend of the geologist James Hutton and in his *Illustrations of the Huttonian Theory of the Earth* (1802) he amplified and explained Hutton's uniformitarian ideas. Hutton's own work had been notoriously hard to follow and Playfair brought uniformitarianism to a considerably larger public. He also pioneered the idea that a river carves out its own valley.

Although he is better known as a geologist Playfair did make contributions of note to mathematics, in particular to geometry. In 1795 he published his *Elements of Geometry* in which he set out an alternative version of Euclid's fifth postulate, which, given the truth of the other postulates, is equivalent to Euclid's original formulation. This postulate is consequently now known as "Playfair's axiom" and asserts that for any line (L) and point (P) not on L there is one and only one line, L′, through P parallel to L.

Playfair, Lyon, 1st Baron

(1818–1898)

BRITISH CHEMIST AND POLITICIAN

Playfair was born at Chumar in India while his father was inspector-general of hospitals in the Bengal area. He traveled to England to be educated and attended St. Andrews University. In 1835 he began studying medicine at the Andersonian Institute, Glasgow, but abandoning medicine because of ill health he later took up the study of chemistry at University College, London, and with Justus von Liebig at Giessen. Playfair had an extremely varied career. As an academic he became professor of chemistry at the Royal Institute, Manchester, in 1842 and he later held the chemistry chair at Edinburgh University (1858–69). In 1868 he was elected a member of parliament for the universities of Edinburgh and St. Andrews and served until 1892. As a politician he was reasonably successful, serving as postmaster general in 1873 and as deputy speaker of the House of Commons (1880–83). He was raised to the British peerage in 1892, becoming 1st Baron Playfair of St. Andrews.

For a short period (1841–43) he was manager of a textile-printing factory in Clitheroe. His main work, however, was as a civil servant and a propagandist for science. In 1853 a new government department of science and art was created with Playfair as joint secretary. He was also a member of Prince Albert's circle and organized the Great Exhibition of 1851.

Playfair's own chemical work included a study of the atomic volume and specific gravity (relative density) of hydrated salts, conducted with James Joule.

Pliny the Elder

(23 AD–79 AD)

ROMAN PHILOSOPHER

> Why it [quartz] is formed with hexagonal faces cannot be easily explained; and any explanation is complicated by the fact that, on the one hand, its terminal points are not symmetrical and that, on the other hand, its faces are so perfectly smooth that no craftsmanship could achieve the same effect.
>
> —*Natural History*

Pliny (full name Gaius Plinius Secundus) was born at Novum Comum, now Como in Italy. His monumental *Natural History* (published in 77 AD), the only survival of his writings, incorporates a summary of the knowledge of his time, the greater part of it based on the works of earlier writers. In many respects Pliny's work is highly uncritical, including, for example, descriptions of monsters, which were in turn copied by subsequent writers; in others he may be said to have been before his time, recognizing, for example, the spherical shape of the Earth. One of the great merits of the *Natural History* is the general theme of wonder it generates about the natural world. The most learned man of his age, Pliny died in true scientific tradition, succumbing to gases while trying to get as close as possible to the great eruption of Vesuvius (79 AD), which destroyed Pompeii and Herculaneum.

Plücker, Julius

(1801–1868)

GERMAN MATHEMATICIAN AND PHYSICIST

Born at Elberfeld in Germany, Plücker (**ploo**-ker) studied in Heidelberg, Berlin, and Paris and became a professor of mathematics at the universities of Halle and Bonn. He became professor of physics at Bonn in 1847.

He did important and pioneering work in analytic geometry in which he suggested taking straight lines rather than points as the basic geometrical concept. This idea led him to the celebrated principle of duality, stating the equal validity of certain equivalent theorems. He used this in a geometrical context but it now has far wider applications.

In about 1847 Plücker turned from mathematics to physics, studying the discharge of electricity through gases. He was the first to find that cathode rays can be deflected by a magnetic field, thus indicating their electric charge.

Later Plücker returned to his mathematical interests and did further work on geometry.

Poggendorff, Johann Christian

(1796–1877)

GERMAN PHYSICIST, BIOGRAPHER, AND BIBLIOGRAPHER

Poggendorff (**poh**-gen-dorf) was born at Hamburg in Germany and, after leaving school, worked for a pharmaceutical chemist, devoting his leisure hours to the study of science. In 1820 he entered the University of Berlin to study physics. In 1824 he became editor of *Annalen der Physik und Chemie* (Annals of Physics and Chemistry), a well-established periodical. He was appointed extraordinary professor at the University of Berlin in 1834 and was named a member of the Prussian Academy of Sciences in 1839.

Poggendorff was esteemed by his contemporaries for his work in the newly developing sciences of electricity and chemistry. He devised various measuring instruments, including a galvanometer (1821) and a magnetometer (1827), and carried out important experiments. With Leibig he introduced subscript figures into chemical formulas.

Poggendorff's lasting influence lies perhaps in his work as a biographer and bibliographer. As editor of *Annalen* he secured many excellent contributions, placed stress on articles with an experimental basis, presented translations of important foreign papers, and gave the journal a prominent position among scientific periodicals. He also wrote on the history of physics and lectured on that subject at the University of

Berlin. In 1863 he produced the first two volumes of *Biographisch-Literarische Handworterbuch zur Geschichte der exakten Wissenschaften* (A Concise Biographical Literary Dictionary on the History of the Exact Sciences; now called "Poggendorff"); these included the dates and bibliographical references for over 8,000 researchers in the exact sciences of all periods and many countries up to 1858. This immensely important reference work is still published and now numbers over twenty volumes.

Pogson, Norman Robert

(1829–1891)

BRITISH ASTRONOMER

Pogson, who was born at Nottingham in England, started his career in 1852 as an assistant at the Radcliffe Observatory in Oxford. While there he discovered four new asteroids: Amphitrite in 1854, Isis in 1856, and Ariadne and Hestia in 1857. He was to discover nine in all, including the first to be discovered on the continent of Asia and consequently called Asia (1891).

In 1860 he was appointed government astronomer at Madras. He remained in India for the rest of his life, conscious of the enormous amount of observational work that could be done there. He constructed star catalogs and a variable star atlas while there.

His most lasting achievement was the introduction of *Pogson's ratio*. It had been realized that the average first-magnitude star is about a hundred times brighter than stars of the sixth magnitude. He therefore proposed that this interval should be represented by five equal magnitudes, that is, one magnitude would equal $\sqrt[5]{100}$, which equals 2.512. This means that stars of increasing magnitude are roughly 2.5 times brighter. The system has survived in the form proposed by Pogson more than a century ago.

Poincaré, (Jules) Henri

(1854–1912)

FRENCH MATHEMATICIAN AND
PHILOSOPHER OF SCIENCE

The mind uses its faculty for creating only
when experience forces it to do so.
—*Science and Hypothesis* (1905)

Mathematical discoveries, small or great...are never born of spontaneous generation. They always presuppose a soil seeded with preliminary knowledge and well prepared by labor, both conscious and subconscious.
—Quoted by A. L. Mackay in *A Dictionary of Scientific Quotations* (1991)

Poincaré (pwan-ka-**ray**) was born at Nancy in eastern France and studied at the Ecole Polytechnique and the School of Mines. At first he had intended to become an engineer, but fortunately his mathematical interests prevailed and he took his doctorate in 1879 and then taught at the University of Caen. He was professor at the University of Paris from 1881 until his death.

As Poincaré is commonly referred to as the great universalist – the last mathematician to command the whole of the subject – an account of his work would have to cover the whole of mathematics. In pure mathematics he worked on probability theory, differential equations, the theory of numbers, and in his *Analysis situs* (1895; Site Analysis) virtually created the subject of topology. He was, however, hostile to the work on the foundations of mathematics carried out by Bertrand Russell and Gottlob Frege. The discovery of contradictions in their systems, disasters to Frege and Russell, was happily welcomed by Poincaré: "I see that their work is not as sterile as I supposed; it breeds contradictions."

He also deployed the powerful weapons of modern mathematics against a number of problems in mathematical physics and cosmology. In 1887 Oscar II of Sweden offered a prize of 2,000 krona for a solution to the question of whether or not the solar system is stable. Will the planets continue indefinitely in their present orbits? Or will some bodies move out of the system altogether, or collide catastrophically with each other? Poincaré published his answer in the monograph *Sur les trois corps et les equations de la dynamique* (1889; On the Three Bodies and

Equations of Kinetics). The title refers to what is now known as the "three-body problem": given three point masses with known initial positions and velocities, to work out their positions and velocities at any future time. The three-body problem had resisted all previous attempts to find a general solution. Poincaré also failed to find an analytical general solution, but he was awarded the prize for making significant advances in the ways of finding approximate solutions.

Poincaré also formulated a famous conjecture, which despite considerable effort and many false alarms remains unsolved. To a topologist an ordinary sphere is a two-dimensional manifold (a 2-sphere) – two-dimensional because, although it looks like a three-dimensional solid, only its surface is significant. A loop placed on its surface can be shrunk to a point, or, in the language of topology, the 2-sphere is "simply connected." This is seen as a defining property of a sphere. A torus, on the other hand, is not a sphere because not all loops placed upon it can be shrunk to points.

What about an n-sphere, the surface of an $n+1$-dimensional body? Poincaré's conjecture is that the n-sphere is the only simply connected manifold in higher dimensions, as the 2-sphere is the only simply connected 2-manifold. Stephen Smale proved in 1969 that the conjecture would hold for all dimensions $n > 4$, and in 1984 Michael Freedman added the case $n = 4$. The case of $n = 3$ remains a conjecture.

Poincaré, in such later books as *Science and Hypothesis* (1905), developed a radical conventionalism. The high-level laws of science, he argued, are conventions, adopted for ease and simplicity and not for "truth." What would happen, he asked, if we found a very large triangle defined by light rays with angles unequal to 180°? As Euclidean geometry is so useful in countless other ways we would more likely sacrifice our physics to preserve our geometry and conclude that light rays do not travel in straight lines.

Poisson, Siméon-Denis

(1781–1840)

FRENCH MATHEMATICIAN AND
MATHEMATICAL PHYSICIST

> At the very end of his [i.e., Poisson's] life, when it had become painful for him
> to speak, I saw him almost weep,...for he had become convinced that our young
> teachers were concerned solely with obtaining a post and possessed no love for
> science at all.
>
> —Antoine Augustin Cournot, *Souvenirs* (1913; Recollections)

Poisson (pwah-**son**), born the son of a local government administrator
at Pithiviers in France, studied at the Ecole Polytechnique, where his
teachers included Pierre Simon Laplace and Joseph Lagrange. He himself later held various teaching posts at the Ecole. His important mathematical work was largely in mathematical physics and he also did a
considerable amount of experimental work on heat and sound. In thermodynamics he played an important role in making the whole subject
amenable to mathematical treatment by showing how to quantify heat
precisely. He is also one of the principal founders of the mathematical
theory of elasticity.

Poisson is possibly best known for his work on probability, and he was
something of a pioneer in applying the techniques of mathematical probability to the social sciences, something that was extremely controversial
at the time. The term "law of large numbers" was introduced by Poisson
in his seminal work, *Recherches sur la probabilité des jugements* (1837;
Researches on the Probability of Opinions), in which he put forward his
discovery of the *Poisson distribution*. This is the distribution that is a special case of the binomial distribution obtained when the probability of
success in a given trial is some constant divided by the number of trials.

Although chiefly an applied mathematician Poisson also made some
significant contributions to pure mathematics, in particular to complex
analysis. It was Poisson who first thought of integrating complex functions along a path in the complex plane.

Polanyi, John Charles

(1929–)

CANADIAN CHEMIST

John Polanyi (pol-**yah**-nee) was the son of the distinguished physical chemist Michael Polanyi. Born in Berlin, Germany, he was educated at Manchester University and at Princeton, where he obtained his PhD in 1952. He moved soon after to Toronto University, being appointed professor of chemistry in 1962.

Beginning in the 1950s Polanyi has sought to throw light on the nature of chemical reactions. What actually happens, he asked, during the reaction $H + Cl_2 \rightarrow HCl + Cl$? The reaction was known to be strongly exothermic; it was not known, however, how this released energy was distributed in the various degrees of freedom of the reaction products. D. Herschbach had begun detailed investigations of reaction mechanics by measuring the velocities and angular distribution of the reaction products using molecular beams. In contrast Polanyi described his own method as one in which "the molecules formed in chemical reaction do the work by signaling to us their state of excitation...through infrared emission."

Initially Polanyi and his coworkers had to work with a detector "only slightly more sensitive than the palms of our hands...a thermocouple." They were soon able to replace this with semiconductor infrared detectors. By analyzing the infrared emission, Polanyi was able to measure how much of the reaction energy was stored as molecular vibration and rotation. In this way he was able to show that in the example cited above two distinct states of the molecule HC1 were formed: one with high vibrational and rotational excitation, but low translational energy; and the less common state with low vibrational and rotational energy but high translational energy. Polanyi has continued to work in the field of reaction dynamics and has developed many new techniques and derived numerous insights into the subject. For his contributions he shared the 1986 Nobel Prize for chemistry with Herschbach and Y. T. Lee.

Polanyi's work in infrared chemical luminescence led to the development of chemical lasers by G. Pimental and J. Kaspar in 1960.

Polanyi, Michael

(1891–1976)

HUNGARIAN–BRITISH PHYSICAL CHEMIST AND PHILOSOPHER

> The pursuit of science can be organized...in no other manner than by granting complete independence to all mature scientists. They will then distribute themselves over the whole field of possible discoveries, each applying his own special ability to the task that appears most profitable to him. The function of public authorities is not to plan research, but only to provide opportunities for its pursuit.
> —*The Logic of Liberty* (1951)

Polanyi, the son of a civil engineer, was educated at the university in his native Budapest, where he qualified in medicine in 1913, and at the Institute of Technology, Karlsruhe. He remained in Germany, working at the Institute for Fiber Chemistry from 1920 to 1923 and in Fritz Haber's institute. In 1933, with the rise of the Nazis, he moved to Manchester University, England, as professor of physical chemistry. From 1948 until his retirement in 1958 Polanyi, whose interests had become more philosophical, occupied a personal chair of social studies at Manchester.

His earliest success came from his work as an x-ray crystallographer on the structure of natural fibers in 1921. He also, in 1923, made the first use of the rotating-crystal apparatus to determine crystal structure. With Haber he worked extensively on the kinetics of chemical reactions, beginning there an important collaboration with Henry Eyring. In 1931 they constructed the first potential energy surface.

Later he became interested in the philosophy of science, exploring in his widely read book *Personal Knowledge* (1958) just how science can reconcile its claim to objective knowledge with the intensely personal and fallible manner in which it operates.

Poncelet, Jean-Victor

(1788–1867)

FRENCH MATHEMATICIAN

Poncelet (pawn-se-**lay**) was born at Metz in eastern France. A military engineer in Napoleon's Russian campaign, he was taken prisoner in 1812 during the retreat from Moscow, having been left for dead by the army. During his two years in Russia as a prisoner of war he set about reconstructing as much as he could remember of the mathematics he had learned as a student. He was able to go beyond merely reconstructing what he had been taught, to do original work.

Poncelet's important contribution to mathematics was in the field of projective geometry. He was one of the first to formulate and make extensive use of the principle of duality – the equivalence of certain related geometric concepts and theorems. He was also the first mathematician to introduce imaginary points into projective geometry.

Pond, John

(1767–1836)

BRITISH ASTRONOMER

Pond, the son of a London businessman, studied at Cambridge University until ill health forced him to leave. In 1798 he began a series of astronomical observations at Westbury in Wiltshire. These and earlier observations showed him that the instruments at the Royal Observatory at Greenwich had become defective. In 1811, on the recommendation of Nevil Maskelyne, he was appointed Astronomer Royal, an office he continued to hold until his resignation in 1835.

Pond is remembered for his major reform of the Royal Observatory, in terms of new instruments, new methods of observation, and a larger staff. He installed a six-foot mural circle in 1812 and a new transit instrument in 1816, both built by Edward Troughton. With these he compiled an accurate catalog of 1,113 stars, published by him in 1833. At a less fundamental level Pond introduced in the same year the Greenwich custom of "timeballs" by which, "every day from the top of a pole from the Easter Turret of the Royal Observatory at Greenwich, at the moment of one o'clock P.M." a ball was, and still is, dropped. This has been described as the world's "first public time signal."

Pond's term of office was far from harmonious. He was forced to suffer a series of attacks from Stephen Lee, assistant secretary of the Royal Society, from 1825, being accused of publishing contradictory and inaccurate data and of making insufficient observations. Although Pond was acquitted of "culpable" negligence, two of his assistants were reprimanded by a Royal Society Committee set up to investigate the observatory.

Ponnamperuma, Cyril Andrew

(1923–1994)

SINGHALESE–AMERICAN CHEMIST

Ponnamperuma (pon-am-pe-**roo**-ma), who was born at Galle (now in Sri Lanka), was educated at universities spanning three continents – namely Madras in India, Birkbeck College, London, and Berkeley in California where, in 1962, he obtained his PhD. After working in the exobiology division of NASA from 1963 he was appointed, in 1971, professor of chemistry and director of the Laboratory of Chemical Evolution at the University of Maryland.

In 1952 Stanley Miller illuminated discussion on the origin of life by showing that simple amino acids could be produced in a laboratory test tube under minimal conditions that might well have existed in the distant past. After Miller chemists were eager to see what other organic molecules could be produced in a variety of supposed primitive terrestrial environments.

In this field Ponnamperuma had a number of significant successes. In 1963, with Ruth Mariner and Carl Sagan, he irradiated adenine, ribose sugar, a nucleic acid, and a phosphate source and detected the formation of ATP (adenosine triphosphate), the basic cellular energy source. Ponnamperuma also managed, with Mariner and Melvin Calvin, to synthesize adenine by exposing a mixture of methane, ammonia, and water to beta particles and, in 1965, he derived various sugars by exposing formaldehyde to ultraviolet light. Such experimental results led Ponnamperuma to conclude, in 1972, that the basic units that constitute nucleic acids and proteins could have been synthesized by the various forms of energy in the early atmosphere.

However, this is but the first of the three necessary stages – construction of molecules from atoms, formation of molecules into polymers, and formation of polymers into organisms. Some simple dipeptides have been made, but beyond this there are major difficulties. Ponnamperuma's views are expressed fully in his *The Origins of Life* (1972).

Pons, Jean Louis

(1761–1831)

FRENCH ASTRONOMER

Born at Peyres in France, Pons (pawns) started his astronomical work in Marseilles before moving to Florence as director of the observatory in 1819. He was an assiduous comet hunter, discovering 37. He is known as the codiscoverer of the *Pons–Winnecke* and the *Pons–Brooks* comets. True fame seems to have missed him, however, for though he did in fact discover the comet with the shortest period of 3.3 years it was named for Encke, who first worked out its orbital period.

Pons, Stanley

(1943–   )

AMERICAN CHEMIST

Born the son of a textile-mill owner in Valdek, North Carolina, Pons was educated at Wake Forest University, North Carolina, and at Ann Arbor, Michigan. Instead of completing his PhD he was induced in 1966 to enter the family business. His interest in chemistry remained too strong and, consequently, he decided in 1975 to return to graduate school. He opted for the University of Southampton in England where he worked under Martin Fleischman, completing his doctorate in 1978. After holding junior posts at Oakland University, Michigan, and Alberta University, Canada, Pons was appointed in 1980 to a professorship in chemistry at the University of Utah, Salt Lake City.

In March 1989 Pons and his former supervisor Fleischman announced that they had achieved fusion of deuterium nuclei in a test tube at room temperature by using an electrolytic process. Their announcement made headline news around the world. However, subsequent work at other laboratories failed to reproduce the results, although Pons and Fleischman continued to insist on the validity of their claim.

Pontecorvo, Guido

(1907–   )

ITALIAN–BRITISH GENETICIST

Pontecorvo (pon-tay-**kor**-voh) was born in Pisa, Italy. Having graduated in agricultural sciences from the university in his native city of Pisa in 1928, he spent the following nine years in Florence, supervising the Tuscany cattle-breeding program. Political conditions caused him to leave Italy in 1938, his intention being to continue with similar work in Peru. However he first accepted an invitation to the Institute of Animal Genetics in Edinburgh, where he met the famous American geneticist Hermann Muller, another visitor at the institute. Under Muller's influence Pontecorvo became increasingly interested in pure genetics and together with Muller he devised an elegant method for investigating the genetic differences between species that produce sterile hybrids on crossing.

Pontecorvo remained in Edinburgh working on *Drosophila* species and gained his PhD in 1941. Two factors then prompted him to change from *Drosophila* genetics to fungal genetics, firstly the dire need for penicillin during World War II and secondly his interest in the structure and function of the gene, a topic more easily investigated in the fungi.

Pontecorvo's work on the fungus *Aspergillus nidulans* led to the discovery, with Joseph Roper, of the parasexual cycle in 1950. This cycle gives rise to genetic reassortment by means other than sexual reproduction and its discovery provided a method of genetically analyzing asexual fungi. Pontecorvo also put forward the idea of the gene as a unit of function, a theory substantiated by Seymour Benzer in 1955. Pontecorvo occupied the first chair of genetics at Glasgow University from 1955 until 1961, when he moved to the Imperial Cancer Research Fund. He retired in 1975.

Pope, Sir William Jackson

(1870–1939)

BRITISH CHEMIST

Pope, born the son of a city merchant in London, was educated at Finsbury Technical College and the Central Institution, London (later to become part of Imperial College). After acting as an assistant to Henry Armstrong, he served as head of the chemistry department at Goldsmith's College, London, from 1897 to 1901. He then occupied the chair of chemistry at Manchester until 1908 when he moved to a similar chair at Cambridge.

Pope's main work was in the field of stereochemistry and the optical activity of chemical compounds. Johannes Van't Hoff had shown in 1874 that the tetrahedral structure of the carbon atom would account for the molecular asymmetry of certain carbon compounds. Between 1898 and 1902 Pope was able to show that there were compounds where the asymmetry did not occur at carbon atoms; he showed, for example, that nitrogen, sulfur, and selenium could also act as asymmetric centers. Pope further demonstrated that compounds containing no asymmetric atoms could still be optically active because of overall asymmetry of the molecule.

During World War I Pope concentrated on developing war gases, particularly mustard gas. He was knighted in 1919.

Popov, Aleksandr Stepanovich

(1859–1906)

RUSSIAN PHYSICIST AND
ELECTRICAL ENGINEER

Popov (po-**pof**), the son of a priest from Bogoslavsky in Russia, was educated in a seminary to prepare him for a clerical profession. His interest however turned to physics and mathematics, which he studied at the University of St. Petersburg between 1877 and 1882. While still a student he worked in 1881 at the Electrotekhinik artel, which operated Russia's first electric power stations. He taught for a short time at the university and then in 1883 joined the staff of the Torpedo School at Kronstadt, where naval specialists were trained in all branches of electrical engineering and where he was able to conduct his own research. He subsequently became head of the physics department and remained there until 1900. Popov returned to St. Petersburg as professor at the Institute of Electrical Engineering in 1901 and was appointed its director in 1905. Later that year Popov's health was undermined by his refusal to take severe action against the political disturbances among his students and he died shortly after.

In 1888 Heinrich Hertz had produced and transmitted electromagnetic waves, arousing the interest of many scientists. Popov began experiments on the transmission and reception of the so-called Hertzian waves (radio waves) somewhat earlier than Marconi. He modified the coherer developed by Oliver Lodge for detecting these waves, making the first continuously operating detector. Connecting his coherer to a wire antenna, he was able in 1895 to receive and detect the waves produced by an oscillator circuit. His interests at this time, however, seemed more toward the investigation of atmospheric phenomena such as thunderstorms and lightning; he used his coherer connected to lightning conductors for this purpose. Stimulated by the 1896 patent awarded to Marconi, Popov again turned his attention to radio transmission and enlisted the help of the Russian navy. In 1897 he was able to transmit from ship to shore over a distance of 3 miles (5 km) and managed to persuade the naval authorities to begin installing radio equipment in its vessels. By the end of 1899 he had increased the distance of his ship to shore transmissions to 30 miles (48 km). He received little encouragement or support from the Russian government and did not commercialize his discoveries.

The Russian claim that Popov invented radio communication is not widely accepted, although he did publish in January 1896 a description of his receiving apparatus that coincides very closely with that described in Marconi's patent claim of June 1896. Popov is credited however with being the first to use an antenna in the transmission and reception of radio waves.

Popper, Sir Karl Raimund

(1902–1994)

AUSTRIAN–BRITISH PHILOSOPHER

Science may be described as the art of systematic oversimplification.
　　—*The Observer* (August 1982)

Our knowledge can only be finite, while our ignorance must necessarily be infinite.
　　—*Conjectures and Refutations* (1963)

Popper was born in the Austrian capital Vienna, where his father was a lawyer with an interest in literature and philosophy. After obtaining his PhD from the University of Vienna in 1928, he taught in a secondary school for some years and then lectured at various universities in England in 1935 and 1936. In 1937 he was appointed to a lectureship in philosophy at the University of New Zealand, Christchurch. After the war Popper returned to England and joined the London School of Economics, where he served as professor of logic and scientific method from 1949 until his retirement in 1969.

Popper's view of science, first fully formulated in his *Logik der Forschung* (1934; The Logic of Scientific Discovery, 1959), has found considerable support among working scientists and rather less from philosophers of science. The logic of science is not an inductive one, Popper claimed. Science does not begin by attempting to formulate laws and theories on the basis of carefully collected observations. Science, in fact, begins not with observations but with problems.

The problems are dealt with by constructing theories, laws, or hypotheses, which for Popper function as conjectures or guesses. But there may well be a multitude of conjectures, all proposing plausible solutions. Here Popper insists that the aim of science is not to attempt to select from the competing hypotheses and theories the one that is true, for such constructs can never be shown to be true. No matter how many observations confirm a theory, it is not possible to say that it is correct. We can, however, frequently show that theories are undoubtedly false.

Popper used this insight to insist that the basic procedure of science consists of strenuously attempting to falsify such conjectures and accepting those that have survived the most severe attempts at falsification. This acceptance does not confer truth on the conjecture. That a hypothesis has so far resisted attempts to falsify it is no guarantee that it will continue to pass future tests.

With such an intellectual framework Popper could easily solve the demarcation problem. Scientific theories can conceive of and describe facts that could falsify them, while what he termed the "pseudo sciences," such as Marxism and psychoanalysis, are able to interpret any event within their theory.

This, for Popper, was a point of more than academic significance. In his *The Poverty of Historicism* (1944–45) and *The Open Society and its Enemies* (1945) he argued strongly against inexorable laws of historical destiny. "There can be no scientific theory of historical development serving as a basis for historical prediction," he concluded.

In Popper's later work, as seen in his *Objective Knowledge* (1972), an attempt was made to develop an evolutionary account of the growth of knowledge. He also introduced his notion of "three worlds," arguing that in addition to the familiar worlds of physical and mental states, there exists also a "third world" populated by "theories...their logical relations...arguments...and problems."

Porter, George, Baron

(1920–)

BRITISH CHEMIST

Should we force science down the throats of those that have no taste for it? Is it our duty to drag them kicking and screaming into the 21st century? I am afraid that it is.

—Speech, September 1986

Born at Stainforth in Yorkshire, Porter was educated at the universities of Leeds and Cambridge, where he obtained his PhD. After working on radar during World War II, he returned to Cambridge until, in 1955, he was appointed professor of chemistry at Sheffield University. From 1966 until 1985 he held one of the leading positions in British science, namely, the directorship of the Royal Institution and the Fullerian Professorship of Chemistry. In 1987 he was appointed professor (from 1990, chairman) of the Centre for Photomolecular Science at Imperial College, London.

In collaboration with his Cambridge teacher, Ronald Norrish, Porter developed from 1949 onward the new technique of flash photolysis. There were good reasons for thinking that the course of a chemical reaction was partly determined by a number of intermediate species too short-lived to be detected, let alone investigated. Porter therefore set out to study what he called the spectroscopy of transient substances.

The apparatus used involved a long glass or quartz tube containing the gas under investigation. This was subjected to a very brief pulse of intense light from flash tubes, causing photochemical reactions in the gas. The free radicals and excited molecules produced have only a transient existence, but could be detected by a second flash of light, directed along the axis of the reaction tube, used to record photographically an absorption spectrum of the reaction mixture. In this way the spectra of many free radicals could be detected.

In addition, it was possible to direct a continuous beam of light down the reaction tube and focus on one particular absorption line of a species known to be present. The change of this line with time allowed kinetic measurements of the rates of very fast gas reactions to be made.

The methods of flash photolysis have since been extended to liquids and solutions, to gas kinetics, and to the study of complex biological molecules such as hemoglobin and chlorophyll. Porter shared the Nobel Prize for chemistry in 1967 with Norrish and with Manfred Eigen for "their studies of extremely fast reactions effected by disturbing the equilibrium by means of very short pulses of energy."

In 1990 Porter was raised to the British peerage as Baron Porter of Luddenham.

Porter, Keith Roberts

(1912–1977)

CANADIAN BIOLOGIST

Porter, who was born at Yarmouth in Nova Scotia, Canada, studied biology at Acadia University and Harvard, receiving his PhD in 1938. After working at the Rockefeller Institute (1939–61) he held chairs of biology, first at Harvard (1961–70) and thereafter at the University of Colorado.

While working with Albert Claude at the Rockefeller Institute, Porter studied the endoplasmic reticulum, a network of membranes within cells. More significant was his study of its equivalent form in muscle fibers, the sarcoplasmic reticulum. Although this had first been discussed by E. Veratti in 1902, it required the development of the electron microscope to permit Porter to describe, in the 1950s, its pervasive character as a network of extremely fine channels enclosing each myofibril. He went on to propose that it served to coordinate and harmonize the complex response of the contractions of millions of fibers.

The actual mechanism of contraction was initiated by the release of calcium ions into the fluid surrounding the muscle fibers. The source of such ions was shown to be the sarcoplasmic reticulum, to which they were quickly returned and stored by what became known as a "calcium pump."

Porter, Rodney Robert

(1917–1985)

BRITISH BIOCHEMIST

Porter was educated at the university in his native city of Liverpool, England, and at Cambridge University where he was a pupil of Frederick Sanger. After working at the National Institute of Medical Research from 1949 to 1960 he moved to the chair of immunology at St. Mary's Hospital, London. Porter remained there until 1967 when he became professor of biochemistry at Oxford.

In 1962 Porter proposed a structure for the important antibody gamma globulin (IgG). Ordinary techniques of protein chemistry revealed that the molecule is built up of four polypeptide chains paired so that the molecule consists of two identical halves, each consisting of one long (or heavy) chain and one short (or light) chain.

Further evidence was obtained by splitting the molecule with the enzyme papain. This split IgG into three large fragments, two similar to each other known as F_{ab} (fragment antigen binding) and still capable of combining with antigen, and a crystalline fragment known as F_c (fragment crystalline) without any activity. This immediately suggested to Porter that, because crystals only form easily from identical molecules, the halves of the heavy chain that make up the F_c fragment are probably the same in all molecules. Thus the complexity is mainly in the F_{ab} fragments where the combining sites are found.

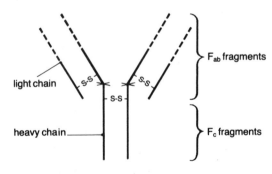

IMMUNOGLOBULIN   The structure of IgG proposed by Rodney Porter.

Linking such insights with results obtained by Gerald Edelman and data derived from electron microscopy allowed Porter to propose the familiar Y-shaped molecule built from four chains joined by disulfide bridges with the variable combining part at the tips of the arms of the Y.

In 1972 Porter shared with Edelman the Nobel Prize for physiology or medicine for their work in determining the structure of an antibody.

Poseidonius

(*c.* 135 BC–*c.* 51 BC)

GREEK PHILOSOPHER, HISTORIAN, AND ASTRONOMER

Poseidonius (pos-I-**doh**-nee-us) was born at Apameia in Syria and studied under the Greek Stoic philosopher Panaetius in Athens. Sometime after 100 BC he became head of the Stoic school of philosophy at Rhodes. Although none of his works have survived it is known that he completed a history of the world. He taught Cicero, who appears to have used some of his ideas in his *Dream of Scipio*.

As an astronomer Poseidonius made an ingenious attempt to measure the circumference of the Earth. Assuming Rhodes and Alexandria to be on the same meridian he noted that while the star Canopus just touches the horizon at Rhodes, it has a meridian altitude of 7 degrees 30 minutes or 1/48th of the circumference of a circle at Alexandria. As the distance between the two was 5,000 stadia, he concluded that the Earth's circumference was 48 × 5,000, which equals 240,000 stadia or, assuming 8.75 stadia to the mile (this value is uncertain), about 27,000 miles. The result was reasonably accurate and in broad agreement with that established by Eratosthenes by a different method. At some stage, however, Poseidonius reduced the figure to the much too low 180,000 stadia, presumably the result of revising the Rhodes–Alexandria distance. It was this figure, transmitted in the *Geography* of Ptolemy, that Columbus used more than 1,000 years later, when considering the feasibility of reaching Asia by sailing westward.

Poseidonius made less successful attempts to measure the size of the Sun and Moon. He also constructed a revolving celestial sphere exhibiting the daily motions of the Sun, Moon, and planets.

Poulton, Sir Edward Bagnall

(1856–1943)

BRITISH ZOOLOGIST

Poulton was born at Reading in southern England, the son of an architect. He spent his entire career at the University of Oxford, first as a student at Jesus College and later (1893–1933) as Hope Professor of Zoology.

Influenced by the writings of Alfred Russel Wallace, Poulton made an intensive and detailed study of the adaptive importance of protective coloring and mimicry in nature. His results, published in *The Colours of Animals* (1890), were strictly Darwinian with an emphasis on the inheritance of factors arising from the continuous variation found in a population.

Poulton maintained this belief despite the rediscovery of the works of Gregor Mendel and the consequent insistence on the role of mutation in evolution. In such works as *Essays on Evolution* (1908) Poulton argued against the growing Mendelian orthodoxy, insisting that adaptations as complex as mimicry could not have been brought about by mutation.

Powell, Cecil Frank

(1903–1969)

BRITISH PHYSICIST

The son of a gunsmith, Powell was born at Tonbridge, Kent, and educated at Cambridge University, where he obtained his PhD in 1927. He spent virtually his entire career at Bristol University where he became

Wills Professor of Physics in 1948 and director of the Wills Physics Laboratory in 1964.

Under Powell Bristol became a leading center for the study of nuclear particles by means of photographic emulsions. In this technique an ionizing particle crossing a sensitive plate coated with grains of silver bromide leaves clear tracks of its passage. From the size and path of the track much information about the nature of the particle can be inferred. In 1947 Powell, in collaboration with Giuseppe Occhialini, published a standard work on the subject, *Nuclear Physics in Photographs*. It was this technique that allowed Powell to discover the pi-meson (or pion) in 1947 in the plates of cosmic rays. The existence of such a particle had been predicted in 1935 by Hideki Yukawa, and Powell's discovery thus went some way to establish a coherent picture of nuclear phenomena.

For his discovery Powell was awarded the 1950 Nobel Prize for physics.

Poynting, John Henry

(1852–1914)

BRITISH PHYSICIST

Poynting was born at Monton, near Manchester in England, and educated at the universities of Manchester and Cambridge (1872–76). He served as professor of physics at Mason Science College (later the University of Birmingham) from 1880 until his death in 1914.

He wrote on electrical phenomena and radiation and is best known for *Poynting's vector*, introduced in his paper *On the Transfer of Energy in the Electromagnetic Field* (1884). In this he showed that the flow of energy at a point can be expressed by a simple formula in terms of the electric and magnetic forces at that point.

In 1891 he determined the mean density of the Earth and made a determination of the gravitational constant in 1893 through the accurate use of torsion balances. His results were published in *The Mean Density of the Earth* (1894) and *The Earth; Its Shape, Size, Weight and Spin* (1913). Poynting was also the first to suggest, in 1903, the existence of the effect of radiation from the Sun that causes smaller particles in orbit about the Sun to spiral close and eventually plunge in. This was developed by the American physicist Howard Robertson and was related to the theory of relativity in 1937, becoming known as the *Poynting–Robertson effect*.

Pratt, John Henry

(1809–1871)

BRITISH GEOPHYSICIST

Pratt was the son of a secretary to the Church Missionary Society; after graduating from Cambridge University in 1833 he went to India as a chaplain with the East India Company. In 1850 he became archdeacon of Calcutta.

An amateur scientist, Pratt became interested in geophysics and in 1854 his most important work was published when he formulated the theory of isostasy. While conducting his triangulation of India the surveyor, George Everest, found a discrepancy in the astrogeodetic and triangulation measurements between two stations – Kaliana and Kalianpur – near the Himalayas. From this Pratt surmised that mountain ranges failed to exert the gravitational pull expected of them and thus distorted measurements made with pendulums. He saw the Himalayas as having a lesser density than the crust below, and generalized that the higher the mountain range, the lower is its density. He compared the raising of mountains to fermenting dough in which the density decreases as the dough rises.

Some of the same ideas were present in a paper submitted just six weeks after Pratt's by George Airy although Airy preferred the image of an iceberg to that of rising dough.

Pratt wrote *Mathematical Principles of Mechanical Philosophy* (1836), a work that was expanded to *On Attractions, Laplace's Functions, and The Figure of the Earth* (1860, 1861, 1865).

Prausnitz, John Michael

(1928–   )

GERMAN–AMERICAN CHEMIST

Prausnitz (**prows**-nits) emigrated to America from his native Berlin in 1937 and became naturalized in 1944. He was educated at the universities of Cornell, Rochester, and Princeton, where he obtained his PhD in

1955. He then joined the Berkeley faculty of the University of California, where he has served since 1963 as professor of chemical engineering.

Prausnitz has worked mainly on the extension of physical chemistry into applications in chemical engineering process design. To this end he has worked on phase equilibria and on molecular thermodynamics. His views are discussed in his book *Molecular Thermodynamics of Fluid Phase Equilibria* (1969).

Praxagoras of Cos

(about 350 BC)

GREEK PHYSICIAN

Little is known of the life of Praxagoras (prak-**sag**-o-ras), except that he was born on the Greek island of Cos, and not much more of his writings other than their titles as recorded by Galen. He was the teacher of Herophilus and wrote works on *Physics*, *Anatomy*, *Diseases*, and *Symptoms*.

He developed the humoral theory of Hippocrates, apparently proposing that the four traditional humors be supplemented with the sweet, acid, salty, and bitter humors among several others. As the bulk of them are suggestive of tastes they could well have been derived from consideration of diet.

Praxagoras is also the first reported to have restricted the pulse to a specific set of vessels, the arteries, and to use it in diagnosis. However he remained committed to the traditional Greek view that the arteries carried not blood but "pneuma" or air. This came from venous blood via the heart and the lungs, continued along the arteries until they joined the neura (meaning for Praxagoras tendons rather than nerves), and ultimately produced muscular action. It was left to his pupil Herophilus to appreciate more fully the nature of the nerves.

Pregl, Fritz

(1869–1930)

AUSTRIAN CHEMIST

Pregl (**pray**-gel), who was born at Laibach (now Ljubljana in Slovenia), was the son of a bank official. He graduated in medicine from Graz (1893) where he became an assistant in physiological chemistry in 1899. In 1910 he became head of the chemistry department at Innsbruck, remaining there until 1913 when he returned to Graz to become director of the Medico-Chemical Institute.

Pregl began research on bile acids in about 1904 but soon found that he could only obtain tiny amounts. This led him to pioneer techniques of microanalysis. Justus von Liebig had needed about 1 gram of a substance before he could make an accurate analysis; through his new techniques Pregl was capable of working with 2.5 milligrams. This was achieved by the careful scaling down of his analytic equipment and the design of a new balance, which was produced in collaboration with the instrument maker W. Kuhlmann of Hamburg. With this he was capable of weighing 20 grams to an accuracy of 0.001 milligram.

The techniques developed by Pregl are of immense importance in organic chemistry and he was awarded the Nobel Prize for chemistry in 1923 for this work.

Prelog, Vladimir

(1906–)

SWISS CHEMIST

Born in Sarajevo (now in Bosnia and Hercegovina), Prelog (**prel**-og) studied chemistry at the Prague Institute of Technology where he received his doctorate in 1929. He then worked in Prague as an industrial chemist until 1935 when he moved to the University of Zagreb. With the German invasion of Yugoslavia in 1941 Prelog joined the staff of the Federal Institute of Technology in Zurich, serving there as professor of chemistry from 1950 until his retirement in 1976.

Prelog's early work was with the alkaloids. His research resulted in the solution of the configuration of *Cinchona* alkaloids (antimalarial compounds), the correction of the formulas for *Strychnos* alkaloids, and the elucidation of many other indole, steroid, and aromatic alkaloid configurations. He later investigated the metabolites of certain microorganisms and in so doing discovered many new natural substances including the first natural compound found to contain boron, boromycin.

Prelog intensively studied the relationship between conformation and chemical activity in medium-sized (8–11 ring members) ring structures. This brought to light a new type of reaction that can occur in such compounds. Prelog next showed that conformation affects the outcome of syntheses where different-sized atoms or groups are being substituted into a compound. The regular way in which this occurs allowed the configurations of many important compounds to be worked out. Applying such work to the reactions between enzymes, coenzymes, and substrates gave interesting results about the stereospecificity of microorganisms.

With Christopher Ingold, Prelog introduced the so-called R–S system into organic chemistry, which allowed, for the first time, enantiomers, or mirror images, to be described unambiguously.

For such wide ranging work on the "stereochemistry of organic molecules and reactions" Prelog was awarded the 1975 Nobel Prize for chemistry, which he shared with John Cornforth.

Prestwich, Sir Joseph

(1812–1896)

BRITISH GEOLOGIST

Prestwich, the son of a London wine merchant, was educated at University College, London. He then spent 40 years in the family wine business before accepting, after his retirement from business in 1874, the chair of geology at Oxford University, a post he held until his final retirement in 1888.

In his spare time Prestwich produced six books and well over 100 papers. He worked on the Quaternary Period of England, Belgium, and France and the Tertiary Period of southeast England, where he established the stratigraphy of the clays of the London basin. These results and other technical work were fully described in his *Geology – Chemical, Physical and Stratigraphical* (2 vols. 1886–88).

In 1859 Prestwich played a more public role than that of technical geologist when he was persuaded to visit Boucher de Perthes's site at Abbeville and to report on the authenticity of the antiquities found there. He concluded that the flint implements were the work of man and that they were associated with the remains of unknown animals. By doing so he was committing himself to the then revolutionary belief in the antiquity of man. Prestwich was knighted in 1896.

Prévost, Pierre

(1751–1839)

SWISS PHYSICIST

Born in Geneva, Switzerland, Prévost (pray-**voh**) was professor of physics at Berlin and then at the university in his native city. In 1792 he published his *Sur l'equilibre du feu* (On the Equilibrium of Heat), which did much to clarify the nature of heat.

If, as was widely believed at the time, heat was a fluid, called caloric, which flowed from hot bodies to colder ones, then it was reasonable to suppose that cold was also a fluid, "frigoric," which flowed from cold bodies to warmer ones. In favor of the existence of frigoric was a body of experimental work that dated back to the 17th century. Thus it was known that if a piece of ice was placed near a thermometer in a room of constant temperature then the temperature of the thermometer would fall. More impressively, if two concave mirrors are arranged so that they face each other and a piece of ice is placed at one focus and a thermometer at the other, then the indicated temperature will fall. Experiments like this readily lent themselves to the interpretation that the fluid frigoric can be emitted and reflected. Prévost argued in 1791 that there is but a single fluid involved. Snow melting in the hand was a case of heat flowing from the hand to the snow rather than conversely. He introduced the idea of dynamic equilibrium in which all bodies are radiating and absorbing heat. When one body is colder than another it absorbs more than it radiates. Its temperature will rise until it is in equilibrium with its surroundings. At this point, it does not stop radiating heat but absorbs just as much as it loses to remain in equilibrium. The idea is known as the *Prévost theory of exchanges.*

Although Prévost was a supporter of the caloric theory of heat, his views influenced a later generation of physicists who introduced the kinetic theory of heat on a quantitative basis toward the end of the 19th century.

Priestley, Joseph

(1733–1804)

BRITISH CHEMIST AND PRESBYTERIAN MINISTER

> It was ill policy in Leo the Tenth to patronize polite literature. He was cherishing an enemy in disguise. And the English [church] hierarchy ... has equal reason to tremble even at an air pump or an electrical machine.
> —*Experiments and Observations on Different Kinds of Air* (1775–86)

Priestley was the greatest British chemist of the 18th century and also one of the century's greatest men. Born in the English city of Leeds, his father was a cloth dresser and a Congregationalist. Priestley was educated at a nonconformist seminary, later becoming a minister at Needham Market in 1755. After a few years in Nantwich in a similar post he went to teach at Warrington Academy in 1761.

On visits to London he met Benjamin Franklin, who aided him in his *History of Electricity* (1767). He moved to Leeds in 1767 and, being near a brewery, "began to make experiments in the fixed air that was continually produced in it." It was around this time that he invented soda water with the ample supply of carbon dioxide ("fixed air") from the brewery. In 1772 he became Lord Shelburne's librarian, which involved only nominal duties and allowed him to do some of his most important work. He left in 1780 to become a minister in Birmingham, where he mixed with such members of the Lunar Society as Erasmus Darwin, James Watt, Josiah Wedgwood, and Matthew Boulton. As a dissenting radical he preached against the discrimination suffered by non-Anglicans and, in reply to Edmund Burke's *Reflections on the French Revolution*, wrote in favor of the principles of the French Revolution. This led a Birmingham mob to break into his home (1791) and burn it, destroying all his books, papers, and instruments. He moved to London for a short while but finding no security there moved to America in 1794 to join his sons who had emigrated there earlier. In Pennsylvania he continued with his scientific and theological work until his death.

Priestley attempted to understand the facts of combustion and respiration. His first insight came from the realization that, since even a small candle uses an enormous amount of pure air, there must be a provision in nature to replace it. After trying various techniques to purify the foul air left after combustion he eventually found that a sprig of mint would revive the air so it could support combustion once more (1771). In the next few years, using a variety of new techniques, he isolated various gases – nitrous oxide, hydrogen chloride, sulfur dioxide – and, in 1774, he produced oxygen. Using a powerful magnifying glass to focus the rays of the Sun, he heated oxides of mercury and lead confined in glass tubes over mercury. He found that they gave off large amounts of a gas in which a candle would burn with an enlarged flame. At first he identified the gas as nitrous oxide but found that, unlike that gas, it was barely soluble in water. He next thought it might simply be ordinary air but on putting mice in it he found that they lived longer than in a similar volume of normal air. Being an ardent believer in the phlogiston theory, he named this gas "dephlogisticated air." Antoine Lavoisier realized the crucial value of this discovery in explaining combustion and named the gas "oxygine."

Priestley continued to discover more compounds. He determined the relative densities of various gases by weighing balloons filled with them and also investigated gaseous diffusion, conductivity of heat in gas, and the effect of electrical discharge on gases at low pressure.

Prigogine, Ilya

(1917–)

BELGIAN CHEMIST

Prigogine (pree-goh-**zheen**) was born in Moscow and educated at the Free University of Belgium where he served as professor of chemistry from 1947 to 1987. He was appointed director of the Statistical Mechanics and Thermodynamics Center of the University of Texas, Austin in 1967.

In 1955 Prigogine produced a seminal and revolutionary work, *Thermodynamics of Irreversible Processes*. In this book he pointed out a serious limitation in classical thermodynamics of being restricted to reversible processes and equilibrium states. He argued that a true thermodynamic equilibrium is rarely attained; a more common state is met with in the cell, which continuously exchanges with its surroundings, or in the solar system with the steady flow of energy from the Sun preventing the atmosphere of the Earth from reaching thermodynamic equilibrium.

A beginning had been made by Lars Onsager to cover nonequilibrium states but this applied only to states not too far away from equilibrium. Prigogine, in a quite radical way, developed machinery to deal with states far from equilibrium. These he called "dissipative structures." He went on to suggest that, "On a broader scale, it is difficult to avoid the feeling that such instabilities related to dissipative processes should play an extensive role in biological processes." Such a possibility Prigogine began to explore in his *Membranes, Dissipative Structures and Evolution* (1975).

Prigogine was awarded the 1977 Nobel Prize for chemistry for his work on "nonequilibrium thermodynamics particularly his theory of dissipative structures."

Pringsheim, Ernst

(1859–1917)

GERMAN PHYSICIST

Pringsheim (**prings**-hIm) was educated at Berlin University, where he gained his PhD in 1882. He later took up an appointment at Breslau as professor of theoretical physics.

Pringsheim did important work on the distribution of radiation from a hot body, and with a colleague at Breslau, Otto Lummer, showed that the formulas of Max Planck and Wilhelm Wien, accounting for black-body radiation, led to certain inconsistencies. This observation was instrumental in the development by Planck of his quantum theory.

Pringsheim, Nathanael

(1823–1894)

GERMAN BOTANIST

Pringsheim, who was born at Wziesko (now in Poland), studied medicine at the universities of Breslau and Leipzig. However, his interest turned to natural science when he moved to the University of Berlin; he gained his PhD in 1848 with a thesis on the growth and thickness of plant cell walls. In 1864 he was appointed professor of botany at the University of Jena but resigned the post in 1868 to conduct private research in a laboratory attached to his home in Berlin.

Pringsheim was one of the leaders in the botanical revival of the 19th century with his contribution to studies of cell development and life history, particularly in the algae and fungi. He was among the first to demonstrate sexual reproduction in algae and observe alternation of generations between the two sexually differentiated motile zoospores and the resting undifferentiated spore that results from their fusion. He further showed that sexual reproduction involves fusion of material of the two sex cells.

From studies (1873) on the complex morphological differentiation in a family of marine algae, the Sphacelariaceae, Pringsheim opposed the Darwinian theory of evolution by natural selection. Like the Swiss botanist, Karl Naegeli, he believed the increase in structural complexity to be a spontaneous morphological phenomenon, conferring no survival value.

Pringsheim's studies of the origin of plant cells contributed evidence for the theory that cells are only produced by the division of existing cells. With Julius von Sachs, Pringsheim also described the plastids, organelles unique to plant cells. In later years he concentrated more on physiology than morphology but his contributions to this field were not acknowledged or developed by other workers.

He was founder of the *Jahrbücher für Wissenschaftliche Botanik* (1858; Annals of Scientific Botany) and the German Botanical Society (1882). He wrote memoirs on *Vaucheria* (1855), *Oedogonium* and *Coleochaete* (1856–58), *Hydrodictyon* (1861), and *Pandorina* (1869).

Pritchard, Charles

(1808–1893)

BRITISH ASTRONOMER

Pritchard, who was born at Alderbury in southern England, was the son of an unsuccessful manufacturer. With the help of family friends he was sent to school and to Cambridge University. He became a fellow of his college in 1832 and headmaster of Clapham Grammar School in 1834 where he remained until 1862 – his school became quite famous and was attended by the sons of John Herschel, George Airy, and Charles Darwin. In 1870 he became Savilian Professor of Astronomy at Oxford where he built and equipped a new observatory. Although he had a small observatory at Clapham, Pritchard is most unusual for a scientist in that most of his work was done in his seventies. In 1881 he introduced a new kind of photometer – the wedge photometer – which he used in estimating the brightness of stars. He observed and calculated the relative magnitude of 2,784 stars from the celestial pole to 10°S, publishing his results in 1885. He also pioneered attempts to determine stellar parallax by photography. In 1886 he exposed 200 plates of 61 Cygni, establishing a parallax of 0.438 seconds of arc. Between 1888 and 1892, when he was 84, he determined the parallax of a further 28 stars by photographic means.

Proclus

(*c.* 410–485 AD)

GREEK PHILOSOPHER

> It is well known that the man who first made public the theory of irrationals perished in a shipwreck in order that the inexpressible and unimaginable should ever remain veiled. And so the guilty man, who fortuitously touched on and revealed this aspect of living things, was taken to the place where he began and there is for ever beaten by the waves.
> —Commentary on Euclid's *Elements*

Proclus (**proh**-klus) was one of the last significant Greek philosophers. He was born at Constantinople (now Istanbul in Turkey) and studied in Athens under Plutarch and Syriacus. He later became head of the Academy, which Plato had founded in Athens centuries earlier. Proclus was largely responsible for the wide dissemination of Neoplatonic thought throughout the Byzantine, Roman, and Islamic worlds. Neoplatonism stemmed from the work of Plotinus, a third-century Roman philosopher, founded on a modified system of Platonism with the addition of mysticism.

Proclus's ideas influenced Arabic thinkers and in the Middle Ages his works became the principal source of the then popular Neoplatonism. He wrote a number of commentaries on Plato's dialogues. He was a distinguished mathematician and wrote an important commentary on the first book of Euclid's *Elements*, which survived through the ages.

Proctor, Richard Anthony

(1837–1888)

BRITISH–AMERICAN ASTRONOMER

Proctor, the son of a London lawyer, worked as a clerk in a bank before going to Cambridge University in 1856 to study law. In 1866 the failure of a bank he had interests in led him to make his living from writing and lecturing. He had become interested in mathematics and astronomy, and most of his books were straightforward accounts of recent advances in astronomy. He also made lecture tours through America and Australia and in 1881 he settled in America where he founded the scientific magazine *Knowledge*.

His most important work as an astronomer was with Mars. In 1867 he published a chart of Mars that introduced the current, if misleading, nomenclature of seas, oceans, islands, and straits. He worked out the rotational period of Mars very accurately as a little more than 24 hours 37 minutes. He also charted the stars in Friedrich Argelander's catalog, and was one of the first to suggest that meteoric bombardment, and not volcanic activity, was the cause of lunar craters.

Prokhorov, Aleksandr Mikhaylovich

(1916–   )

RUSSIAN PHYSICIST

Prokhorov (**proh**-ko-rof) graduated in 1939 from the faculty of physics of the Leningrad State University, where he later became a doctor of physics, mathematics, and science (1946). During World War II he served in the Russian army.

Subsequently, working at the Physics Institute of the Soviet Academy of Sciences with Nikolai Basov, Prokhorov performed fundamental work in microwave spectroscopy, which led to the development of the maser in 1955, and later the laser. Basov and Prokhorov, together with the American physicist Charles Townes, received the 1964 Nobel Prize for physics for their development of the maser principle, and were pioneers of the new science of quantum radio physics (now referred to by the broader term, quantum electronics).

Proudman, Joseph

(1888–1975)

BRITISH MATHEMATICIAN AND OCEANOGRAPHER

> The quickest way to get a lot of things done is to do one thing at a time.
> —Maxim

Proudman, who was born at Unsworth, near Manchester in England, studied mathematics and physics at Liverpool University. After graduating in 1910 he continued his studies at Cambridge University. Subsequently Proudman returned to Liverpool (1913) in the capacity of lecturer in mathematics and remained associated with this university for the rest of his career. In 1919 he became the first professor of applied mathematics and in 1933 a chair in oceanography was created specifically for him. He remained at Liverpool, serving also as pro-vice-chancellor (1940–46), until his retirement in 1954.

Proudman's abiding scientific interest was in the study of the tides and other aspects of the sea. He made fundamentally important contributions of both a practical and theoretical nature to oceanography. In 1916 Horace Lamb was asked to prepare a report on tidal research and Proudman contributed to this a paper on the harmonic analysis of tidal observations. In 1919 he founded an institute in Liverpool devoted to research on tidal phenomena, which, after several changes of name, eventually became known as the Bidston Laboratory of the Institute of Oceanographic Sciences. He worked closely on tidal phenomena with another member of the institute, Arthur Doodson. Proudman's work pioneered the mathematical study of the tides, and only as a result of his work did a unified mathematical approach to oceanography become possible. His works included *Dynamical Oceanography* (1953).

Proust, Joseph Louis

(1754–1826)

FRENCH CHEMIST

Proust (proost) was born the son of an apothecary at Angers in northwest France. He studied in Paris and became chief apothecary at the Saltpêtrière Hospital. In 1789 he went to Madrid to become director of the Royal Laboratory under the patronage of Charles IV. After the invasion of Spain by Napoleon, the fall of his patron, and the destruction of his laboratory by the invading army, he returned to France in 1808. He lived in poverty for some years before being awarded a pension by Louis XVIII.

In 1799 Proust formulated his law of definite proportions. He pointed out that copper carbonate must always be made from the same fixed proportions of copper, carbon, and oxygen. From this he generalized that all compounds contained elements in certain definite proportions. Proust's law was not immediately accepted by all chemists; in particular, his proposal led to a long and famous controversy with Claude-Louis Berthollet who argued that elements could combine in a whole range of different proportions. It is now clear that Proust was talking about compounds whereas Berthollet was thinking of solutions or mixtures. Berthollet eventually admitted his error.

The strength of Proust's law was seen a few years later when John Dalton published his atomic theory. The law and the theory fitted exactly – Proust's definite proportions being in fact a definite number of atoms joining together to form molecules.

Prout, William

(1785–1850)

BRITISH CHEMIST AND
PHYSIOLOGIST

Prout was born at Horton in England and studied medicine at Edinburgh, graduating in 1811. He established himself as a physician in London and became a pioneer of physiological chemistry, in which he lectured. He wrote on the stomach and urinary diseases and on the chemistry of the blood, urine, and kidney stones. In 1818 he prepared urea for the first time and in 1824 he identified hydrochloric acid in stomach secretions. He was also one of the first to divide food components into the groups of fats, carbohydrates, and protein.

Prout's fame also rests on a paper he published anonymously in 1815, *On the Relation between the Specific Gravities of Bodies in Their Gaseous State and the Weight of Their Atoms*. In this he formulated what has since been called *Prout's hypothesis*: the atomic weight of all atoms is an exact multiple of the atomic weight of hydrogen. Determination of atomic weights had made this view plausible. At the time there was considerable interest in the hypothesis as it implied that elements were themselves "compounds" of hydrogen, and Prout suggested that hydrogen was the *prima materia* (basic substance) of the ancients. However, more accurate determinations of atomic weight, particularly by Jean Stas, showed that many were not whole numbers. Stas described the hypothesis as "only an illusion" although he also remarked that there was "something at the bottom of it." Interest was revived with the publication of Dmitri Mendeleev's periodic table, although Mendeleev described the idea of a *prima materia* as "a torment of classical thought." The discovery of isotopes in the 20th century resolved the position.

Ptolemy

(about 2nd century AD)

EGYPTIAN ASTRONOMER

Virtually nothing is known about the life of Ptolemy (**tol**-e-mee; full name Claudius Ptolemaeus). He was probably a Hellenized Egyptian working in the library at Alexandria. He produced four major works, the *Almagest*, the *Geography*, the *Tetrabiblos* (Four Books), and the *Optics*. The first work – the culmination of five hundred years of Greek astronomical and cosmological thinking – was to dominate science for 13 centuries. Ptolemy naturally relied on his predecessors, especially Hipparchus, as in classical times borrowing the work of others was normal practice. A work of such staggering intellectual power and complexity could never be created by one person alone. The basic problem he faced was to try to explain the movements of the heavens on the assumption that the universe is geocentric and all bodies revolve in perfectly circular orbits moving with uniform velocity. As the heavenly bodies move in elliptical orbits with variable velocity around a center other than the Earth some quite sophisticated geometry is called for to preserve the basic fiction. Ptolemy used three complications of the original scheme: epicycles, eccentrics, and equants. These devices worked reasonably well except that they did not lead to particularly accurate predictions. Nor did they permit Ptolemy to develop a system of the universe as a whole. He could give a reasonable account of the orbit of Mars, and of Venus, and of Mercury, and so on, taken separately, but if they were put together into one scheme then the dimensions and the periods would start to conflict. Whatever its faults the system remained intact for 1,300 years until it was overthrown by Copernicus in the 15th century.

In the *Geography* Ptolemy explains fully how lines of latitude and longitude can be mathematically determined. However no longitudes were astronomically determined and only a few latitudes had been so calculated. Positions of places were located on this dubious grid by reducing distances measured on land to degrees. Distances over seas were simply guessed at. As he had put the Canaries 7° east of their true position his whole grid was thrown out of alignment. The *Geography* had almost as great (and as enduring) an influence on the western world-view as the *Almagest*. Columbus might never have sailed without Ptolemy's erroneous view that Asia was closer (westward) than it really is, a view endorsed by the map-makers contemporaneous with Columbus.

The only book of Ptolemy's that is readily available today and still widely read is the *Tetrabiblos*, which is a work on astrology. The work is long and comprehensive and is probably as well argued as the case for astrology can be. It is naturalistic in that he supposes that there might be some form of physical radiation from the heavens that affects mankind. Most of the concepts and arguments of modern astrology can be traced back to this Ptolemaic work.

The final major work of Ptolemy, the *Optics*, in which he sets out and demonstrates various elementary principles, is in many ways the most successful of all his works. Although he understood the principles of reflection reasonably well his understanding of refraction seems to be purely empirical. He gives tables he has worked out for the refraction of a ray of light passing from light into water for various angles of incidence.

His main work was known in Greek as the *Syntaxis*; it was the Arabs who named it the *Almagest* from the Arabic definite article "al" and their own pronunciation of the Greek word for "great." Such was the tribute posterity has paid to Ptolemy.

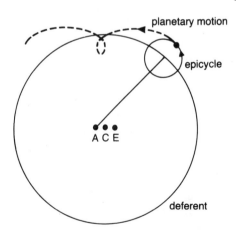

PTOLEMAIC SYSTEM   The motion of planets as described by Ptolemy.

Puck, Theodore Thomas

(1916–)

AMERICAN BIOLOGIST

Born in Chicago, Illinois, Puck was educated at the university there, obtaining his PhD in 1940. He later moved to the University of Colorado in 1948 as professor of biophysics, remaining there until his retirement in 1986.

In 1956 Puck and his students at Colorado extended the technique of cloning (culturing colonies of identical cells) to mammalian cells. The technique has had a profound impact on many areas of biological activity, both theoretical and practical.

Purbach, Georg von

(1423–1461)

AUSTRIAN ASTRONOMER AND MATHEMATICIAN

Purbach (or Peurbach; **poor**-bahk or **poir**-bahk) took his name from his birthplace in Austria. He had traveled in Italy and studied under Nicholas of Cusa before becoming professor of mathematics and astronomy at the University of Vienna in about 1450. Purbach's main aim as a scholar was to produce an accurate text of Ptolemy's *Almagest*. The most common available text was that of Gerard of Cremona, which was a Latin translation of an Arabic translation and was nearly 300 years old. Purbach began by writing a general introduction to Ptolemy that described accurately and briefly the constructions of the *Almagest*. Unfortunately he died before he could embark on the translation. His place was taken by his pupil, Regiomontanus, who completed a textbook begun by Purbach but failed to produce the edition and translation of Ptolemy so much wanted by Purbach.

One of his most significant works, the fruit of much observational and theoretical work, was a very thorough table of lunar eclipses, which he published in 1459. Purbach wrote a textbook, *Theoricae novae planetarum* (New Theories about Planets), which became an influential exposition of the Ptolemaic theory of the solar system, a theory whose influence lasted until Tycho Brahe finally disproved the existence of the solid spheres postulated by Ptolemy. Such was the accuracy of Purbach's set tables that they were still in use almost two hundred years later. He also compiled a table of sines, using Arabic numerals, and was one of the first to popularize their use instead of chords in trigonometry.

Purcell, Edward Mills

(1912–   )

AMERICAN PHYSICIST

Purcell was born at Taylorville, Illinois. He gained his BSc degree in electrical engineering at Purdue University, Illinois (1933) and his masters degree and PhD from Harvard (1938), having also spent a year in Germany at the Technische Hochschule, Karlsruhe. At Harvard his career advanced from instructor in physics (1938), to associate professor (1946), full professor (1949), and professor emeritus (1980). During the war years 1941–45 he was a group leader at the Massachusetts Institute of Technology Radiation Laboratories.

Purcell's research has spanned nuclear magnetism, radio astronomy, radar, astrophysics, and biophysics. In the field of nuclear magnetism, he was awarded the 1952 Nobel Prize for physics (shared with Felix Bloch) for his work in developing the nuclear magnetic resonance (NMR) method of measuring the magnetic fields of the nuclei of atoms. As a result of these experiments, measurements of nuclear magnetic moment could now be performed on solids and liquids, whereas previously they had been confined to molecular beams of gases. Nuclear magnetic resonance is now commonly applied in chemical analysis.

Purcell's major contribution to astronomy was the first detection of microwave emission from neutral hydrogen in interstellar space at the wavelength of 21 centimeters (1420 Hz). The phenomenon had been predicted theoretically by Hendrik van de Hulst and others and was first observed in 1951 by three independent groups of radio astronomers – American, Dutch, and Australian – the American group being the first to report their findings. This, and the subsequent observation of the corresponding absorption line by the Dutch group in 1954, has made possible the mapping of a large part of our own galaxy, and allowed the calculation of the excitation temperature in interstellar space. Purcell was also aware of the possible future implications of his discovery for interstellar communications.

Purkinje, Johannes Evangelista

(1787–1869)

CZECH PHYSIOLOGIST

> With boundless eagerness I investigated within the shortest time all areas of plant and animal histology, and concluded that this new field was inexhaustible.
> —Letter to Rudolph Wagner (1841)

Born at Libochovice (now in the Czech Republic), Purkinje (**puur**-kin-yay or pur-**kin**-jee) began studying to be a priest but changed to medicine and graduated MD from Charles University, Prague, in 1819. He became professor of physiology and pathology at the University of Breslau in 1823 but returned to Charles University in 1850 to take the chair of physiology, which he held until his death. Purkinje's most celebrated research was concerned with the eye, although he also did valuable work on the brain, muscles, sweat glands, digestion, animal and plant cells, and embryology. He explored various aspects of vision, drawing attention, for example, to the fact that in subdued light blue objects appear brighter to the eye than red objects – the *Purkinje effect*. He located *Purkinje cells* in the middle layer of the brain's cerebellar cortex and was the first to apply the term "protoplasm" to the living embryonic material contained in the egg. He also discovered, in the inner walls of the ventricles of the heart, the *Purkinje fibers*, which transmit the pacemaker stimulus. His comparative studies of cellular structure in plants and animals were continued by Matthias Schlieden and Theodor Schwann and led to subsequent increased knowledge of the factors involved in inheritance. Purkinje was among the first to use a microtome for preparing thin slices of tissue for microscopic examination, and may have been the first to teach microscopy and microscopical technique as part of his college courses. He also realized that fingerprints can be used as a method of identification.

Pythagoras

(*c.* 580 BC–*c.* 500 BC)

GREEK MATHEMATICIAN AND PHILOSOPHER

Number is the ruler of forms and ideas, and the cause of gods and demons.
—Quoted by Robert Graves in *The White Goddess* (1948)

All that is known of the life of Pythagoras (pI-**thag**-or-as) with any certainty is that he left his birthplace, Samos, in about 520 BC to settle in Croton (now Crotone) in southern Italy and, as a result of political trouble, made a final move to Metapontum in about 500.

In Croton Pythagoras established his academy and became a cult leader. His community was governed by a large number of rules, some dietary, such as those commanding abstinence from meat and from beans, and others of obscure origin, such as the commands not to let a swallow nest under the roof or not to sit on a quart measure.

The movement was united by the belief that "all is number." While the exact meaning of this may be none too clear, that it led to one of the great periods of mathematics is beyond doubt. Not only were the properties of numbers explored in a totally new way and important theorems discovered, of which the familiar theorem of Pythagoras is the best example, but there also emerged what is arguably the first really deep mathematical truth – the discovery of irrational numbers with the realization of the incommensurability of the square root of 2.

Pytheas of Massalia

(about 4th century BC)

GREEK NAVIGATOR AND ASTRONOMER

> Neither land nor sea nor air but a mixture of all, like a sea-lung, in which sea and land and everything swing and which may be the bounds of all, impassable by foot or boat.
> —Description of the hostile sea conditions around Thule (probably Iceland)

Pytheas (**pith**-ee-as) is famous for providing the first account of the seas of northern Europe. He sailed to the tin mines of Cornwall, circumnavigated Britain (without mentioning Ireland), and sailed further north to a land he called Thule, which may have been Iceland. He may also have sailed to the mouth of the Vistula River and visited Heligoland.

His reports were on the whole disbelieved by later geographers, such as Strabo, largely because the lands of the far north were allegedly frigid and uninhabitable. His accuracy in noting that the pole star does not mark the pole makes it probable that he did sail much further north than any Greek before him.

Quetelet, Adolphe

(1796–1874)

FLEMISH ASTRONOMER,
MATHEMATICIAN, AND
SOCIOLOGIST

Quetelet (kay-te-**lay**), born the son of a municipal official in Ghent (now in Belgium), was educated at the lycée there. When only 19 he was appointed as an instructor in mathematics at the city's Royal College. In 1819 he moved to Brussels to take the chair of mathematics at the Athenaeum, a post he held until his appointment in 1828 as director of the newly established Royal Observatory.

It is, however, as a statistician and not as an astronomer that Quetelet is remembered. In this field he appeared to have an obsession with the collection and analysis of the variations found in natural phenomena. Thus in 1825 he began by preparing a table of births and deaths in Brussels that was later extended to cover the whole of Belgium. He soon branched out to cover the statistics of crime and tried to show their relationship to such variables as sex, age, climate, and education.

In various influential works Quetelet argued for the use of statistics in the establishment of a social science and for the discovery of social laws. This idea, together with his concept of the "average man" (*l'homme moyen*) caused much controversy.

Rabi, Isidor Isaac

(1898–1988)

AUSTRIAN–AMERICAN PHYSICIST

There isn't a scientific community. It is a culture. It is a very undisciplined organization.
—Quoted by D. S. Greenberg in *The Politics of Pure Science* (1967)

Rabi (**rah**-bee) and his parents emigrated to America from Rymanow in Poland, where he was born, while he was still young. He subsequently grew up in a Yiddish-speaking community in New York, where his father ran a grocery store. He was educated at Cornell, graduating in 1919, and Columbia, where he obtained his PhD in 1927. After two years in Europe he returned to Columbia where he spent his whole career until his retirement in 1967, being appointed professor of physics in 1937 and the first University Professor (a position with no departmental duties) there in 1964.

While in Germany (1927) Rabi had worked under Otto Stern and was impressed with the experiment Stern had performed with Walter Gerlach in which the use of molecular beams led to the discovery of space quantization (1922). Consequently Rabi began a research program at Columbia where he invented the atomic- and molecular-beam magnetic-resonance method of observing atomic spectra, a precise means of determining the magnetic moments of fundamental particles. Using his techniques after World War II, experimentalists were able to measure the magnetic moment of the electron to nine significant figures, thus providing a powerful tool for the testing of theories in quantum electrodynamics. The method had wide applications to the atomic clock, to nuclear magnetic resonance, and to the maser and laser. For this work Rabi was awarded the Nobel Prize for physics in 1944.

During the war Rabi worked on the development of microwave radar. In the postwar years he was a member of the General Advisory Committee of the Atomic Energy Commission, serving as its chairman (1952–56) following the resignation of J. Robert Oppenheimer. As a member of the American delegation to UNESCO he originated the movement that led to the foundation of the international laboratory for high-energy physics in Geneva known as CERN.

Rainwater, (Leo) James

(1917–1986)

AMERICAN PHYSICIST

Born in Council, Idaho, and educated at the California Institute of Technology, Rainwater went on to gain his BS, MA, and PhD from Columbia University. At Columbia he progressed through physics assistant (1939–42), to instructor (1946), assistant professor (1947), and associate professor (1949), to become full professor of physics in 1952. In the intervening war years he worked for the Office of Scientific Research and Development and on the Manhattan (atom bomb) project.

Rainwater's principal academic achievement was in explaining the structure and behavior of the atomic nucleus. At the time, two independent models existed, each explaining some of the properties of the atom – the "shell" model of independent particles, and the "liquid-drop" model of collective motion. Rainwater, in collaboration with Aage Bohr, showed how these theories could be unified (1950).

Rainwater, Bohr, and Benjamin Mottelson (Bohr's principal collaborator in Denmark) are credited with developing a unified theory that reconciled the individual motions of the nuclear particles with the collective behavior of the nucleus. For this the three men shared the 1975 Nobel Prize for physics.

From 1951 until 1953 and again in the period 1956–61, Rainwater was director of the Nevis Cyclotron Laboratory. From 1965 he spent much of his time supervising the conversion of the synchrocyclotron there.

Raman, Sir Chandrasekhara Venkata

(1888–1970)

INDIAN PHYSICIST

Raman (**rah**-man) was born at Trichinopoly (now Tiruchirappalli) in India and educated at the University of Madras. However, although he revealed considerable talent, he was unable to pursue his education overseas because of ill health. Instead, he chose to enter the civil service where he worked as an auditor for ten years while continuing with his own private research. In 1917 he took up an appointment as professor of physics at the University of Calcutta. In 1933 he moved to Bangalore where he first headed the physics department at the Indian Institute of Science and later, in 1948, became founding director of the Raman Institute.

In 1928 he discovered a spectral effect for which, in 1930, he was awarded the Nobel Prize for physics, thus becoming not only the first Indian but the first Asian to be so honored. The *Raman effect* (as it is now known) occurs when visible radiation is scattered by the molecules in the medium. Not only will the original frequency of the incident light be found but in addition specific new-frequency lines will be detected as a result of the interaction of photons with the molecules. From these new lines in the spectrum (Raman lines) information can be deduced about the molecular structure. The effect is similar to that found by Arthur Compton for x-rays and had in fact been predicted by Werner Heisenberg some years earlier.

Ramanujan, Srinivasa Iyengar

(1887–1920)

INDIAN MATHEMATICIAN

Ramanujan (rah-**mah**-nuu-jan), the son of a clerk, was born into a poor Brahmin family in Erode near Madras, India. Sometime in 1903, while a student at Kumbakonam High School, he acquired a copy of G. S. Carr's *Synopsis of Elementary Results in Pure Mathematics*. Carr is an unusual work, normally of use as a reference work for a professional mathematician: it consists of about 6,000 theorems presented without comment, explanation, or proof. Ramanujan set himself the task of demonstrating all the formulas, a task only a natural-born mathematician would contemplate, let alone pursue. Indifferent to other subjects, Ramanujan failed every exam he entered. For a time he was supported by Ramachandra Rao, a senior civil servant and secretary of the Indian Mathematical Society (IMS). In 1912 he took a clerical position with the Madras Port Trust. At the same time it was suggested that he should seek the advice of a number of British mathematicians about his work and career.

In January 1913 Ramanujan sent a letter to a number of British mathematicians containing a number of formulas. The only one to respond was the Cambridge mathematician G. H. Hardy. Hardy noted that, while some of the formulas were familiar, others "seemed scarcely possible to believe." Some he thought he could, with difficulty, prove himself; others, he had never seen anything like before, and they defeated Hardy completely. Despite this, it was obvious to Hardy that the formulas must be true and could only come from a mathematician of the very highest class. With Hardy's backing, Ramanujan was awarded a scholarship by the University of Madras and invited to visit Cambridge.

There were, however, religious problems facing the devout Ramanujan but these were resolved when the goddess Namagiri appeared in a dream to Ramanujan's mother absolving him from his traditional obligations. By June 1913 Ramanujan was in Cambridge working with Hardy.

They collaborated on five important papers. Ramanujan was elected to the Royal Society in 1918, the first Indian to be honored in this way, and was made a fellow of Trinity College, Cambridge, in 1919. By this time his health had begun to fail. He returned to India in 1919 and died soon after from TB.

Some of Ramanujan's most distinctive work in collaboration with Hardy was on partitions. The partition of a number n, $p(n)$, is the number of ways it can be expressed as a sum of smaller numbers. Thus as the number 4 can be expressed as 5 summands: 4, 3+1, 2+2, 2+1+1, and 1+1+1+1, so p(4)=5. As $p(n)$ grows rapidly as n increases (p(50) for example is 204,266), some way other than counting is needed to determine its value. In 1918 Hardy and Ramanujan established a complicated formula that produced for p(100) the figure 190,569,291.996 while the true figure is 190,569,292. A similar accuracy applied to p(200).

Part of Ramanujan's mathematical ability came from his ability to do mental calculations extremely quickly. It is said that he was traveling in a cab with Hardy when Hardy observed that the number of the cab in front, 1729, was a dull number. "No," replied Ramanujan, "it is a very interesting number; it is the smallest number expressible as a sum of two cubes in two different ways." ($1,729 = 1^3+12^3$ and 9^3+10^3.)

Ramón y Cajal, Santiago

(1852–1934)

SPANISH HISTOLOGIST

The son of a country doctor from Petilla in Spain, Ramón y Cajal (rah-**mon** ee kah-**hahl**) embarked on medical studies only after being apprenticed first to a barber and then to a shoemaker. He obtained his license to practice in 1873, and after a year's service in the army in Cuba returned to Madrid and graduated as a doctor of medicine in 1877.

He is remembered for his research into the fine structure of nervous tissue. Before the development of the nerve-specific silver nitrate stain by the Italian cytologist Camillo Golgi in 1873, it was difficult (in neuro-histological preparations) to distinguish true nervous elements from the surrounding supporting tissue (neuroglia). Ramón y Cajal refined Golgi's staining technique and subsequently used it to show the intricacy of the structure and connections of cells in the gray matter of the brain and spinal cord. He also used the stain to elucidate the fine structure of the retina of the eye, and the stain has proved useful in the diagnosis of brain tumors.

In 1906 Ramón y Cajal (together with Golgi) was awarded the Nobel Prize for physiology or medicine for establishing the neuron as the fundamental unit of the nervous system – a finding basic to the present understanding of the nerve impulse. He also advanced the neuron theory, which states that the nervous system is made up of numerous discrete cells and is not a system of fused cells.

Between 1884 and 1922 Ramón y Cajal held professorships successively at the universities of Valencia, Barcelona, and Madrid and in 1900 became director of the newly established Instituto Nacional de Higiene. In 1920 the Institute Cajal was commissioned by King Alfonso XIII of Spain and here Ramón y Cajal worked until his death.

Ramsay, Sir William

(1852–1916)

BRITISH CHEMIST

[Ramsay was] a great general who wanted an able chief-of-staff. All his best work was done with a colleague.
—Morris William Travers, letter to Frederick Soddy, 10 October 1949

Ramsay came from a scientific background in Glasgow, Scotland, his father being an engineer and one of his uncles a professor of geology. He studied at Glasgow University (1866–69) and returned there as an assistant in 1872 after postgraduate work in chemistry at Tübingen, where he studied under Robert Bunsen. He was appointed professor of chemistry at University College, Bristol, in 1880 and moved to a similar post at University College, London (1887–1912).

Ramsay's early research was mainly in the field of organic chemistry but in 1892 he came across some work of Lord Rayleigh that dramatically changed the direction of his work. Rayleigh reported that nitrogen obtained from the atmosphere appeared to be denser than nitrogen derived from chemical compounds. Rayleigh's original view of this was that the synthetic nitrogen was probably contaminated with a lighter gas. Ramsay, however, predicted that the atmosphere contained some unknown denser gas. He favored this view for he remembered some experiments performed by Henry Cavendish in 1785 in which he showed that present in the air, after removal of all its oxygen and nitrogen, there remained an unabsorbable 1/20th part of the original. Ramsay experimented with methods of totally removing the oxygen and nitrogen from samples of air and found (1894) that a bubble of gas remained. The gas was identified as a new element by Sir William Crookes from the lines in its spectrum. Ramsay and Rayleigh announced the discovery of the element in 1898, naming it argon from the Greek "inert."

In the following year Ramsay heard that in America a strange gas had been discovered by heating uranium ores. Ramsay obtained some of the gas from the mineral cleveite and Crookes was able to establish spectroscopically that this was in fact helium, the element whose spectrum had first been observed in a solar eclipse by Pierre Janssen in 1868.

From the positions of argon and helium in the periodic table of elements it appeared that three more gases should exist. In 1898 Ramsay began the search for these, assisted by Morris Travers. They liquefied argon and by its fractional distillation were able to collect three new gases, which they named neon, krypton, and xenon, from the Greek for "the new," "the hidden," and "the strange." Ramsay completed his work on the inert gases when, in 1904, with R. Whytlaw-Gray he discovered niton (now known as radon), the radioactive member of the series.

In 1903, with Frederick Soddy, Ramsay demonstrated that helium is continually produced during the radioactive decay of radium. The significance of this was not apparent for some time but its explanation by Ernest Rutherford was to lead to the foundation of the new discipline of nuclear physics.

Ramsay was knighted in 1902 and in 1904 was awarded the Nobel Prize for chemistry. His published works included *The Gases of the Atmosphere* (1896) and his two-volume *Modern Chemistry* (1900).

Ramsden, Jesse

(1735–1800)

BRITISH INSTRUMENT MAKER

The son of an innkeeper, Ramsden was born at Halifax in England and spent the years 1751–55 as apprentice to a clockmaker. In 1755 he moved to London, where he served a further apprenticeship before setting up his own business in 1762 in the Haymarket, and from 1775 at 199 Piccadilly.

Ramsden became the leading maker of astronomical instruments in Europe in the latter half of the 18th century and at the height of his fame customers were prepared to wait three years for the delivery of one of his sextants, theodolites, or micrometers. His most significant innovation was described in his *Description of an Instrument for Dividing Mathematical Instruments* (1777) for which he received £615 from the Longitude Board. This improved the accuracy of instruments by calibrating both linear and circular scales mechanically – a process previously done with compass and dividers.

Ramsey, Norman Foster

(1915–   )

AMERICAN PHYSICIST

Born in Washington DC, Ramsey was educated at Columbia and at Harvard, where he obtained his PhD. He has served as professor of physics at Harvard since 1947.

Ramsey was a student of Isidor Rabi and worked with him on the rotational magnetic moments of molecules, showing how these depend on the mass of the nuclei. During World War II he worked first on radar, and later at the Los Alamos Laboratory. His subsequent work was on both high-energy particle scattering and on low-energy magnetic resonance.

In 1947 he began work on a new, more accurate, molecular-beam resonance technique using two separate radiofrequency fields. This was used to measure nuclear magnetic moments and nuclear quadrupole moments and also to investigate the magnetic interactions within simple molecules. Ramsey used the idea of magnetic shielding to interpret the chemical shifts found in nuclear magnetic resonance spectra.

Ramsey, along with D. Kleppner and H. M. Goldenberg, also developed the hydrogen maser. This used a molecular beam of hydrogen atoms and depended for its action on the hyperfine splitting of energy levels (splitting caused by interaction of electron energy levels with the nuclear magnetic moment). It was a highly accurate device, capable of measuring frequency to 1 part in 10^{12}.

Ramsey has also worked on the thermodynamics and statistical mechanics of systems at low temperatures, pointing out that there is a possibility of certain nuclear spin systems having a negative thermodynamic temperature (i.e., a temperature below absolute zero).

For his work on molecular beams Ramsey was awarded the 1989 Nobel Prize for physics, which he shared with H. Dehmelt and W. Paul. He is also the author of a standard work on the subject, *Molecular Beams* (Oxford, 1963).

Randall, Sir John Turton

(1905–1984)

BRITISH PHYSICIST

The son of a nurseryman, Randall was born at Newton-le-Willows in northern England and educated at the University of Manchester. He began work with General Electric at their Wembley laboratory, originally seeking to develop luminescent powders. He was subsequently appointed in 1937 to a Royal Society Fellowship at Birmingham University to conduct research into luminescence.

But the coming of the war stopped all such nonmilitary work and Randall, along with his Birmingham colleagues, began work on improving current radar techniques. By 1943, in collaboration with Boot, he had developed the cavity magnetron, one of the most vital inventions of the war.

With the end of the war in sight Randall was appointed professor of natural philosophy in 1944 at St. Andrews in Scotland. In 1946 he accepted the post of head of a new department of biophysics set up by the Medical Research Council at King's College, London. Under him were Maurice Wilkins and Rosalind Franklin, two scientists intimately connected with the elucidation in 1953 of the structure of DNA.

Randall himself worked on the structure of collagen, an important protein giving the skin its elasticity; it was found to consist of three helices coiled into a superhelix. On his retirement to Edinburgh in 1970 Randall continued to work with an informal research group on problems in biophysics.

Rankine, William John Macquorn

(1820–1872)

BRITISH ENGINEER AND PHYSICIST

Rankine was the son of an engineer from the Scottish capital Edinburgh and he himself trained as a civil engineer. He spent four years in Ireland working on surveys and in 1855 became professor of civil engineering and mechanics at Glasgow University.

He is best known for his work in thermodynamics, especially his formulation of the *Rankine cycle*, the theoretically ideal process for the operation of turbines and steam engines, in which a condensing vapor is the working fluid. This was contained in his *Manual of the Steam Engine and*

Other Prime Movers (1859), and was the first systematic theory for steam engines. He also published studies of soil mechanics and of metal fatigue.

Rankine was the first president of the Institute of Engineers in Scotland and was elected a fellow of the Royal Society in 1853.

Ranvier, Louis-Antoine

(1835–1922)

FRENCH HISTOLOGIST

Ranvier (rahn-**vyay**), the son of a businessman, studied medicine in his native city of Lyons and in Paris, where he qualified as a physician in 1865. He worked initially as an assistant to Claude Bernard at the Collège de France where he served as professor of general anatomy from 1875 until his retirement in 1900.

Ranvier wrote *Traité technique d'histologie* (1875–82; Technical Treatise on Histology), which served as the leading histological textbook for a generation. He is, however, better known for his description in 1871 of the so-called *nodes of Ranvier*. These are regular gaps in the myelin sheath covering medullated nerves.

He clearly had some insight into the transmission of nerve impulses for in 1878 he went on to compare the function of the myelin sheath with that of the insulation surrounding an underwater telegraph cable. It was, however, left to Ralph Lillie in 1925 to suggest that the nerve impulse was transmitted in a saltatory fashion from node to node; this was later confirmed by I. Tasaki, among others, in the 1930s.

Raoult, Francois-Marie

(1830–1901)

FRENCH CHEMIST

Raoult (rah-**ool**) came from a poor background in Fournes-en-Weppes, France. He obtained his PhD in 1863 from the University of Paris and was 37 years old when he took up his first academic appointment at the University of Grenoble, where he was made professor of chemistry in 1870.

Raoult is noted for his work on the properties of solutions, in particular the effect of a dissolved substance in the lowering of freezing points. In 1882 he showed (*Raoult's law*) that the depression in the freezing point of a given solvent was proportional to the mass of substance dissolved divided by the substance's molecular weight. He later showed a similar effect for the vapor pressure of solutions. Measurement of freezing-point depression became an important technique for determining molecular weights.

Raoult's work was also important in validating Jacobus van't Hoff's theory of solutions. Also of significance in his work was his observation that the depression of the freezing point of water caused by an inorganic salt was double that caused by an organic solute (given the same molecular weight). This was one of the anomalies whose explanation led Sven Arrhenius to formulate his theory of ionic dissociation.

Ratcliffe, John Ashworth

(1902–1987)

BRITISH PHYSICIST

Born at Bacup in northern England, Ratcliffe was educated at Cambridge University, where he later lectured in physics (1927–60) and held the title of reader (from 1947). During World War II he was with the Telecommunications Research Establishment, Malvern. In 1960 he was appointed director of the Radio and Space Research Station at Slough, a position he retained until his retirement in 1966.

Ratcliffe worked extensively in the field of atmospheric physics, beginning with his research in the 1920s with Edward Appleton. They established that radio waves are reflected from the Heaviside layer by electrons and not ions. Details of his researches were published in *Magneto-Ionic Theory and Its Applications to the Ionosphere* (1959) and in his more general work, *Sun, Earth, and Radio* (1970).

Not the least of his achievements lay in his role as one of the founding fathers of radioastronomy in Cambridge. Not only did he maintain the tradition of radio research in the Cavendish Laboratory but encouraged many other scientists in the field, including the young Martin Ryle, who worked on solar radio waves. From such beginnings later emerged the Mullard Radio Astronomy Observatory.

Ratzel, Friedrich

(1844–1904)

GERMAN GEOGRAPHER AND ETHNOGRAPHER

Ratzel (**raht**-sel) was the son of an official at the court of the grand duke of Bavaria. He was born in Karlsruhe in Germany and educated at the universities of Heidelberg, Jena, and Munich. After a tour of America

(1874–75) he taught geography at the Technical University of Munich (1875–86) before being appointed in 1886 to the chair of geography at Leipzig, where he remained until his death.

In his two-volume *Anthropogeographie* (1882; 1891; Human Geography) he laid the foundations for the modern study of human geography. He attempted to describe the distribution of human populations and its relation to migration, and to show the relationship between man and his environment.

Ratzel introduced in his *Politische Geographie* (1897; Political Geography) the concept of *lebensraum*, or "living space," which was to have a powerful attraction for the German Nazi regime. The book was written under the influence of Herbert Spencer, and in its Ratzel developed the idea of *lebensraum* as part of his theory of the state and society as an organism. The state, he argued, was a spatial entity, which sought to grow and develop to its natural limits.

Ratzel was a prolific author; in addition to a short but much reprinted work on the geography of Germany he also produced a comprehensive statement of his views in his *Die Erde und das Leben: Eine vergleichende Erdkunde* (1901–02; Earth and Life: A Comparative Geography).

Raup, David Malcolm

(1933–   )

AMERICAN PALEONTOLOGIST

Born in Boston, Massachusetts, Raup was educated at the University of Chicago and at Harvard, where he obtained his PhD in 1957. After a brief spell at the California Institute of Technology, Raup spent the period from 1957 to 1965 at Johns Hopkins, Baltimore, and from 1966 to 1978 as professor of geology at the University of Rochester, New York. In 1980 Raup returned to the University of Chicago as professor of geophysics.

Much of Raup's work has been devoted to the problem of extinction. In 1983, in collaboration with John Sepkoski, Raup proposed the controversial thesis that extinction rates were cyclical, peaking periodically every 26 million years. The evidence for the hypothesis was derived from a large body of data collected by Sepkoski.

Initially Raup offered no explanation for such periodicity, other than to suggest that an extraterrestrial cause was more likely than a terrestrial one. Physicists were quick to take up the challenge with Richard Muller proposing the existence of a companion star of the sun, later named

Nemesis, with a 26-million-year orbit, bringing with it periodic asteroid showers. Raup described the controversy which developed in his *The Nemesis Affair* (New York, 1986).

But, writing later in his *Extinction* (Oxford, 1993), he has noted that most astronomers have rejected the Nemesis and similar hypotheses. As to the 26-million-year periodicity, expert opinion is apparently evenly divided.

Raup has also published, with S. M. Stanley, a widely used textbook, *Principles of Paleontology* (San Francisco, 1978).

Ray, John

(1627–1705)

ENGLISH NATURALIST AND TAXONOMIST

> Diseases are the tax on pleasures.
> —*English Proverbs*

Ray, a blacksmith's son from Black Notley, Essex, attended Braintree Grammar School, where he benefited from a trust established to finance needy scholars at Cambridge University. He graduated in 1648 and became a fellow the following year, but his university career ended with the Restoration; as a Puritan, he refused to take the oath required by the Act of Uniformity and he lost his fellowship in 1662.

His activities as a naturalist were funded thereafter by friends from Cambridge, in particular by Francis Willughby, who helped him with the ambitious project of describing all known living things. From 1663 to 1666 Ray and Willughby traveled through Europe, widening their knowledge of the flora and fauna. On their return Ray moved into Willughby's house so that they could collaborate in writing up the work. In 1667 Ray published a catalog of British plants. In the same year he was elected a fellow of the Royal Society.

Willughby died in 1672 but left money in his will to enable Ray to continue their project. Between 1686 and 1704 Ray published *Historia plantarum* (History of Plants), a three-volume encyclopedia of plants describing 18,600 species. In it he emphasized the importance in classification of distinguishing between the monocotyledons and the dicotyledons but more importantly he fixed the species as the basic unit in the taxonomic hierarchy.

Ray also attempted to classify the animal kingdom. In 1693 he published a system based on a number of structural characters, including internal anatomy, which provided a more natural classification than those being produced by his contemporaries.

Ray is also remembered for his theological writings, in which he used the homologies he had perceived in nature as evidence for the necessity of an omniscient creator.

Rayleigh, John William Strutt, 3rd Baron

(1842–1919)

BRITISH PHYSICIST

> Some proofs command assent. Others woo and charm the intellect. They evoke delight and an overpowering desire to say "Amen, Amen."
> —Quoted by H. E. Hunter in *The Divine Proportion* (1970)

Rayleigh, born at Witham in England, succeeded to his father's title in 1873. He graduated in mathematics from Cambridge University in 1865 and remained at Cambridge until his marriage, in 1871, to Evelyn Balfour, sister of the statesman Lord Balfour. In the following year poor health, which had also disrupted his schooling as a child, necessitated a break from academic life and recuperation in a warmer climate. During this convalescence, which was spent traveling up the Nile in a houseboat, Rayleigh wrote *The Theory of Sound*, which remains a classic in writings on acoustics.

On his return to England, Rayleigh built a laboratory next to his family home. Apart from the period 1879–84, when he succeeded James Clerk Maxwell as Cavendish Professor of Experimental Physics at Cambridge, Rayleigh carried out most of his work in this private laboratory. Of his early work the best known is his equation to account for the blue color of the sky, which (confirming John Tyndall's theory) concerned light scattering by small particles in the atmosphere. The amount of scattering depends on the wavelength of the light, and this causes the blue color. From this theory came the scattering law, an important concept in studies of wave propagation. Rayleigh also did a vast amount of work on other problems in physics, particularly in optics and acoustics.

While serving as Cavendish Professor, Rayleigh concerned himself with the precise measuring of electrical standards. He invented the *Rayleigh potentiometer* for precise measurement of potential difference. He extended this precision to the determination of the density of gases, and made the seemingly strange observation that nitrogen from air is always slightly denser than nitrogen obtained from a chemical compound. This led to his collaboration with William Ramsay that resulted in the discovery of argon. Rayleigh received the Nobel Prize for physics for this work in 1904; in the same year Ramsay was awarded the chemistry prize.

Read, Herbert Harold

(1889–1970)

BRITISH GEOLOGIST

Read, the son of a dairy farmer from Whitstable in Kent, was educated at Imperial College, London, graduating in 1912. After service in World War I he worked with the British Geological Survey of Scotland until 1931 when he was appointed to the chair of geology at Liverpool University. In 1939 he returned as professor of geology to Imperial College, serving there until his retirement in 1955.

Read is best known for his research on the origins of granite. His chief work on this was *The Granite Controversy* (1957), a collection of related papers published during the period 1939–54, in which he argued, in his famous phrase of 1948, "there are granites and granites," or in other words, many different processes had led to a uniform final product. From his fieldwork in the Scottish Highlands, the Shetland Islands, and in Ireland he grouped together the metamorphic, migmatitic, and granitic rocks as plutonic.

Read also proposed a granite series beginning with the early deep-seated autochthonous granites (granites occurring in the same region in which they were formed) and followed by the para-autochthonous, intruded magmatic, and plutonic granites. His work destroyed the simplistic view, dating back to James Hutton, that granites are simple igneous rocks.

Réaumur, René Antoine Ferchault de

(1683–1757)

FRENCH ENTOMOLOGIST, PHYSICIST, AND METALLURGIST

The crocodile is certainly a fierce insect, but I am not in the least disturbed about calling it one.
—On his broad use of the term "insect"

From the time of Aristotle to the present day I know of but one man who has shown himself Mr. [Charles] Darwin's equal in one field of research – and that is Réaumur.
—Thomas Henry Huxley. Quoted by Leonard Huxley in *Life and Letters of Thomas Henry Huxley* (1901)

Born at La Rochelle in western France, Réaumur (ray-oh-**muur**) traveled to Paris in 1703 and was admitted to the French Academy of Sciences in 1708. He was commissioned by Louis XIV (1710) to compile a report on the industry and arts of France, published as the *Description des arts et métiers* (Description of the Arts and Skilled Trades).

Réaumur made contributions to many branches of science and industry. He developed improved methods for producing iron and steel; the cupola furnace for melting gray iron was first built by him (1720). In 1740 he produced an opaque form of porcelain, still known as *Réaumur porcelain*. Réaumur also devised a thermometer (1731), using a mixture of alcohol and water, with its freezing point of water at 0° and its boiling point at 80° (the *Réaumur temperature scale*). He also investigated digestion and established that this was a chemical rather than a mechanical process and he isolated gastric juice in 1752.

Perhaps his greatest individual achievement was the six-volume *Mémoires pour servir à l'histoire des insectes* (1734–42; Memoirs Serving as a Natural History of Insects), the first serious and comprehensive entomological work.

Reber, Grote

(1911–   )

AMERICAN RADIO ASTRONOMER

Reber, who was born in Wheaton, Illinois, studied at the Illinois Institute of Technology and became a radio engineer. His work in radio astronomy has taken him to many places including Washington DC in the late 1940s where he was chief of the Experimental Microwave Research Section, Hawaii, in 1951, and Tasmania in 1954 where he joined the Commonwealth Scientific and Industrial Research Organization. From 1957 to 1961 he worked at the National Radio Astronomy Observatory in Virginia and then returned to Tasmania to complete the studies he had started there.

Reber built the first antenna to be used specifically for extraterrestrial radio observations and was largely responsible for the early developments in radio astronomy. For many years he was probably the world's only radio astronomer. His interest was aroused in 1933 by the work of Karl Jansky. In 1937 he built, in his own backyard, a 9.4-meter steerable parabolic bowl-shaped radio reflector with an antenna at its focus. Working at a shorter wavelength than Jansky, 60 centimeters instead of 15 meters, he began to spot emission peaks in the Milky Way. These were the intense radio sources in the constellations Cygnus, Taurus, and Cassiopeia. He published his results from 1940 onward and these came to the attention of many astronomers who, although unable to follow him immediately owing to the war, recognized the value of his work. Over the years Reber has constructed several telescopes so that he could map the radio sky at different wavelengths. His Hawaiian instrument operated at 5.5–14 meters while in Tasmania he used radio waves of 144 meters.

It was reading Reber's results that stimulated Jan Oort to pose the problem that led to Hendrik van de Hulst's discovery of the 21-centimeter hydrogen emission.

Redfield, William C.

(1789–1857)

AMERICAN METEOROLOGIST

Redfield, who was born in Middletown, Connecticut, worked initially as a saddle and harness maker, studying science in his spare time. He then moved to New York in the 1820s to develop steam transport on the Hudson River.

Redfield's most important contribution to meteorology was contained in his 1831 paper *Remarks on the Prevailing Storms of the Atlantic Coast*. By carefully examining ships' logs in addition to his own direct observations of the effects of storms, he concluded that they blow counterclockwise around a center that moves in the direction of the prevailing winds. This conflicted with the view of James Espy that storms are systems of radially convergent winds and caused a bitter controversy between the two men.

He also worked on, and published an account of, the fossil fish of the American sandstone. In 1848 he was made the first president of the American Association for the Advancement of Science.

Redi, Francesco

(1626–1697)

ITALIAN BIOLOGIST, PHYSICIAN, AND POET

Redi (**ray**-dee), who was born at Arezzo in Italy, studied medicine and philosophy at the University of Pisa, graduating in 1647. He was employed as personal physician to Ferdinand II and Cosimo III, both grand dukes of Tuscany. Intellectually, Redi displayed a variety of talents, being a noted poet, linguist, literary scholar, and student of dialect. On the scientific side, he laid the foundations of helminthology (the study of parasitic worms) and also investigated insect reproduction.

As a biologist he is best known for his experiments to test the theory of spontaneous generation. These were planned to explore the idea, put forward by William Harvey, that flies and similar vermin do not arise spontaneously but develop from eggs too small to be seen. Redi prepared eight flasks of various meats, with half left open to the air and half sealed. Maggots were found only in the unsealed flasks where flies had been able to enter and lay their eggs. That this effect was not due to the presence or absence of fresh air was shown by a second experiment in which half the flasks were covered with fine gauze. Again, no maggots developed in these. This was one of the earliest examples of a biological experiment planned with proper controls. Redi still believed, however, that spontaneous generation occurred in such animals as intestinal worms and gall flies, and it was not until the time of Louis Pasteur that the theory of spontaneous generation was finally discredited.

Reed, Walter

(1851–1902)

AMERICAN PHYSICIAN

> Walter Reed, medical graduate of Virginia, the Army Surgeon who planned and directed in Cuba the experiments that have given man control over that fearful scourge, yellow fever.
> —Citation on the conferment of an honorary degree from Harvard University (1902)

Born in Belroi, Virginia, Reed trained as a doctor at the University of Virginia and at Bellevue Hospital, New York, graduating in 1870. He joined the Army Medical Corps in 1874, spending many years in various frontier posts before being appointed professor of bacteriology at the Army Medical Center, Washington, in 1893.

In the 1890s Reed achieved some success in the investigation of epidemic diseases. For example he was able to show in 1896 that the outbreak of malaria in Washington was not due to bad water and in 1899 he proved that *Bacillus icteroides*, proposed by the Italian bacteriologist Giuseppe Sanarelli as the pathogen of yellow fever, in fact caused hog cholera. Accordingly, in 1900, Reed was appointed to direct a commission to investigate yellow fever in Cuba. The commission began by testing the assumption that yellow fever was spread by infected clothing and bedding. Three nonimmune American volunteers spent 20 nights in a building with tightly screened windows, effectively excluding the entry of insects, sleeping on bedding used by patients with yellow fever. None of the volunteers contracted the disease. They next tested the hypothesis of Carlos Finlay, that the disease was transmitted by the mosquito *Aedes aegypti*. For the initial trial healthy nonimmune volunteers were bitten by infected mosquitoes; five of the six contracted the disease, while the sixth turned out to have been bitten by a mosquito incapable of transmitting yellow fever. Equally significant was the fact that none of the seven nonimmune members of the group who had not been bitten contracted the disease. Reed thus concluded that an attack of yellow fever could be readily induced in healthy subjects by the bite of *Aedes aegypti* mosquitoes that had previously been fed with the blood of yellow fever patients. (However, the trials were not carried out without tragedy, for in the course of them the entomologist of the commission, Jesse Lazear, died of the disease.) In 1901 Reed, in collaboration with James Carroll, the bacteriologist of the expedition, succeeded in establishing the nature of the actual yellow fever pathogen. By showing it to be a microorganism similar to that first discovered by Martinus Beijerinck in 1898, they were the first to implicate a virus in human disease.

Shortly after his return to America Reed died of appendicitis.

Regiomontanus

(1436–1476)

GERMAN ASTRONOMER AND MATHEMATICIAN

The motion of the stars must vary a tiny bit on account of the motion of the earth.
—Remark in a letter anticipating Copernicus's idea of a moving earth (1472)

Regiomontanus (ree-jee-oh-mon-**tay**-nus), as befitted a Renaissance humanist, changed his name, Johann Müller, for a Latin version of the name of his home town Königsberg (now Kaliningrad in Russia). His father was a miller. He was educated at Leipzig and Vienna where he was a pupil of Georg von Purbach. One of the ambitions of Purbach had been to produce a good text of Ptolemy's *Almagest* based on the original Greek rather than translations from Arabic at third or fourth hand. He had intended to go to Italy in quest of manuscripts of Ptolemy and other ancient scientists with the great Greek scholar Cardinal Bessarion. The death of Purbach in 1461 allowed Regiomontanus to take his place and spend six years in Italy searching for, translating, and editing manuscripts. After his return he settled in Nuremberg where his wealthy benefactor, Bernard Walther, built him an observatory and provided him with instruments. In 1475 he was called to Rome by the pope, Sixtus IV, to help in the reform of the calendar but died of the plague (or, possibly, poison) in 1476.

Regiomontanus was one of the key figures of 15th-century science. In the 1460s he wrote *De triangulis* (On Triangles), a work not printed until 1533 but that was, together with *Tabulae directionum* (1475; Tables of Direction), the main channel for the introduction of modern trigonometry into Europe. In the latter work he broke away from the ancient tradition of chords and instead gave tables of sines for every minute and tangents for every degree.

Regnault, Henri Victor

(1800–1878)

FRENCH PHYSICIST AND CHEMIST

Regnault (re-**nyoh**) came from a poor background in Aachen (now in Germany) and started work as a draper's assistant. He entered the Ecole Polytechnique in 1830 and later worked under Justus von Liebig at Giessen. He was successively professor of chemistry at the University of Lyons and the Ecole Polytechnique (1840). He became professor of physics at the Collège de France (1841) and finally director of the Sèvres porcelain factory in 1854.

Regnault's main work was in physics on the properties of gases and in particular the more accurate determination of many physical and chemical effects. Through his meticulous studies he showed, for example, that the law of Pierre Dulong and Alexis Petit was only approximately true when pure samples were taken and temperatures carefully measured. He also worked on the properties of gases – Joseph Gay-Lussac had claimed that a gas will increase by 1/266 of its volume for each increase of temperature of 1°C but Regnault showed that the true increase was 1/273. In addition he made accurate measurements of specific and latent heats and reliable determinations of atomic weights. Regnault is credited with the invention of the air thermometer.

In chemistry, Regnault discovered various organic chlorides that have since become important industrially, including vinyl chloride and carbon tetrachloride. He also took samples of air from different parts of the world and demonstrated that wherever it comes from it contains about 21% oxygen.

Reich, Ferdinand

(1799–1882)

GERMAN MINERALOGIST

Reich (rIk), who was born at Bernburg in Germany, studied at the University of Göttingen and taught at the Freiberg Mining Academy. In 1863 he obtained a yellow precipitate from some local zinc ores. Convinced that it contained a new element he asked his assistant Hieronymus Richter to examine it spectroscopically (he himself was color blind). Richter found a new line in the dark blue region that confirmed Reich's original conviction; the new element was named "indium" after the bright indigo line characteristic of its spectrum.

Reichenbach, Hans

(1891–1953)

AMERICAN PHILOSOPHER

> His impact on his students was that of a blast of fresh, invigorating air; he did all he could to bridge the wide gap of inaccessibility and superiority that typically separated the German professor from his students.
>
> —Carl Gustav Hempel

The son of a prosperous Hamburg wholesaler, Reichenbach (**rI**-ken-bahk) trained originally as an engineer at the Technical High School, Stuttgart. Further study took him to the universities of Berlin, Göttingen, Munich, and Erlangen, where he gained his PhD for a thesis on probability theory. Soon after he joined the Signals Corps, serving with them on the Russian front. He worked briefly in the radio industry after the war but found time to attend Einstein's seminar on relativity given in Berlin. The two became good friends. In 1920 Reichenbach returned to Stuttgart where he taught radio, surveying, and philosophy. In 1926 he applied for the philosophy of science chair in Berlin. Many, however, were opposed to him because of his well-known indifference to metaphysics. It took the intervention of Einstein, with the accusation, "And what would you have done if the young Schiller had applied?", to win the post for Reichenbach. But in 1933, following the rise of Hitler, Reichenbach was dismissed. He had in fact already fled Germany for Turkey where he served as professor of philosophy at Istanbul University from 1930 to 1938, when he moved to a similar position at the University of California, Los Angeles.

Reichenbach was a logical empiricist. Thus he argued in his *Theory of Probability* (Los Angeles, 1949) that probability statements are about measurable frequencies. That is, to say the probability of a die showing a six is 1/6 means that, in the long run, it will show a six one-sixth of the time. The problem facing the frequency theorist is to explain precisely what is meant by "in the long run." And how it might be applied to such claims as "there is probably life on Mars."

Reichenbach also tackled the problem of induction, favoring the pragmatic theory, with the claim that while we could not show that inductive arguments are probable, we can show that no other method is better.

Toward the end of his life Reichenbach's interest turned to the nature of space and time and his ideas are to be found in two posthumously published works, *The Philosophy of Space and Time* (New York, 1953) and *The Direction of Time* (Los Angeles, 1956).

Reichenbach and Carnap founded the important journal *Erkenntnis* (Perception) in 1930, the house organ of the Vienna circle, which somehow managed to survive in Nazi Germany until 1938.

Reichstein, Tadeus

(1897–1996)

POLISH–SWISS BIOCHEMIST

Reichstein (**rIk**-shtIn or **rIk**-stIn), the son of an engineer, was born in Wloclawek, Poland, and educated at the Federal Institute of Technology, Zurich, where he obtained his PhD in 1922. After some years in industry, Reichstein returned to work on the staff of the Institute in 1929. In 1938 he moved to the University of Basel, becoming in 1946 head of the Institute of Organic Chemistry, a position he held until his retirement in 1967.

In the 1930s Reichstein began to investigate the chemical role of the adrenal cortex. These are small glands, found on the kidneys, whose removal is invariably fatal. Beginning with a ton of beef adrenals he managed to reduce it to a mere ten grams of biologically active material.

From such samples he had, by 1946, isolated 29 different steroids, six of which he found would prolong the life of an animal with its adrenal gland removed. Of these, aldosterone, corticosterone, and hydrocortisone later proved the most active. Reichstein managed a partial synthesis of desoxycorticosterone, which for many years was the only corticoid that lent itself to large-scale production. At that time it was also the most effective treatment for Addison's disease.

Similar work was being done in America by Edward Kendall who shared with Reichstein the 1950 Nobel Prize for physiology or medicine together with Philip Hench.

In 1933 Reichstein succeeded in synthesizing ascorbic acid, vitamin C, at about the same time as Norman Haworth in England. He found a better technique for making the vitamin later that year, and this method is still used in commercial production.

Reid, Harry Fielding

(1859–1944)

AMERICAN GEOLOGIST

Reid, who was born in Baltimore, Maryland, was educated at Johns Hopkins University there, gaining his PhD in 1885. After a brief period at Chicago, he returned to Johns Hopkins in 1894 and remained there until his retirement in 1930, having served as professor of geology since 1900.

Reid is best known for his work on earthquakes and for his formulation of the *elastic rebound theory*. Rocks, he noted, are elastic and can store energy in the same way as a compressed spring. Elastic strains are caused by movements of the Earth's crust. If these are greater than the rock can bear, it ruptures, and the rock rebounds to relieve the elastic stresses. Reid formulated his theory in his *The California Earthquake of April 19, 1906* (1910).

Reines, Frederick

(1918–   )

AMERICAN PHYSICIST

Born at Paterson in New Jersey, Reines was educated at the Stevens Institute of Technology and gained his PhD in theoretical physics at New York University in 1944. From 1944 to 1959 he was a group leader at the Los Alamos Scientific Laboratory, concerned with the physics and effects of nuclear explosions.

He was also concerned with investigations into the neutrino, and with Clyde Cowan performed the first experiments that confirmed its existence in the intense radiations from nuclear reactors. The first tentative observation was in 1953, but more definitive experiments were carried out at the Savannah River nuclear reactors in 1956. Detection of the neutrino is difficult because it can travel very long distances through matter before it interacts. Reines subsequently refined the techniques of detection and measurement.

Reines later turned his attention to looking for the relatively small numbers of natural neutrinos originating in cosmic radiation, and to this end constructed underground detectors looking for signs of interactions in huge vats of perchloroethylene. In the course of this work he devised a method of distinguishing cosmic-ray neutrinos from the muons they produce in traveling through the atmosphere.

From 1959 Reines was head of the physics department at the Case Institute of Technology, Cleveland, going on to become professor of physics and dean of physical sciences at the University of California at Irvine in 1966, positions he held until his retirement in 1988. For his codiscovery of the neutrino Reines shared the 1995 Nobel Prize for physics with Martin Perl.

Reinhold, Erasmus

(1511–1553)

GERMAN ASTRONOMER AND MATHEMATICIAN

Erasmus Reinhold, my teacher…a man well-versed not only in mathematics but in universal philosophy, and very careful besides.
—Kaspar Peucer

Little is known about the life of Reinhold (**rIn**-hohlt) other than that he was born at Saalfeld in Germany and became a student at Wittenberg, where he was appointed professor of astronomy in 1536 and rector of the university in 1549. He died a few years later from bubonic plague.

In 1542 Reinhold published a commentary on the *Theoricae novae planetarum* (New Theories about Planets) of Georg von Purbach, a traditional Ptolemaic text dating from about 1454. He is best known, however, for his *Tabulae Prutenicae* (Prussian Tables, 1551), the first work to provide astronomical tables based upon the new heliocentric system of Copernicus. He referred to Copernicus as "a second Atlas, a second Ptolemy," but went on to complain that the computations in Copernicus did not agree with Copernicus's own observations. Comparison between the two based upon recalculations with a computer have established that the accuracy of Reinhold's calculations systematically exceeds that of Copernicus. Although Reinhold's work did much to extend Copernican views, Reinhold made no reference to heliocentric assumptions in his tables.

Remak, Robert

(1815–1865)

POLISH–GERMAN EMBRYOLOGIST AND ANATOMIST

Remak (**ray**-mahk), born the son of a shopkeeper in Posen (now in Poland), obtained his MD from the University of Berlin in 1838. Although he spent most of his career there and despite his considerable scientific achievements Remak was denied appropriate promotion and a teaching position because he was a Jew.

In 1838 Remak finally disposed of the ancient myth, probably dating back to Alcmaeon of Croton, that nerves were hollow tubes. In the long history of medicine they had been authoritatively described by centuries of observant anatomists as carrying various spirits, fluids, and airs. Even the introduction of the microscope in the 17th century made no difference. It was left to Remak to point out that the nerve fiber is not hollow, but solid and flat.

In 1844 Remak discovered ganglion cells in the heart, thus showing that it could maintain a rhythmic beat independently of the central nervous system. He further noted that certain fibers of the nervous system, the sympathetic fibers, have a distinctly gray color rather than the more common white. They in fact lack the myelin sheath enclosing other nerve fibers.

In the mid 1840s, in collaboration with Johannes Müller, Remak made a major revision to the orthodox embryology of Karl von Baer. They reduced the four germ layers of von Baer to three by taking the two middle layers as only one. They also at this point introduced the modern terminology of endoderm, mesoderm, and ectoderm.

It was also Remak who, in 1841, first fully described the process of cell division. He went on to insist that the nucleus was a permanent feature of the cell even though it did become less noticeable after cell division. By 1855 Remak was ready to assert the general conclusion implicit in much of the early cell theory: that the production of nuclei or cells is really only division of preexisting nuclei or cells.

Remsen, Ira

(1846–1927)

AMERICAN CHEMIST

Born in New York City, Remsen was educated at the Free Academy and at the College of Physicians and Surgeons, where he qualified as a physician in 1867. He then studied chemistry in Germany, obtaining his PhD from Göttingen in 1870, and spent the period 1870–72 as assistant to Rudolph Fittig at Tübingen. He returned to America in 1872 and after teaching joined Johns Hopkins University as the first professor of chemistry in 1876. He spent the rest of his career there, serving as president from 1901 to 1913.

Remsen did much to introduce into America the new, rigorous, and professional chemistry that he had learned in Germany. In 1873 he translated Friedrich Wöhler's *Outline of Organic Chemistry* and followed this with his own *Theoretical Chemistry* (1877) and numerous other books, popular and educational as well as advanced. He also founded the *American Chemical Journal* in 1879.

His numerous editorial, writing, teaching, and administrative duties made it impossible for him to pursue a very active research life and he is today best remembered as initiating the discovery of saccharin. In 1879 he gave Constantin Fahlberg, one of his research students, the task of oxidizing the sulfamide of toluene with potassium permanganate. The resulting compound was 500 times sweeter than cane sugar. Fahlberg patented the process, naming the compound saccharin; although Remsen had a part in the discovery he never contested Fahlberg's patent.

Retzius, Anders Adolf

(1796–1860)

SWEDISH ANATOMIST

Retzius (**ret**-si-us) was born in Lund, Sweden, where his father was a professor of natural history at the university; he himself was educated there before he went to the University of Copenhagen. On his return to Sweden he held the chair of anatomy at the Stockholm Karolinska Institute from 1824 until his death.

As a comparative anatomist Retzius did important work on *Amphioxus lanceolatus*, the primitive chordate and key link between the invertebrates and vertebrates. He is, however, best known for his work on human races, which arose from dissatisfaction with the system developed by Johann Blumenbach. In 1842 he introduced the idea of a cephalic index, defined as the ratio between a skull's length and width. Using this he classified skulls into brachycephalic and dolichocephalic, or long and short, types defined precisely in terms of the cephalic index. Retzius has thus been claimed as the father of both craniometry and physical anthropology.

Revelle, Roger

(1909–1991)

AMERICAN OCEANOGRAPHER

Born in Seattle, Washington, Revelle was educated at Pomona College, California, and at the University of California, where he obtained his PhD in 1936. At the same time he joined the Scripps Institute of Oceanography, La Jolla, California, serving as director from 1951 until 1964. He then moved to Harvard as director of the Center for Population Studies, a post he held until 1976.

Revelle was responsible for directing much of the work at Scripps that eventually led to the discovery of sea-floor spreading and magnetic reversals. He also turned in the 1950s to what was then the far from fashionable topic of global warming.

The issue had first been raised by Arrhenius in 1895. He had calculated that a doubling of atmospheric carbon dioxide would raise the temperature by about 10°C. This would, in theory, occur because energy from the Sun arrives at the Earth's surface in the form of light and ultraviolet radiation, which are not absorbed by carbon dioxide. The energy is radiated by the Earth as infrared radiation, which is absorbed by carbon dioxide. The atmosphere thus acts in a similar way to the glass in a greenhouse, and the consequent warming is known as the "greenhouse effect." Revelle lobbied for real measurements and as a result gas recorders were set up in 1957 at Mauna Loa, Hawaii, and at the South Pole. By 1990 the carbon dioxide concentration had risen to 350 parts per million, an increase of 11%.

Revelle was also largely responsible for the foundation of the San Diego campus of the University of California in 1959, and was appointed to be its first dean of science. He returned to San Diego in 1976 as professor of science and public policy.

Reynolds, Osborne

(1842–1912)

IRISH ENGINEER AND PHYSICIST

In my boyhood, I had the advantage of the constant guidance of my father, also a lover of mechanics and a man of no mean attainments in mathematics and their application to physics.
—Quoted by H. Lamb in his obituary notice of Reynolds in
Proceedings of the Royal Society (1912–13)

Reynolds was born in Belfast, now in Northern Ireland; after gaining experience in workshop engineering, he went to Cambridge University, graduating in 1867. In 1868 he became the first professor of engineering at Owens College, Manchester. Reynolds made valuable contributions to hydrodynamics and hydraulics. He is best known for the *Reynolds number*, which he introduced (1883–84) as a dimensionless parameter that determines whether fluid flow is smooth or turbulent. His studies of condensation and heat transfer led to a radical revision of boiler and condenser design. He formulated theories of lubrication and of turbulence, helped to develop the idea of group velocity of waves, explained how radiometers work, and determined the mechanical equivalent of heat.

Reynolds became a fellow of the Royal Society in 1877 and a Royal Society medalist in 1888.

Rhazes

(*c.* 865 AD–*c.* 925 AD)

ISLAMIC PHYSICIAN

> Truth in medicine is an unattainable goal, and the art as described in books is far beneath the knowledge of an experienced and thoughtful physician.
> —Quoted by Max Neuburger in
> *History of Medicine*

Little is known about the life of Rhazes (**ray**-zeez), although there are numerous traditional stories about him. Born at Rayy (now in Iran), he was chief physician at his local hospital and also, at some time, physician at the new hospital in Baghdad. Several of his works on medicine were translated into Latin and he had considerable influence on medical science in the middle ages.

The *Fihrist*, a tenth-century source, lists 113 of his works, some of which survived and were available to the medieval West. His *Kitab al-Mansuri*, known as the *Liber almansuris* (The Book by al-Mansuri) in the West, is mainly a compilation of earlier writings of such authorities as Hippocrates and Galen and as such was important in making such texts more widely available. Another encyclopedic work, *Kitab al-hawi*, or *Liber continens* (The Complete Book), went through five editions. His most original work, though, was his *Treatise on the Small Pox and Measles*, which contains what is thought to be the first description of smallpox.

Rheticus

(1514–1576)

AUSTRIAN ASTRONOMER AND MATHEMATICIAN

The planets show again and again all the phenomena which God desired to be seen from the Earth.
—Quoted by O. Neugebauer in *The Exact Sciences in Antiquity* (1957)

Rheticus (or Rhäticus; **ray**-tee-kuus) was born Georg Joachim von Lauchen in Feldkirch, Austria, but, in the manner of the time, he adopted a professional name from the Latinized form of his birth district, Rhaetia. After traveling in Italy and after attending several German universities, Rheticus was appointed professor of mathematics at Wittenberg in 1536; the chair of astronomy at the time was held by Reinhold. Both were Copernicans and both knew that the doctrine was opposed by the authorities, Protestant and Catholic alike.

Nevertheless the Protestant Rheticus traveled to Catholic Poland in 1539 to see Copernicus. As it happened Copernicus had completed the manuscript of his *De revolutionibus* (On Revolutions) many years before but, for a number of reasons, was unwilling to publish the work. Rheticus was a man of some charm and consequently persuaded Copernicus to allow a brief summary of his work to appear. The result was the *Narratio Prima of Rheticus* (Danzig, 1539; Basel, 1541; The First Narrative of Rheticus). It caused no major reactions and consequently Copernicus released the manuscript of the *De revolutionibus* to Rheticus.

A brief stay of a few weeks was extended to two years as Rheticus first copied the manuscript and then prepared the text for publication. By May 1542 Rheticus was ready to take the manuscript to the Nuremberg printers. When the work finally appeared in 1543 Copernicus failed to acknowledge the help of Rheticus in any way at all.

By this time Rheticus, reportedly because of his homosexuality, was no longer acceptable at Wittenberg and moved accordingly to the Leipzig chair of mathematics in 1542. But in 1550 he was once more forced into flight charged with indulging in "Italian perversions." Thereafter Rheticus seems to have practiced medicine and is occasionally met with in the service of some noble house.

During the latter part of his life Rheticus had, with the assistance of several calculators, prepared a massive set of trigonometrical tables. Whereas previous workers had expressed the functions in terms of arcs of circles, Rheticus introduced the modern practice of defining them as ratios between the sides of right triangles. Ten-place tables were computed for all six trigonometric functions for every 10″ of arc. The work was incomplete at his death and Rheticus needed his own disciple to publish his manuscript. It finally appeared in 1596 edited by Valentin Otho as the *Opus palatinum de triangulis* (The Imperial Work on Triangles).

Ricci, Matteo

(1552–1610)

ITALIAN ASTRONOMER AND MATHEMATICIAN

Ricci (**reet**-chee), a Jesuit, was born the son of a pharmacist in Macerata, Italy. He received a rigorous education from the Jesuits in Rome, including classes in mathematics and astronomy from Christopher Clavius. After a few years' missionary work in India he arrived in Macao in 1582 to wait his chance to gain admission to the centralized xenophobic Ming China. The policy of the Celestial Empire incorporated a generalized contempt for all foreigners as uncultured barbarians together with the not unreasonable claim that the least offensive place for such creatures was their own country. If foreigners themselves were despised, foreigners who presumed to possess a superior religion and culture were beyond comprehension. Thus Ricci's options were very limited, forcing him to gain entry in the only practical way, that is, by becoming an unofficial Chinese. To gain respect and influence he had to go further and become a Chinese scholar. It took 20 years for Ricci to reach Peking, for first he had to master Chinese culture, language, and literature.

Once accepted as a scholar he found many in the Mandarinate who were keen to learn western mathematics and astronomy. Thus he translated the first six books of Euclid into Chinese in 1607, together with works of his teacher Clavius. The Chinese scholars appreciated the many fields in which Ricci was their superior. This had the effect that Chinese science after 1600 ceased to exist as an independent tradition, for although the door could be closed against the Bible and Christianity, it was impossible to shut one's mind to Euclid. Thus Chinese science, because of Ricci, at last became part of universal science. One ironical aspect of this was that Ricci introduced the astronomy of Ptolemy into China with all its medieval accretions just as it was being rejected in Europe.

Ricci had one further advantage that gained for him his ten years' residence in Peking. He had brought with him a magnificent clock with "self-sounding bells" for the emperor Wan Li. As the Chinese scholars were largely ignorant of their own horological tradition, Ricci and the Jesuits were charged with its installation, its upkeep, and the training of eunuchs to care for it. Such was the respect the emperor felt for Ricci, though they never met, that on Ricci's death, land was made available on which his tomb could be built.

Riccioli, Giovanni Battista

(1598–1671)

ITALIAN ASTRONOMER

Born at Ferrara in Italy, Riccioli (reet-**choh**-lee) was a Jesuit priest who spent most of his life at Bologna where he was professor of astronomy. In 1651 he produced his famous work *Almagestum novum* (The New Almagest). It is in this work that the system of naming craters and mountains on the Moon after famous astronomers was introduced. Although the work is not Copernican – Riccioli presents no less than 77 arguments against Copernicus – it is not, despite the title, Ptolemaic either. Riccioli was a follower of Tycho Brahe, naming the largest lunar crater after him. As an observational astronomer he found that Mizar was a double star. He was also a skilled and patient experimenter who attempted to work out the acceleration due to gravity or *g*. He first tested Galileo's claim for the isochronicity of the pendulum and the relationship between the period and the square of the length. To measure the time a falling body takes he needed a pendulum that would beat once a second or 86,400 times per sidereal day. This led to the farce of using a team of Jesuits day after day to count the beats of his pendulum but the magic figure of 86,400 escaped them. Eventually the fathers could no longer tolerate staying up night after night counting pendulum beats and he was left with his pupil Francesco Grimaldi having to accept a less than perfect pendulum. He then performed with Grimaldi the type of experiment Galileo is supposed to have done from the leaning tower of Pisa. He dropped balls of various sizes, shapes, and weights from the 300-foot (92-m) Torre dei Asinelli in Bologna. He succeeded in confirming Galileo's results and establishing a figure for *g* of 30 feet (9.144 m) per second per second, which is close to the value of 9.80665 meters per second per second accepted today.

Richard of Wallingford

(*c.* 1291–1336)

ENGLISH ASTRONOMER AND MATHEMATICIAN

After the death of his father, a blacksmith of Wallingford, Oxfordshire, Richard was adopted by the prior of Wallingford. He was at Oxford University as a student from 1308 to 1314 and taught there from 1317 to 1326 before becoming the abbot of St. Albans. He is thought to have contracted leprosy in early life and there is a manuscript illustration of him in the British Museum that shows him with a spotty or scarred face.

Oxford at this time had gone through a minor renaissance. There were a number of scholars including Richard who were profoundly aware of the limitations imposed by traditional mathematical methods in dealing with virtually any problem of physics. It was Richard who introduced trigonometry into England in its modern form and in a series of manuscripts he produced the basic texts that could have initiated a mathematical revolution. (He was, however, two centuries too soon. The political troubles of the next 200 years and the Black Death were sufficient to smother any premature intellectual birth.) He was not just a theoretical mathematician for he designed and made his own instruments and, above all, he designed a marvelous clock for his abbey. It has been suggested that he introduced the work "clock" into the English language, from the Latin "clocca" for bell. His clock, the plans for which survive, probably predated that of Giovanni de Dondi in the use of an escapement. It showed the position of the Sun, the Moon, the stars, the state of the tide – in fact, it seemed, like most of the medieval clocks, to do just about everything except tell the time.

Richards, Dickinson Woodruff

(1895–1973)

AMERICAN PHYSICIAN

Richards, who was born in Orange, New Jersey, was educated at Yale and Columbia, where he obtained his MD in 1922. After a period of postgraduate work in London, Richards worked at various New York hospitals. From 1945 until his retirement in 1961 he served as professor of medicine at Columbia University.

In 1931 Richards began an important collaboration with André Cournand, which led to the successful development of cardiac catheterization, first used by Werner Forssmann in 1929. In the 1940s Richards demonstrated the use of catheterization as both a research and a diagnostic tool. He showed how it could detect congenital heart defects, measure the effects of drugs acting on the heart, and be used to assess the results of heart surgery.

On a more fundamental level he studied (with Cournand) the blood flow to the lungs and began a major study of changes produced in the circulatory system by traumatic shock.

For his discoveries concerning heart catheterization and pathological changes in the circulatory system Richards shared the 1956 Nobel Prize for physiology or medicine with Cournand and Forssmann.

Richards, Theodore William

(1868–1928)

AMERICAN CHEMIST

Richards came from an artistic background in Germantown, Pennsylvania: his father was a well-known painter and his mother a writer. He originally had ambitions in astronomy but his poor eyesight and the influence of his professor, Josiah P. Cooke, turned him to chemistry. After obtaining his doctorate from Harvard (1888) he continued his studies in Germany before returning to Harvard to take up a professorship in chemistry (1894).

In his doctoral work Richards made an accurate measurement of the ratio of the atomic weight of oxygen to that of hydrogen. His career continued to be devoted almost exclusively to the more accurate determination of atomic weights. He obtained the atomic weights of approximately 60 elements, improving considerably on those achieved by Jean Stas in the 1860s. His determination of the atomic weight of silver, for example, lowered this from Stas's 107.93 to 107.88. In 1913 his team showed that lead present in uranium had a lower atomic weight than normal specimens of lead, thus supporting the idea that it was formed by radioactive decay. In 1914 Richards was awarded the Nobel Prize for chemistry for his work on atomic weights.

In the latter half of his life he became interested in more theoretical problems. In 1902 he published an article which seemed to anticipate some of the ideas of the heat theorem of Nernst; he also worked on the compressibility of the elements.

Richardson, Lewis Fry

(1881–1953)

BRITISH METEOROLOGIST

Big(ger) whirls have little whirls
That feed on their velocity,
And little whirls have lesser whirls,
And so on to viscosity.
—Summarizing his paper *The Supply of
Energy from and to Atmospheric
Eddies* (1920)

Richardson, the son of a farmer, was born in Newcastle-upon-Tyne in northeast England and educated at Durham College and Cambridge University, graduating in 1903. In 1913 he became superintendent of the meteorological observatory at Eskdalemuir, Scotland. His work was interrupted by World War I and he resigned from the Meteorological Office in 1920. He was head of the physics department at Westminster Training College, London, until in 1929 he became principal of Paisley Technical College, Scotland, where he remained until his retirement in 1940.

Richardson was the first to try to apply mathematical techniques to weather prediction, publishing his ideas in *Weather Prediction by Numerical Process* (1922). In this he argued that the state of the atmosphere is defined by its temperature, pressure, and velocity. Once these were known, he believed that equations could be used to predict future weather conditions. The main problem with implementing his program was the time taken for computation, and it also suffered from a shortage of information. This was partially resolved with the advent of electronic computers following World War II.

The *Richardson number*, a value involving the gradients of temperature and wind velocity, is named for him.

Richardson also attempted to apply a mathematical framework to the study of the causes of war, publishing his work in *Generalized Foreign Politics* (1939), *Arms and Insecurity* (1949), and *Statistics of Deadly Quarrels* (1950).

Richardson, Sir Owen Willans

(1879–1959)

BRITISH PHYSICIST

Richardson, the son of a woollen manufacturer from Dewsbury in the north of England, was educated at Cambridge University and at London University, where he became a DSc in 1904. He taught at Princeton in America from 1906 to 1913, when he returned to England to become Wheatstone Professor of Physics at King's College, London, where he remained until his retirement in 1944.

Richardson is noted for his work on the emission of electrons from hot surfaces – the phenomenon first observed by Thomas Edison and used by Edison, John Fleming, Lee de Forest, and others in electron tubes. Richardson proposed an explanation of what he named "thermionic emission," suggesting that the electrons came from within the solid and were able to escape provided that they had enough kinetic energy to overcome an energy barrier at the surface – the work function of the solid. Thus thermionic emission of electrons is analogous to evaporation from a liquid. The *Richardson law* (1901) relates the electron current to the temperature, and shows that it increases exponentially with increasing emitter temperature.

Richardson published an account of his extensive work on thermionic emission in his book *The Emission of Electricity from Hot Bodies* (1910). His work was important for the development of electron tubes used in electronic devices, and he was awarded the 1928 Nobel Prize for physics for this work. During World War II he worked on radar.

Richer, Jean

(1630–1696)

FRENCH ASTRONOMER

> Now several astronomers, sent into remote countries to make astronomical ob-
> servations, have found that pendulum clocks do accordingly move slower near
> the equator than in our climates...In the year 1672, M. Richer took notice of it
> in the island of Cayenne.
>
> —Isaac Newton, *Principia* (1687)

Richer (ree-**shay**) is a rather anonymous figure who is known only through his work with others. In 1671 he went on a scientific mission to Cayenne, where it was intended that he should observe meridian transits of the Sun and also measure the distance of Mars from any nearby stars while Giovanni Cassini performed similar observations in Paris. Apart from the obvious advantage of having two observers making the same measurements with a long base line, there was also the hope that Cayenne, 5° from the equator, would provide better viewing and that, because of its equatorial position, meridian sightings would be subject to less atmospheric refraction than in Paris.

But more important discoveries were to be made. The observations of Mars were made successfully, allowing Cassini to use the parallax obtained to give a distance of the Sun from the Earth of 86 million miles (138 million km). This was not particularly accurate – being 7% out – but at least it was properly determined and could easily be improved. What, however, really surprised Richer was that his pendulum timings were all slightly different from what they would have been in Paris; the pendulum was running slow, even at sea level. Cassini, at first, seems to have doubted the competence of Richer's observations but was eventually convinced. It was this work that provided Newton with the essential information in working out the size and shape of the Earth. If the pendulum slowed down then there must be a smaller gravitational force operating on it. The only way this could reasonably happen was if Cayenne was further from the center of the Earth than Paris; that is, if the Earth bulged at the equator, or to be precise, is an oblate spheroid.

Richet, Charles Robert

(1850–1935)

FRENCH PHYSIOLOGIST

> I possess every good quality, but the one that
> distinguishes me above all is modesty.
> —*The Natural History of a Savant*

Richet (ree-**shay**), the son of a distinguished Parisian surgeon, studied medicine at the University of Paris. After graduation in 1877 he worked at the Collège de France before he returned to the University of Paris where he served as professor of physiology from 1887 until his retirement in 1927.

Richet worked on a wide variety of problems, which ranged from heat regulation in mammals to the unsuccessful development of an anti-TB serum. His most important work began, however, with his investigation of how dogs react to the poison of a sea anemone. He found that he could induce a most violent reaction in dogs that had survived an original injection without any distress. If 22 days later he gave them a second injection of the same amount then they immediately became extremely ill and died in 25 minutes. Richet had discovered the important reaction of anaphylaxis, a term he coined in 1902 to mean the opposite of phylaxis or protection.

By 1903 he was able to show that the same effect could be produced by any protein whether toxic or not as long as there was a crucial interval of three to four weeks between injections. His work was to have profound implications for the newly emerging science of immunology and won for Richet the 1913 Nobel Prize for physiology or medicine.

Richter, Burton

(1931–)

AMERICAN PHYSICIST

Richter (**rik**-ter) was joint winner of the 1976 Nobel Prize for physics. A New Yorker by birth, he studied first at the Massachusetts Institute of Technology, gaining his BS in 1952 and his PhD in physics in 1956. His interest in the physics of elementary particles took him subsequently to Stanford University's high-energy physics laboratory where he became a member of the group building the first pair of electron-storage rings. In this machine, intense beams of particles were made to collide with each other in order to study the validity of quantum electrodynamic theory.

In the 1960s, Richter designed the Stanford Positron Electron Accelerating Ring (SPEAR), which was capable of engineering collisions of much more energetic particles. It was on this machine that, in November 1974, Richter and his collaborators created and detected a new kind of heavy elementary particle, which they labeled psi (ψ). The discovery was announced in a 35-author paper (typical of today's high-energy research teams) in the journal *Physical Review Letters*. The particle is a hadron with a lifetime about one thousand times greater than could be expected from its observed mass. Its discovery was important as its properties are consistent with the idea that it is formed from a fourth type of quark, thus supporting Sheldon Glashow's concept of "charm."

Almost simultaneously, another group led by Samuel Ting 2,000 miles away at the Brookhaven Laboratory, Long Island, made the same discovery independently in a very diffferent experiment. Richter and Ting met to discuss their findings, and confirmation came quickly from other laboratories when they knew the energy of the new particle and were able to tune their own machines accordingly. Ting called the new particle J; it is now usually referred to as the J/psi in recognition of the simultaneity of its discovery. The discovery led to the finding of many other similar particles as a "family" and has stimulated new attempts to rationalize the

underlying structure of matter. Within only two years, Richter and Ting
were to be the recipients of the Nobel Prize for physics.

Richter has been a full professor at Stanford University since 1967,
taking a sabbatical year at the European Organization for Nuclear Research (CERN) in Geneva (1975–76). He became director of the Linear
Accelerator Center in 1984.

Richter, Charles Francis

(1900–1985)

AMERICAN SEISMOLOGIST

Born in Hamilton, Ohio, Richter was educated at the University of
Southern California, Stanford, and the California Institute of Technology, where he obtained his PhD in 1928. He worked for the Carnegie Institute (1927–36) before being appointed to the staff of the California
Institute of Technology. He became professor of seismology in 1952.

Richter developed his scale to measure the strength of earthquakes in
1935. Earlier scales had been developed by de Rossi in the 1880s and by
Giuseppe Mercalli in 1902 but both used a descriptive scale defined in
terms of damage to buildings and the behavior and response of the population. This restricted their use to the measurement of earthquakes in
populated areas and made the scales relative to the type of building
techniques and materials used.

Richter's scale is an absolute one, based on the amplitude of the
waves produced by the earthquake. He defined the magnitude of an
earthquake as the $\log_{10}$ of the maximum amplitude, measured in microns.
This means that waves whose amplitudes differ by a factor of 100 will
differ by 2 points on the Richter scale. With Beno Gutenberg he tried to
convert the points on his scale into energy released. In 1956 they showed
that magnitude 0 corresponds to about 10^{11} ergs (10^4 joules), while magnitude 9 equals 10^{24} ergs (10^{17} joules). A one unit increase will mean
about 30 times more energy being released. The strongest earthquake so
far recorded had a Richter-scale value of 8.6. In 1954 Richter and Gutenberg produced one of the basic textbooks on seismology, *Seismicity of
the Earth.*

Richter, Hieronymous Theodor

(1824–1898)

GERMAN CHEMIST

Born at Dresden in Germany, Richter was assistant to Ferdinand Reich at the Freiberg School of Mines. In 1863 they noticed a brilliant indigo line in the spectrum of some zinc-ore samples they were examining. This led to the discovery of a new element, which they named "indium." Richter later succeeded Reich to become director of the School of Mines at Freiberg (1875).

Ricketts, Howard Taylor

(1871–1910)

AMERICAN PATHOLOGIST

Ricketts brought facts to light with brilliance and accuracy and indicated by the methods he used most of the major lines of development subsequently employed in the study of rickettsial diseases.
—Obituary notice of Ricketts (1910)

Rickets was born at Findlay, Ohio, and graduated in medicine from the Northwestern University Medical School in 1897. Five years later he became associate professor in pathology at the University of Chicago.

Shortly before his death he became professor of pathology at the University of Pennsylvania.

His research was concerned with the transmission of disease by insects, and in 1906 he showed that the bite of the wood tick was responsible for the transmission of Rocky Mountain spotted fever. After a further three years' study he was able to describe the microorganism that caused the disease. This is an unusual microorganism because it is smaller than a bacterium and resembles a virus in that it can grow only inside living cells. Ricketts went on to study the related disease typhus and showed that it was transmitted by the body louse. Unfortunately he contracted the disease, but after his death the microorganisms causing typhus and related diseases were given the name *rickettsia* in his honor.

Riddle, Oscar

(1877–1968)

AMERICAN BIOLOGIST

Born in Cincinnati, Ohio, Riddle was educated at Indiana University and at Chicago, where he obtained his PhD in 1907. After serving on the Chicago faculty from 1904 to 1911, he joined the research staff of the Carnegie Institution at their Station for Experimental Evolution, Cold Spring Harbor, New York, where he remained until his retirement in 1945.

In 1928 it was found that an extract from the anterior pituitary would stimulate milk secretion in rabbits. Riddle and his colleagues soon succeeded in isolating the hormone, which he named prolactin in 1932, and began a prolonged study of its physiological effects. He discovered that it would stimulate the growth of the crop sac in pigeons and inhibit gonadal growth in a number of animals.

His most dramatic and controversial finding, however, was that he could induce maternal behavior in hens by the injection of prolactin. Rats too were shown to adopt such normal maternal behavior as licking and retrieving despite their virgin state.

Rideal, Sir Eric (Keightley)

(1890–1974)

BRITISH CHEMIST

Rideal, born the son of a consultant chemist in London, was educated at Cambridge University, England, and at the University of Bonn where he obtained his doctorate in 1912. After active service in World War I he taught at the University of London (1919–20) before returning to Cambridge. He became professor of colloid science there (1930–46). Rideal moved to the Royal Institution, London, in 1946 as Fullerian Professor of Chemistry but returned to university chemistry in 1950 when he accepted the chair of physical chemistry at King's College, London, where he remained until his retirement in 1955.

Rideal worked on catalysis, producing with Sir Hugh Taylor one of the first comprehensive works on the subject, *Catalysis in Theory and Practice* (1919). He later worked on other problems in surface chemistry, particularly in its relation to biology.

Riemann, (Georg Friedrich) Bernhard

(1826–1866)

GERMAN MATHEMATICIAN

> Therefore, either the reality on which our space is based must form a discrete manifold, or else the reason for the metric relationships must be sought for, externally, in the binding forces acting upon it.
> —Lecture on the foundations of geometry. Quoted in *Nature*, 22 March 1990

Riemann (**ree**-man) was born at Breselenz in Germany and, before studying mathematics in earnest, studied theology in preparation for the priesthood at his father's request. Fortunately he was able to persuade his father, a Lutheran pastor, that his real talents lay elsewhere than in theology. He attended the University of Göttingen and his mathematical abilities were such that his doctoral thesis won the rarely given praise of Karl Friedrich Gauss. After gaining his doctorate Riemann worked on the inaugural lecture necessary in order to gain the post of *Privatdozent* at Göttingen and this too gained Gauss's praise. Eventually Riemann succeeded his friend, Lejeune Dirichlet, as professor of mathematics at Göttingen in 1859 but by then his health had begun to decline and he died of tuberculosis while on holiday in Italy.

Riemann's work ranges from pure mathematics to mathematical physics and he made influential contributions to both. His work in analysis was profoundly important. The *Riemann integral* is a definite integral formally defined in terms of the limit of a summation of elements as the number of elements tends to infinity and their size becomes infinitesimally small.

One of Riemann's most famous pieces of work was in geometry. This was initiated in his inaugural lecture of 1854 that so impressed Gauss, entitled "Concerning the Hypotheses that Underlie Geometry." What Riemann did was to consider the whole question of what a geometry was from a much more general perspective than anyone had previously done. Riemann asked questions, such as how could concepts like curvature and distance be defined, in such a way as to be applicable to geometries that were not Euclidean. Janós Bolyai and Nikolai Lobachevsky (and, at the time unknown to everyone, Gauss) had developed particular non-Euclidean geometries, but Riemann went further and opened up the possibility of a range of geometries different from Euclid's. This work had far-reaching consequences, not just in pure mathematics but also in the theory of relativity.

Riemann was also interested in applied mathematics and physics and was a coworker of Wilhelm Weber.

Righi, Augusto

(1850–1920)

ITALIAN PHYSICIST

Righi (**ree**-gee) studied in his native city of Bologna, firstly at the technical school and later at the university. For seven years, from 1873, he taught physics at the Bologna Technical School. In 1880 he was appointed professor of experimental physics at the University of Palermo and in 1885 professor of physics at the University of Padua. He returned to Bologna in 1889 as professor at the Institute of Physics of the university, remaining there until his death.

Righi's early work included investigations on the action and efficiency of disk-type electrostatic machines and analysis of the composition of vibrational motion as described by Jules Antoine Lissajous. In 1880 he described magnetic hysteresis – the lagging of magnetic induction behind magnetizing field in ferromagnetic substances. He studied the photoelectric effect and in 1888 demonstrated that two electrodes exposed to ultraviolet radiation act like a voltaic couple. However, Righi is best remembered for his studies on electrical oscillations. He made improvements to Hertz's vibrator and showed that at least the shorter Hertzian waves displayed the phenomena of reflection, refraction, polarization, and interference. This demonstrated that radio waves differed from light in wavelength rather than in nature and helped to establish the existence of the electromagnetic spectrum.

Ritchey, George Willis

(1864–1945)

AMERICAN ASTRONOMER

Ritchey, who was born in Tupper's Plains, Ohio, was the son of an amateur astronomer and instrument maker. He completed his studies at the University of Cincinnati in 1887, taught at the Chicago Manual Training School from 1888 to 1896, and for a further three years was an optician. He joined the Yerkes Observatory in 1901 as chief optician. In 1906 he moved with George Hale to Mount Wilson as head of instrument construction, working on both the 60-inch (1.5-m) and 100-inch (2.5-m) reflecting telescopes. Shortly after the war Ritchey and the observatory became involved in a serious dispute and he was actually dismissed for supposedly exceeding his authority. He thus spent the period 1923–30 working in Paris for the National Observatory but returned to America to become director of photographic and telescopic research at the U.S. Naval Observatory where he remained until his retirement in 1936.

While in Paris Ritchey worked with Henri Chrétien on a new design for the optics of a reflecting telescope. *Ritchey–Chrétien optics*, first used by Ritchey in 1930 and again in 1936, have since become one of the standard optical configurations of reflectors.

Apart from his strictly instrumental work Ritchey is also remembered for his astronomical observations, especially for his photographs in 1917 of novae in spiral nebulae. In the hands of Heber Curtis these were to become the basis of a new method for determining the distance of nebulae.

Ritter, Johann Wilhelm

(1776–1810)

GERMAN SCIENTIST

Ritter (rit-er), who was born at Samnitz (now in Poland), left school at the age of fourteen and became an apothecary's apprentice. In 1795 he received a modest inheritance that allowed him to enter the University of Jena the following year. Between 1796 and 1804 he studied and taught at Jena and at Gotha. In 1804 he became a member of the Bavarian Academy of Science and moved to Munich.

Ritter was one of the first investigators to collect hydrogen and oxygen separately from the newly discovered electrolysis of water (1800). In 1802 he built the first dry voltaic pile. He believed in the electrical nature of chemical combination, and explained galvanic and voltaic effects in chemical terms. He was the first to present an electrochemical series (a series of the relative chemical activity of elements based on electrochemical properties). Ritter also examined the effect of light on chemical reactions. His identification of ultraviolet radiation (1801) came after investigating its darkening effects on silver chloride.

Robbins, Frederick Chapman

(1916–   )

AMERICAN VIROLOGIST AND PEDIATRICIAN

Robbins was born in Auburn, Alabama, the son of plant physiologist William Robbins. He obtained his MD from Harvard Medical School in 1940 and from 1942 to 1946 headed the virus and rickettsial section of the U.S. army's 15th medical general laboratory. Here he worked on the isolation of the parasitic microorganisms causing Q fever, which are also responsible for certain kinds of typhus.

After the war Robbins became assistant resident at the Children's Hospital, Boston. In 1948 he became a National Research Fellow in virus diseases, working with John Enders and Thomas Weller. By 1952 Robbins and his coworkers had managed to propagate the poliomyelitis virus in tissue cultures. They established that the polio virus can multiply outside nerve tissue and, in fact, exists in the extraneural tissue of the body, only later attacking the lower section of the brain and parts of the spinal cord.

This research enabled the production of polio vaccines, the development of sophisticated diagnostic methods, and the isolation of new viruses. In recognition of this work, Robbins, together with Enders and Weller, received the Nobel Prize for physiology or medicine in 1954.

Robbins was director of the pediatrics and contagious diseases department at Cleveland Metropolitan General Hospital, and professor of pediatrics at the Case Western Reserve University, from 1952 until his retirement in 1980. He is married to Alice Havemeyer Northrop, daughter of the Nobel Prize winner John Northrop.

Robert of Chester

(*c.* 1110–*c.* 1160)

ENGLISH TRANSLATOR OF SCIENTIFIC WORKS

Robert of Chester was an important figure in the development of medieval science in general and mathematics in particular, not because of any significant discoveries of his own but because he was the first to translate into Latin many important Arab scientific works. Of the scientific texts that thus became available to European scholars for the first time, one of the most important was the *Algebra* of al-Khwarizmi. Robert of Chester was also the first European to translate the Koran from Arabic. He is known to have spent some time in Spain, where he acquired his knowledge of Arabic.

Roberts, John D.

(1918–　)

AMERICAN CHEMIST

Born in Los Angeles, California, Roberts was educated at the university there, obtaining his PhD in 1944. Having taught at the Massachusetts Institute of Technology from 1946 until 1953, he moved to the

California Institute of Technology as professor of organic chemistry, a post he held until his retirement in 1988.

Roberts worked on a number of problems in organic chemistry, including the use of carbon–14 tracers in studying the mechanism of reactions, the effect of substituted groups on organic acids, the molecular-orbital theory of organic molecules, and the mechanisms of cycloaddition reactions.

His most important research was on the application of nuclear magnetic resonance to various problems in organic chemistry using absorption of radiofrequency radiation by hydrogen nuclei. He also extended the NMR technique to resonance absorption by naturally occurring isotopes present in molecules, such as nitrogen–15 and carbon–13, which have a net magnetic moment.

Roberts's books include *Nuclear Magnetic Resonance* (1958) and *At the Right Place at the Right Time* (1990).

Roberts, Richard

(1943–)

BRITISH MOLECULAR BIOLOGIST

Born in Derby, England, Roberts was educated at the University of Sheffield where he gained his PhD in 1968. He moved soon after to America and, after spending a year at Harvard, he moved to the Cold Spring Harbor Laboratory, New York, in 1971. He is currently serving as research director at New England Biolabs, Beverly, Massachusetts.

By the late 1970s it had become clear that the cells of some organisms seemed to have far too much DNA. Prokaryotic cells, i.e., cells without a nucleus, such as the bacteria *Escherichia coli*, have a single chromosome consisting of about 3 million DNA bases. A protein of about 300 amino acids will require 900 base pairs. Consequently a prokaryotic cell should be able to produce about 3,000 proteins, a figure in reasonable agreement with experience. Eukaryotic cells, however, i.e., cells with a nucleus, as in mammals, have a genome of 3–4 billion base pairs, capable of producing some 3 million proteins, a number far in excess of the 150,000 or so proteins found in mammals. The disparity was solved in 1977 when Roberts, working with adenoviruses, stumbled upon the phenomenon of split genes. While all the DNA of prokaryotic cells was transcribed into messenger RNA (mRNA), which was then used as a template upon which amino acids could be assembled into proteins, something quite different seemed to be happening in the nuclei of eukaryotic cells. Only a part of the DNA, sometimes as little as 10%, was actually transcribed into mRNA. DNA appeared to be composed of several stretches, termed "introns," serving no known purpose, but which separated the active DNA sequences, soon to be called "exons." In the process of transcription the introns were neatly excised and the exons consequently spliced together to form the mature mRNA responsible for the production of protein.

The work of Roberts was independently confirmed by Phillip Sharp, with whom he shared the 1993 Nobel Prize for physiology or medicine.

Robertson, John Monteath

(1900–1989)

BRITISH X-RAY
CRYSTALLOGRAPHER

Robertson was born in Auchterarder, Scotland, and educated at Glasgow University where he obtained his PhD in 1926. From 1928 until 1930 he studied at the University of Michigan and then worked at the Royal Institution throughout the 1930s. After brief periods at the University of Sheffield and with Bomber Command of the Royal Air Force, he returned to Glasgow in 1942 and served as professor of chemistry until his retirement in 1970.

Robertson was one of the key figures who, centered on the Braggs and the Royal Institution, developed x-ray crystallography in the interwar period into one of the basic tools of both the physical and life sciences.

He established structures for a large number of molecules, including accurate measurements of bond length in naphthalene, anthracene, and similar hydrocarbons. He also worked on the structure of the important pigment phthalocyanine (1935), durene (1933), pyrene (1941), and copper salts (1951). A notable contribution to the technique was his development of the heavy-atom substitution method, which he used in his investigation of phthalocyanine. This involves substituting a heavy atom into the molecule investigated. The change in intensity of diffracted radiation gives essential information on the phases of scattered waves.

In 1953 Robertson published a full account of his work in his *Organic Crystals and Molecules* in which he demonstrated the growing success in applying the new techniques of x-ray crystallography to complex organic molecules.

Robertson, Sir Robert

(1869–1949)

BRITISH CHEMIST

Robertson, born the son of a dental surgeon in Cupar, Scotland, was educated at St. Andrews University. After graduating in 1890 he served briefly from 1890 to 1892 in the City Analyst's Office, Glasgow, before entering government service on the staff of the Royal Gunpowder Factory, Waltham Abbey. In 1900 he became chemist in charge, but moved to the Royal Arsenal, Woolwich, in 1907 to serve as superintendent chemist of the research department. In 1921 he became government chemist in charge of the Government Chemical Laboratory in the Strand, London. Robertson remained there until his retirement in 1936 but returned to public service during World War II, which he spent working on explosives at the University of Swansea.

Robertson made a number of advances in the chemistry and technology of explosives. He carried out early work on the decomposition of gun cotton and also improved the process of TNT manufacture. More important was his introduction in 1915 of amatol, a mixture of up to 80% ammonium nitrate to 20% TNT, an explosive more efficient and much cheaper than conventionally produced TNT. It was in fact said of amatol by the director of artillery that it "won the war."

As a pure chemist Robertson was one of the first to see the value of infrared spectroscopy for determining molecular structure. He consequently used it to explore ammonia and arsine (AsH_3).

Robinson, Sir Robert

(1886–1975)

BRITISH CHEMIST

Robinson's father was a manufacturer of surgical dressings and one of the inventors of cotton wool. Robinson, who was born at Chesterfield in Derbyshire, England, was educated at the University of Manchester where he obtained a DSc in 1910. From 1912 to 1930 Robinson held chairs in organic chemistry successively at Sydney (1912–15), Liverpool (1915–20), St. Andrews (1921–22), Manchester (1922–28), and University College, London (1928–30). In 1930 he was appointed to the chair of chemistry at Oxford, a post he occupied until his retirement in 1955.

Early in his career, while working with William Perkin Jr. at Manchester, Robinson became interested in the natural dyes brazilin and hematoxylin. Important advances were achieved in understanding the chemistry of these compounds and their derivatives, which eventually led to his syntheses of anthocyanins and flavones, important plant pigments. Robinson also worked on the physiologically active alkaloids and established the structure of morphine (1925) and strychnine (1946). For his "investigations of plant products of biological importance, especially the alkaloids" Robinson was awarded the 1947 Nobel Prize for chemistry.

From 1945 to 1950 Robinson was president of the Royal Society.

Roche, Edouard Albert

(1820–1883)

FRENCH MATHEMATICIAN

Roche (rohsh) studied at the university in his native city of Montpellier, obtaining his doctorate there in 1844. After further study in Paris he returned to Montpellier in 1849 and served as professor of pure mathematics from 1852 until his retirement in 1881.

Roche's name is still remembered by astronomers for his proposal in 1850 of the limiting distance since named for him. He calculated that if a satellite and the planet it orbited were of equal density then the satellite could not lie within 2.44 radii, the *Roche limit*, of the larger body without breaking up under the effect of gravity. As the radius of Saturn's outermost ring is 2.3 times that of Saturn it was naturally felt that the rings could well consist of broken-down fragments of a former satellite that had transgressed the forbidden limit. It is now thought, however, that the Roche limit has prevented the fragments from aggregating into a satellite.

Roche later worked on the nebular hypothesis of Pierre Simon de Laplace, submitting it to a rigorous mathematical analysis and concluding in 1873 that a rapidly rotating lens-shaped body was in fact unstable. He also published work on the structure and density of the Earth and produced a generalization of Taylor's theorem, much used in mathematics.

Rodbell, Martin

(1925–   )

AMERICAN BIOCHEMIST

Rodbell was educated at the University of Washington where he gained his PhD in 1954. He first worked at the National Institute of Health, Bethesda, Maryland. In 1985 he was appointed Scientific Director of the National Institute for Environmental Health Sciences, North Carolina.

Rodbell has sought to show at the molecular level how cells respond to such chemical signals as hormones and neurotransmitters. It had been shown by Earl Sutherland in 1957 that hormones, also known as "first messengers," do not actually penetrate into the cell but rather stimulate the production of a so-called second messenger, cAMP (cyclic adenosine monophosphate). But, Rodbell asked, how does the binding of a hormone to its receptor stimulate the production of cAMP?

The process proved to be quite complex. In the late 1960s Rodbell found that at least two other factors, referred to as an amplifier and a transducer, were essential. The first extra factor, the amplifier, was needed to initiate the production of cAMP. It was identified as the enzyme AC (adenylate cyclase), which converted the energy-rich molecule ATP (adenosine triphosphate) into the second messenger cAMP. For the second extra factor, the transducer, Rodbell found that no reaction would occur without the presence of a complex energy-rich molecule GTP (guanine triphosphate). The GTP reacted in some way with the AC to initiate cAMP production. If either were absent the cell simply would not respond to such external stimuli as insulin or adrenaline.

For his work on what later became known as G proteins Rodbell shared the 1994 Nobel Prize for physiology or medicine with Alfred Gilman.

Roget, Peter Mark

(1779–1869)

BRITISH PHYSICIAN AND ENCYCLOPEDIST

Roget (roh-**zhay** or ro-**zhay**) was born in London, where his father, a Swiss pastor of the French protestant church in Soho, died when Roget was only four. He was brought up by his mother and uncle, Sir Samuel Romilly (1757–1818), a well-known politician and law reformer. He was educated at the University of Edinburgh where he became a qualified MD in 1798.

Roget began to practice medicine in 1804 at the Manchester Public Infirmary. Before this he had spent the period 1789–99 in Bristol where he learned something of the new "pneumatic medicine" from the famous quack Thomas Beddoes and from Humphry Davy. He moved to London in 1800 and worked with Jeremy Bentham on a plan to build a "frigidarium" or ice house for the preservation of food. But Bentham lost interest after a while and in 1802 Roget set off on a European tour as tutor-companion to the sons of John Phillips, a Manchester mill owner. It was an exciting, although dangerous, time to tour Europe. The Treaty of Amiens, signed in 1802, seemed to offer peaceful times, but was soon ignored and in 1803 Napoleon ordered that all British of military age should be immediately interned. Roget managed to delay the authorities by claiming Swiss, and thereby French, citizenship. While his claim was being investigated he succeeded in escaping over the border to Germany.

On his return to England Roget began to practice medicine, first in Manchester, and from 1809 in London. This, however, was only part of his life. Roget also wrote much, including contributions to the *Encyclopedia Britannica Supplement* (6 vols., London, 1816–24). In one entry, "Cranioscopy", he attacked the then fashionable phrenology, arguing that it lacked direct proof and relied excessively on dubious analogies. Another entry, on Bichat, was still being used in the 1967 14th edition. Other works of Roget include *Animal and Vegetable Physiology* (1834) and *Outline of Physiology* (1839).

Roget also devoted much of his time to the administration of British science, most notably as secretary of the Royal Society (1827–49). It was a difficult time in the Society's history. Reformers like Charles Babbage and Michael Faraday argued that the Society had fallen into the hands of nonscientists and did little to promote science. Although Roget weathered this storm, a later dispute in 1845 about the award of the Royal Medal to Thomas Beck for his work on nerves of the uterus led to his resignation in 1849.

Although nearly seventy, Roget's release from the Royal Society at last gave him the freedom to work on the book with which he has become famous. Roget had actually begun to compile words for his *Thesaurus* in 1805 and continued intermittently until he began to construct the final version in 1848. It was published in 1852 and went through a further 25 editions before Roget's death in 1869; thereafter it has continued to sell in great quantities – by 1990 well over 20 million copies had been sold. In his classification of words into categories, Roget was influenced by the success of Linnaeus's classification of plants and animals. He hoped that his classification of language might prove a useful tool for the study of language.

Roget also displayed an interest in scientific inventions. He spent much time trying to develop a calculating machine. Though unsuccessful in this field he had in 1814 invented the log-log scale for use on the slide rule. It was for this innovation that Roget was elected to the Royal Society.

Rohrer, Heinrich

(1933–   )

SWISS PHYSICIST

Born at Buchs in Switzerland, Rohrer (**rohr**-er) was educated at the Federal Institute of Technology, Zurich, where he obtained his PhD in 1960. After two years' postdoctoral work at Rutgers, New Jersey, he returned to Zurich in 1963 to join the staff of the IBM Research Laboratory, Roschliken.

The conventional electron microscope developed by Ruska in the 1930s could present a two-dimensional image only. Further, while atoms have a diameter of 1–2 angstroms (1 angstrom = 10^{-10} meter), electron microscopes could not resolve images below 5 angstroms. Consequently, the surface structure at the atomic level was beyond the range of any existing microscope. To overcome this limitation Rohrer, in collaboration with his IBM colleague, Gerd Bining, began work in 1978 on a scanning tunneling microscope (STM).

In the STM a fine probe passes within a few angstroms of the surface of the sample. If a positive voltage is applied to the probe, electrons can move from the sample to the probe by the tunnel effect, and a current can be detected. This current is sensitive to distance from the surface; a slight change in distance will produce a significant change in current. Consequently, in theory at least, a feedback mechanism should be able to keep the probe at a constant distance from the surface, or, in other words, trace the surface's contours. If the tip is allowed to scan the surface by sweeping through a path of parallel lines, a three-dimensional image of the surface can be constructed.

Inevitably practice proved less straightforward than theory. A major difficulty was to eliminate vibration. As the magnification required was of the order of 100 million, any interference would grossly distort the image produced. The microscope was suspended on springs and placed in a vacuum, and further vibrations were dampened by resting the microscope on copper plates positioned between magnets. If the copper plates begin to move an eddy current will be induced by the magnetic field and the interaction between current and field will, in turn, damp the motion of the plates. Vibration was so reduced as to allow a vertical resolution of 0.1 angstrom; the lateral resolution, depending upon the sharpness of the probe, was initially no better than 6 angstroms.

The STM has proved useful in the study of the surfaces of semiconductors and metals. It is also hoped that with increased lateral resolution it will be applicable to biological samples such as viruses. For their work in this field Rohrer and Bining shared the 1986 Nobel Prize for physics with Ruska.

Rokitansky, Karl

(1804–1878)

AUSTRIAN PATHOLOGIST

Rokitansky (roh-kee-**tahn**-skee) was born at Königgrätz (now Hradec Králové in the Czech Republic), the son of a local government official. He studied philosophy at the University of Prague, later moving to Vienna to study medicine. After graduating in 1828 he accepted a post at the Pathological Institute where he later served as professor of pathological anatomy from 1844 until his retirement in 1875.

He was thus a key figure in the revival of Viennese medicine, making the General Hospital one of the leading centers for medical research in the world. In his *Handbuch der pathologischen Anatomie* (3 vols. 1842–46; Handbook of Pathological Anatomy), based on many thousands of autopsies, he attempted to introduce new standards and criteria of pathology.

Despite the more than 30,000 autopsies personally performed by him, Rokitansky still presented an admittedly modified humoral theory of disease in his Handbook, which led to criticism from Rudolf Virchow. Rokitansky saw sickness as fundamentally due to an imbalance of various substances in the blood, mainly serum proteins such as albumin. Such ideas were omitted from the second edition.

Rokitansky nonetheless distinguished between lobar and lobular pneumonia, described acute yellow fever of the liver, and made fundamental studies of spondylolisthesis, endocarditis, and gastric ulcers.

Ironically, while the eminent pathologist was struggling to modernize the theories of traditional medicine, there worked in his hospital a lowly Hungarian, Ignaz Semmelweis, who by the late 1840s had already achieved considerable success with what was later to develop into the germ theory of disease. Rokitansky was one of the very few physicians to support Semmelweis's work.

Romer, Alfred Sherwood

(1894–1973)

AMERICAN PALEONTOLOGIST

Romer, who was born at White Plains, New York, and educated at Amherst College and Columbia University, established his reputation with a PhD on comparative myology (musculature), which remains a classic in its field. The impetus for subsequent paleontological fieldwork and research came with his appointment as associate professor in the University of Chicago's department of geology and paleontology, where he was able to study the collections of late Paleozoic fishes, amphibians, and reptiles. Professor of biology at Harvard from 1934, Romer then became Harvard's director of biological laboratories (1945) and director of the Museum of Comparative Zoology (1946).

One of the major figures in paleontology since the 1930s, Romer spent the greater part of his career researching the evolution of vertebrates, based on evidence from comparative anatomy, embryology, and paleontology, and his work has had considerable influence on evolutionary thinking, especially with regard to the lower vertebrates. He paid particular attention to the relationship between animal form and physical function and environment, tracing, for example, the physical changes that occurred during the evolutionary transition of fishes to primitive terrestrial vertebrates. He made extensive collections of fossils of fishes, amphibians, and reptiles from South Africa and Argentina and from the Permian deposits in Texas. His best-known publication is *Man and the Vertebrates* (1933), subsequently revised as *The Vertebrate Story* (1959).

Römer, Ole Christensen

(1644–1710)

DANISH ASTRONOMER

Born at Aarhus in Denmark, Ole (or Olaus) Römer (**ru(r)**-mer) was professor of astronomy at the University of Copenhagen when Jean Picard visited Denmark to inspect Tycho Brahe's observatory at Uraniborg. Picard recruited him and Römer joined the Paris Observatory in 1671. In Paris, working on Giovanni Cassini's table of movements of the satellites of Jupiter, he noticed that whether the eclipses happened earlier or later than Cassini had predicted depended on whether the Earth was moving toward or away from Jupiter. Römer realized that this anomaly could be explained by assuming that the light from the satellite had a longer (Earth moving away from Jupiter) or shorter (Earth moving toward Jupiter) distance to travel. As Cassini had recently established the distance between the Earth and Jupiter, Römer realized that he had all the information needed to calculate one of the fundamental constants of nature – the speed of light. In 1676 he announced to the French Academy of Sciences that the speed of light was, in modern figures, 140,000 miles (225,000 km) per second. This value is too small but was an excellent first approximation. In 1681 Römer was made Astronomer Royal and returned to Copenhagen where he designed and developed the transit telescope.

Röntgen, Wilhelm Conrad

(1845–1923)

GERMAN PHYSICIST

Pride in one's profession is demanded, but not professional conceit, snobbery or academic arrogance, all of which grow from false egotism.
—Address on becoming rector of Würzburg University (1894)

Röntgen (**ru(r)nt**-gen or **rent**-gen), who was born at Lennep in Germany, received his early education in the Netherlands; he later studied at the Federal Institute of Technology, Zurich. After receiving his doctorate in 1869 for a thesis on *States of Gases*, he held various important university posts including professor of physics at Würzburg (1888) and professor of physics at Munich (1900). Röntgen researched into many branches of physics including elasticity, capillarity, the specific heat of gases, piezoelectricity, and polarized light. He is chiefly remembered, however, for his discovery of x-rays made at Würzburg on 8 November 1895.

In 1894 Röntgen had turned his attention to cathode rays and by late 1895 he was investigating the fluorescence caused by these rays using a Crookes tube. In order to direct a pencil of rays onto a screen, he covered a discharge tube with black cardboard and operated it in a darkened room. Röntgen noticed by chance a weak light on a nearby bench and found that another screen, coated with barium platinocyanide, was fluorescing during the experiment. He had already established that cathode rays could not travel more than a few centimeters in air, and as the screen was about a meter from the discharge tube he realized that he had discovered a new phenomenon. During the succeeding six weeks he devoted himself, feverishly and exclusively, to investigating the properties of the new emanations, which, because of their unknown nature, he called "x-rays". On 28 December 1895 he announced his discovery and gave an accurate description of many of the basic properties of the rays: they were produced by cathode rays (electrons) at the walls of the discharge tube; they traveled in straight lines and could cause shadows; all bodies were to some degree transparent to them; they caused various substances to fluoresce and affected photographic plates; they could not be deflected by magnetic fields. Röntgen concluded that x-rays were quite different from cathode rays but seemed to have some relationship to light rays. He conjectured that they were longitudinal vibrations in the ether (light was known to consist of transverse vibrations). Their true nature was finally established in 1912.

Röntgen's discovery immediately created tremendous interest. It did not solve the contemporary wave–particle controversy on the nature of radiation but it stimulated further investigations that led, among other things, to the discovery of radioactivity; it also provided a valuable tool for research into crystal structures and atomic structure, and x-rays were soon applied to medical diagnosis. Unfortunately their danger to health only became understood very much later; both Röntgen and his technician suffered from x-ray poisoning.

Although Röntgen was subjected to some bitter attacks and attempts to belittle his achievements, his discovery of x-rays earned him several honors, including the first ever Nobel Prize for physics (1901).

Roozeboom, Hendrik Willem Bakhuis

(1856–1907)

DUTCH CHEMIST

Roozeboom (**roh**-ze-bohm) was born at Alkmaar in the Netherlands. Having worked for some time in a butter factory, he became assistant to Jakob van Bemmelen, professor of chemistry at the University of Leiden, from which he graduated in 1884. He succeeded Jacobus van't Hoff as professor of chemistry in the University of Amsterdam in 1886.

Roozeboom's great achievement was the dissemination of Josiah Willard Gibb's phase rule. Gibbs had published his results in the *Transactions of the Connecticut Academy of Sciences* (a journal not read by many European scientists) in the period 1876–78. Roozeboom heard of the work from Johannes van der Waals and saw it as a major break-through in chemical understanding. Not only did he bring it to the attention of Europe, but he also demonstrated its validity and showed its applicability and usefulness, areas in which Gibbs was weak. He showed, for instance, that it had practical applications in the chemistry of alloys and that it led to the discovery of many new ones.

Roscoe, Sir Henry Enfield

(1833–1915)

BRITISH CHEMIST

> The best of the thing is that vanadium will turn out to be a most valuable substance for calico-printers and dyers – as by its means an aniline-black can be prepared which is far superior to that obtained with copper salts.
> —On the industrial application of vanadium.
> Letter to Robert Bunsen (1876)

The son of a London barrister, Roscoe was educated at University College, London, and at Heidelberg where he studied under Bunsen. On his return to England he was appointed in 1857 to the professorship of chemistry at Owens College, Manchester, the precursor of Manchester University.

Roscoe's main chemical researches were devoted to the study of vanadium and its compounds. Earlier workers, he demonstrated, had used interstitial oxides and nitrides of vanadium rather than the pure metal. Roscoe succeeded for the first time in isolating the pure metal by passing hydrogen over the dichloride. He went on to show that vanadium was a member of Group V of the periodic table.

Not the least of his achievements was the cultivation of science in Victorian Manchester. Owens College was in a state of decline when he arrived in 1857, with few students and little local support. When only 19 students enrolled, Roscoe took his case to local manufacturers and local politicians. To the local politicians he stressed the role of chemistry in sanitary matters, and to the industrialists he spoke of the economies possible from a correct understanding of the chemistry involved in many manufacturing processes. Before long, the Manchester community came to see the need to offer their citizens a scientific education and training. The enrollment at Owens began to grow and long before Roscoe's retirement the college had become a thriving center for teaching and research.

Roscoe made other contributions to public affairs. He was Liberal member of parliament for South Manchester from 1885 to 1889 and served on a large number of Royal and other commissions. He was also the author of the frequently revised and reprinted *Lessons in Elementary Chemistry* (1869).

Rose, William Cumming

(1887–1984)

AMERICAN BIOCHEMIST

Born in Greenville, South Carolina, Rose was educated at Davidson College, North Carolina, and at Yale, where he obtained his PhD in 1911. He taught at the University of Texas from 1913 to 1922, when he moved to the University of Illinois as professor of physiological chemistry; from 1936 until his retirement in 1955 he was professor of biochemistry there.

In the late 1930s Rose was responsible for a beautifully precise set of experiments that introduced the idea of an essential amino acid into nutrition, demonstrating its effect on both human and rodent diet. It had been known for a long time to nutritionists that rats fed on a diet in which the only protein was zein (found in corn), despite enrichment with vitamins, would inevitably die. Rose worked with the constituent amino acids rather than proteins; he still found, however, that whatever combination of amino acids he tried the rats died. However, if the milk protein, casein, was added to their diet the ailing rats recovered.

It was obvious from this that casein must contain an amino acid, not present in zein and then unknown, that was essential for life. Rose began a long series of experiments extracting and testing various fragments of casein until at last he found, in 1936, threonine, the essential amino acid that provided a satisfactory rodent diet when added to the other amino acids. Rose argued that if there was one essential amino acid there could well be others. Over several years he therefore continued to manipulate the rodent diet and finally established the primary importance of ten amino acids: lysine, tryptophan, histidine, phenylalanine, leucine, isoleucine, methionine, valine, and arginine, in addition to the newly discovered threonine. With these in adequate quantities the rats were capable of synthesizing any of the other amino acids if and when they were needed.

In 1942 Rose began a ten-year research project on human diet. By persuading students to restrict their diet in various ways Rose eventually established that there are eight essential amino acids for humans: unlike rats we can survive without arginine and histidine. Since then, however, it has been suggested that these two amino acids are probably required to sustain growth in infants.

Ross, Sir Ronald

(1857–1932)

BRITISH PHYSICIAN

I find Thy Cunning seeds,
O million-murdering Death.
I know this little thing
A myriad men will save
O Death where is thy sting?
Thy victory, O Grave?
　　—Describing his discovery in 1897 of
　　the life-cycle of the malaria parasite

The son of an Indian Army officer, Ross was born in Almora, India. He originally wished to be an artist but his father was determined that he should join the Indian Medical Service. Consequently, after a medical education at St. Bartholomew's Hospital, London, Ross entered the Indian Medical Service in 1881.

Much of Ross's early career was spent in literary pursuits, writing poetry and verse dramas; he published some 15 literary works between 1883 and 1920. It was also during this first period in India that Ross developed his passion for mathematics. This was a lifelong interest and he published some seven titles between 1901 and 1921; in his *Algebra of Space* (1901) he claimed to have anticipated some of the work of A. N. Whitehead.

On leave in England in 1889, Ross took a diploma in public health and attended courses in the newly established discipline of bacteriology. He became interested in malaria and in 1894 approached Patrick Manson with a request to be shown how to detect the causative parasite of malaria, first described by Charles Laveran in 1880. With his guidance and encouragement, Manson turned out to be the major influence in Ross's scientific career. It was Manson who suggested to Ross that mosquitoes might be the vectors of malaria, and when Ross returned to India he spent the next four years researching this theory.

His first strategy, to try and demonstrate the transmission of the disease from mosquitoes to man, met with little success: attempts to infect a colleague with bites from a mosquito fed on malaria patients failed, possibly because the species he used was not a carrier of the disease. He therefore decided to study the natural history of the mosquito in more detail and by 1897 had succeeded in identifying malaria parasites (plasmodia) in the bodies of *Anopheles* mosquitoes fed on blood from infected patients. Ross then attempted to show what happened to the parasite in the mosquito and how it reached a new human victim. He decided to work with avian malaria and its vector *Culex fatigans*, giving him a control over his experimental subjects impossible to attain with man. By 1898 he had succeeded in identifying the *Proteosoma* parasite responsible for avian malaria in the salivary glands of the mosquito, thus proving that the parasite was transmitted to its avian host by the bite of the mosquito. Manson was able to report Ross's work to the meeting of the British Medical Association in Edinburgh and by the end of the year Italian workers under Giovanni Grassi had been able to show similar results in the *Anopheles* mosquito, the vector of human malaria.

In 1899 Ross resigned from the Indian Medical Service and accepted a post at the Liverpool School of Tropical Medicine, remaining there until 1912, when he moved to London to become a consultant. During this period he spent much time on the problem of mosquito control, advising many tropical countries on appropriate strategies.

For his work on malaria Ross was awarded the 1902 Nobel Prize for physiology or medicine.

Rossby, Carl-Gustaf Arvid

(1898–1957)

SWEDISH–AMERICAN METEOROLOGIST

Rossby was born the son of an engineer in Stockholm and educated at the university there. In 1919 he joined the Geophysical Institute at Bergen, which at the time, under Vilhelm Bjerknes, was the world's main center for meteorological research. In 1926 he emigrated to America and was appointed professor of the first meteorology department in America at the Massachusetts Institute of Technology in 1928. After two years as assistant head of the Weather Bureau he became professor of meteorology at the University of Chicago in 1941.

Rossby carried out fundamental work on the upper atmosphere, showing how it affects the long-term weather conditions of the lower air masses. Measurements recorded with instrumented balloons had demonstrated that in high latitudes in the upper atmosphere there is a circumpolar westerly wind, which overlays the system of cyclones and anticyclones lower down. In 1940 Rossby demonstrated that long sinusoidal waves of large amplitude, now known as *Rossby waves*, would be generated by perturbations caused in the westerlies by variations in velocity with latitude. Rossby also showed the importance of the strength of the circumpolar westerlies in determining global weather. When these are weak, cold polar air will sweep south, but when they are strong, the normal sequence of cyclones and anticyclones will develop.

Rossby is credited with having discovered the jet stream. He also devised mathematical models to predict the weather which were simpler than those of Lewis F. Richardson. His school provided the "dynamic meteorology" that allowed, with the coming of computers and weather satellites, the long-term prediction of weather.

Rosse, William Parsons, 3rd Earl of

(1800–1867)

IRISH ASTRONOMER AND
TELESCOPE BUILDER

The eldest son of the 2nd Earl of Rosse, William Parsons was born at York in England. He was educated at Trinity College, Dublin, and Oxford University, where he graduated in 1822. He was a member of parliament from 1822 until 1834, when he resigned to devote himself to science.

Rosse's main aim was to build a telescope at least as large as those of William Herschel. As Herschel had left no details of how to grind large mirrors, Rosse had to rediscover all this for himself. It was not until 1839 that he had made a 3-inch (8-cm) mirror; this was followed by mirrors of 15 inches (38 cm), 24 inches (61 cm), and 36 inches (91 cm) until, in 1842, he felt confident enough to start work on his 72-inch (183-cm) masterpiece. He was only successful on the fifth casting. It weighed 8,960 pounds (4,064 kg), cost £12,000, and became known as the "Leviathan of Corkstown." Its tube was over 50 feet (15 m) long and because of winds it had to be protected by two masonry piers 50 feet (15 m) high and 23 feet (7 m) apart in which it was supported by an elaborate system of platforms, chains, and pulleys.

The giant reflector suffered, despite the cost and time, from two major defects. The climate of central Ireland is such that very few nights of viewing are possible during the year. Also, viewing (when possible), was restricted by the piers to a few degrees of the north–south meridian. Despite this Rosse made a couple of discoveries. He was the first to identify a spiral nebula and went on to discover 15 of them. He also named and studied the Crab nebula, which has been so important to contemporary astronomy. The telescope was finally dismantled in 1908. More than the individual discoveries made by Rosse, the Leviathan was important in the warnings it gave telescope builders. Good big mirrors were needed but they were by no means sufficient; in addition a good site and an adequate mounting were necessary.

Rossi, Bruno Benedetti

(1905–1994)

ITALIAN–AMERICAN PHYSICIST

Rossi (**ros**-ee), born the son of an electrical engineer in Venice, Italy, was educated at the universities of Padua and Bologna. He first taught at the universities of Florence and Padua before emigrating to America in 1938. There he worked at Chicago and Cornell universities and in 1943 moved to Los Alamos to work on the development of the atom bomb. After World War II he was appointed, in 1946, to the chair of physics at the Massachusetts Institute of Technology where he remained until his retirement in 1970.

Rossi's main work was in the field of cosmic rays. These had first been detected by Victor Hess in 1911 but, by 1930, there was little agreement on their real nature; it was not even certain whether or not they were charged particles. To answer this question most physicists had been inconclusively searching for a variation in intensity with latitude.

Instead, in 1930 Rossi proposed an experimental arrangement that would search for any east–west asymmetry. Charged particles coming from outer space would be deflected by the Earth's magnetic field eastward if positively charged and westward if negatively charged. To detect them Rossi suggested that two or more Geiger counters be arranged pointing eastward with their centers arranged in a straight line. A similar arrangement should be set up pointing westward. Thus only particles coming from the direction along the axis of the counters would register simultaneously on both or all of them. In 1934 Rossi set up his counters in the mountains of Eritrea and found a 26% excess of particles traveling eastward, thus showing that the majority of cosmic-ray particles are positively charged.

Rossi was the author of several books, including *Cosmic Rays* (1964), which has been used by generations of physics students.

Rossini, Frederick Dominic

(1899–1994)

AMERICAN PHYSICAL CHEMIST

Rossini, who was born at Monongahela, Pennsylvania, was educated at the Carnegie Institute of Technology (now the Carnegie–Mellon University), Pittsburgh, and the University of California where he obtained his PhD in 1928. He worked at the National Bureau of Standards, Washington DC, from 1928 to 1950, serving as head of the Thermochemistry and Hydrocarbon section from 1936. In 1950, however, he returned to

Carnegie as professor of chemistry and director of the Petroleum Research Laboratory, moving later to chairs of chemistry at Notre Dame in 1960 and Rice University in 1971, in which latter position he remained until his retirement in 1978.

Rossini worked mainly in the fields of thermodynamics and the chemistry of hydrocarbons. On the former subject he published a textbook, *Chemical Thermodynamics* (1950); on the latter he edited and contributed to a standard work, *Hydrocarbons from Petrol* (1953), which described the fractionation, analysis, isolation, purification, and properties of petroleum hydrocarbons.

Rotblat, Joseph

(1908–   )

POLISH–BRITISH PHYSICIST

Rotblat was educated at the University of Warsaw. In 1939 he was appointed to a research fellowship at the University of Liverpool to work on neutron fission in the laboratory of James Chadwick. Like many other Europeans, he worked during World War II at Los Alamos on the development of the atom bomb. But unlike most other scientists as soon as it was clear in early 1945 that Germany was defeated and would be unable to produce a nuclear weapon in time, Rotblat felt unable to justify working any longer on the development of such weapons. He was also alarmed by the attitude of some of his senior colleagues. General Groves, for example, the head of the Manhattan Project, was overheard by Rotblat insisting that the real purpose of the bomb was to subdue Soviet Russia.

Consequently he resigned from Los Alamos, arousing the deep suspicion of the security officers who suspected him of being a Soviet agent, and returned to Liverpool in early 1945. He remained at Liverpool until 1950 when he was appointed professor of physics at Bart's Hospital Medical College, a position he held until his retirement in 1976. Rotblat's scientific work was mainly concerned with radiation medicine.

He did, however, concern himself with other matters. After the explosion of the Bikini H-bomb on Bikini atoll, the Atomic Energy Commission reported that the fallout from this and all other explosions was no more damaging to the individual than the exposure received from a single x-ray. The announcement did nothing to reassure Rotblat. The Bikini bomb, he worked out independently, would have been much more dangerous than the authorities admitted. Further, he reasoned, chest x-rays screen only chests; nuclear bombs radiated the whole body including wombs, ovaries, and testicles.

Rotblat was determined not to let the matter rest. He drafted an appeal for peace, backed by Bertrand Russell and Albert Einstein among others, to be delivered to world leaders. He realized, however, that something more permanent and constructive was needed. Consequently he set about raising money to hold a series of conferences in which technical matters could be debated, authoritative proposals made, and contacts established between scientists from different disciplines and countries.

The American millionaire Cyrus Eaton offered to finance the first conference as long as it was held in the Nova Scotian fishing village of Pugwash, Eaton's birthplace. The first conference was held in 1957 and was attended by 22 scientists. Known as Pugwash conferences, ever since they have continued to be held around the world. Rotblat served as the Secretary-General of Pugwash from its inception until 1973. Since 1988 he has held the office of Pugwash President.

Rotblat was awarded the 1995 Nobel Peace Prize, an award he shared with the organization he helped to found, the Pugwash Conferences on Science and World Affairs. The award was made, the Nobel committee announced, to mark the 50th anniversary of Hiroshima and Nagasaki and to protest against the French nuclear tests in the Pacific.

Rouelle, Guillaume François

(1703–1770)

FRENCH CHEMIST

His [Rouelle's] eloquence was not a matter of words; he presented his ideas the way nature does her productions, in a disorder which was always pleasing and with an abundance which was never wearisome.
　　　　　　　　　　—Vicq d'Azyr

Rouelle (roo-**el**) came from a farming background in Mathieu, France. He studied at the University of Caen and in Paris, becoming an apothecary in 1725. During the period 1742–68 he was chemical demonstrator at the Jardin du Roi and earned a reputation for being an enthusiastic lecturer. He was a follower of Georg Stahl and was one of the first to teach phlogiston theories in France. His students included most of the French chemists of the late 18th century and Antoine Lavoisier was probably his most famous pupil. Rouelle's own work included a classification of salts.

Rouelle's brother, Hilaire Martin Rouelle, acted first as his assistant and then succeeded him in 1768.

Rous, Francis Peyton

(1879–1970)

AMERICAN PATHOLOGIST

Rous was born in Baltimore, Maryland, and educated at Johns Hopkins University, obtaining his MD in 1905. After working as a pathologist at the University of Michigan, he moved in 1908 to the Rockefeller Institute of Medical Research in New York, remaining there until his official retirement in 1945. Unofficially, Rous continued to work in his laboratory until his death at the age of 90.

In 1909 Rous began to investigate a particular malignant tumor of connective tissues in chickens – later to be known as *Rous chickensarcoma*. He ground up the tumor and passed it through a fine filter, extracting what would normally be accepted as a cell-free filtrate. On injection of this filtrate into other chickens, identical tumors developed. In 1911 Rous published his results in a paper with the significant title *Transmission of a Malignant New Growth by means of a Cell-free Filtrate*, significant because nowhere in the title (or even in the paper) does the expected term "virus" occur.

It was well known by 1911 that only a virus could be present in such a filtrate, but Rous was unwilling to use the term for fear of offending his more senior colleagues. Scientists were reluctant to accept that cancer could be caused by viruses since the epidemiology of the disease was obviously different from that of such viral infections as influenza. Rous persisted with his work, however, and by the late 1930s it was widely accepted that a number of animal cancers were caused by viruses. In 1966 Rous was awarded the Nobel Prize for physiology or medicine for the discovery he had announced some 55 years earlier.

Rous also worked on the development of a number of culture techniques for both viruses and cells, techniques that have since become standard laboratory practice.

Roux, Paul Emile

(1853–1933)

FRENCH MICROBIOLOGIST

Roux (roo), who was born at Conforens in France, was educated at the universities of Clermont-Ferrand and Paris, where he obtained his MD in 1881. Before this he had worked as an assistant in the laboratory of Louis Pasteur. In 1888 Roux joined the newly created Pasteur Institute and in 1904 became the director, a post he retained until his death.

Roux worked with Pasteur on most of the latter's major medical discoveries; he assisted him at Pouilly-la-Fort in 1882 with the testing of the anthrax vaccine. He also did much of the early work on the development of a rabies vaccine, but later came to disagree with Pasteur on the speed with which the vaccine was applied to humans and consequently withdrew from the project.

His most important work, however, was done quite independently of Pasteur and led to the development of a successful antitoxin against diphtheria. He demonstrated in 1885, with the Swiss bacteriologist Alexandre Yersin, that the menace of diphtheria lay not in the bacteria themselves but in a lethal poison produced by them. Roux and Yersin produced large amounts of the diphtheria bacillus in a liquid culture medium. After 42 days they carefully separated the germs from the liquid using fine porcelain filters and injected the germ-free liquid into experimental animals. This liquid contained a toxin so powerful that one ounce (28 grams) of it could kill over half a million guinea pigs.

The next step was to develop a means to neutralize the toxin. Emil von Behring had achieved some early success in this by inoculating guinea pigs with diphtheria toxin and collecting the serum, which contained an antitoxin to the poison. Roux himself used horses, which enabled the extraction of much larger quantities of serum. By 1894 he was ready to try his serum on patients in the Enfants Malades Hospital in Paris. Within four months mortality fell from 51% to 24%.

In 1903 Roux achieved some success, in collaboration with Elie Metchnikoff, in transmitting syphilis to a chimpanzee. Such work greatly facilitated the laboratory investigation of syphilis and the search for a cure.

Rowland, Frank Sherwood

(1927–   )

AMERICAN CHEMIST

The work is going well, but it looks like the end of the world.
—On his researches into the destruction of the ozone layer

Born in Delaware, Ohio, Rowland was educated at Wesleyan University, Ohio, and at the University of Chicago, where he gained his PhD in 1952. After holding teaching posts at Princeton and Kansas, Rowland moved to the University of California, Irvine, in 1964 as professor of chemistry.

Shortly before Christmas 1973, Mario Molina took to Rowland, his postdoctoral adviser, some calculations suggesting that CFCs (chlorofluorocarbons), widely used in aerosol propellants, will rise to the upper atmosphere and destroy the ozone layer, located 8 to 30 miles above the Earth. As the layer protects us from harmful ultraviolet rays, its destruction could have disturbing consequences.

Rowland and Molina published their preliminary results in June 1974. They pointed out that in the lower atmosphere CFCs were relatively inert compounds. But at a height of about 15 miles (25 km) in the stratosphere they begin to absorb ultraviolet radiation in the 1,900–2,250 angstrom range and decompose, releasing chlorine atoms which will attack ozone (O_3) atoms in a chain reaction:

$Cl\bullet + O_3 \rightarrow ClO + O_2$

$ClO + O\bullet \rightarrow Cl\bullet + O_2$

In the first part of the reaction a chlorine atom attacks an ozone molecule and forms chlorine monoxide and normal oxygen; in the second stage of the reaction, involving oxygen atoms, the chlorine is regenerated and is free to enter once more into the first reaction, destroying an ozone molecule in the process. The result is that a relatively small amount of CFC can destroy a large amount of ozone.

Rowland discovered that 400,000 tons of CFCs had been produced in the United States in 1973, and that the bulk of this was being discharged into the atmosphere. He calculated that at the then current production rate there would be a long-term steady-state ozone depletion of 7–13%. The CFC industry responded by pointing out there was no actual proof of Rowland's hypothesis. Further, they argued, even if the hypothesis was true, other atmospheric processes could offset the effects of the reaction. In 1974 it seemed that Rowland had found just such a process with the possible formation of chlorine nitrate ($ClONO_2$) in the atmosphere. Thus it seemed possible that the reaction:

$ClO + NO_2 \rightarrow ClONO_2$

would remove chlorine monoxide, leaving less chlorine to react with ozone. More detailed analysis revealed that chlorine nitrate might change the distribution of ozone in the atmosphere without significantly minimizing its depletion rate. The National Academy of Sciences published a report in September 1976 supporting the work of Rowland and Molina, and in October 1978 CFC use in aerosols was banned in the United States. Final confirmation came when Joe Farman discovered in late 1984 a 40% ozone loss over Antarctica.

For his work on CFCs Rowland shared the 1995 Nobel Prize for chemistry with Mario Molina and Paul Crutzen.

Rowland, Henry Augustus

(1848–1901)

AMERICAN PHYSICIST

He who makes two blades of grass grow where one grew before is the benefactor of mankind, but he who obscurely worked to find the laws of such growth is the intellectual superior as well as the greater benefactor of mankind.
—Quoted by D. S. Greenburg in *The Politics of Pure Science* (1967)

Born at Honesdale in Pennsylvania, Rowland graduated in engineering from the Rensselaer Polytechnic, New York, in 1870, and worked for a time as a railroad engineer. He then taught at Wooster, Ohio, before returning to Rensselaer to take up a professorial appointment in 1874. Following a year's study in Berlin under Hermann von Helmholtz, Rowland returned to America and joined Johns Hopkins University as their first professor of physics (1876).

While in Berlin Rowland contributed to electromagnetic theory by showing that a magnetic field accompanies electric charge. The strength of the magnetic field equals the velocity of the charge multiplied by its quantity, and the phenomenon is anlogous to an electric current flowing in a conductor. At Johns Hopkins, Rowland worked toward achieving more accurate values for units.

Rowland is best remembered for his design, in 1882, of the concave diffraction grating, which enables spectra to be photographed without the need for lenses or prisms. Moreover the grating (with 20,000 grooves to the inch) gave a greater resolving power and dispersion, and it has since been used in many areas of spectroscopy.

Rubbia, Carlo

(1934–)

ITALIAN PHYSICIST

Born at Gorizia, Trieste, Rubbia (roo-**bee**-a) was educated at the University of Pisa, where he obtained his PhD in 1958. After spending a year each at Columbia, New York, and Rome, he took up an appointment in 1960 at the European Laboratory for Particle Physics (CERN), Geneva, becoming its director-general in 1989. He has also held since 1972 a professorship of physics at Harvard.

Rubbia is noted for his work in high-energy physics using the considerable accelerator capacity of CERN. He set himself an ambitious target in the mid 1970s, namely, the discovery of the intermediate vector bosons. Forces operate by interchanging particles. Thus the electromagnetic force works by exchange of virtual photons. The weak interaction would, therefore, require a comparable particle; in actual fact three such particles would be needed, W^+, W^-, and Z^0. Further, as the weak force acts at distances below about 10^{-13} centimeters, and as the shorter the distance the larger the particle would have to be, the bosons would have to be massive, some 80 times bigger than a proton.

To produce such particles in an accelerator requires enormous energies and it was not expected that CERN would be able to obtain such energies for more than a decade. Rubbia proposed in 1976 that the existing super proton synchroton should be changed from a fixed-target accelerator to one producing collisions between beams of protons and antiprotons traveling in opposite directions. If feasible, and given that a particle's kinetic energy increases as the square of its velocity, much higher energies would be attained. As redesigned by his CERN colleague, Simon van der Meer, the SPS produced energies of 540 billion electronvolts (540 GeV) – the equivalent of the 155,000 GeV achieved by striking a stationary target.

Rubbia faced two further problems: how to produce enough antiprotons, and how to recognize the W and Z particles. Antiprotons were produced by accelerating protons in the SPS and firing them at a metal target. A new detector, designed by Charpak, was built. To detect a W particle the experimenters looked for its characteristic interactions. They should see antiprotons collide with protons and emit a W particle, which in 10^{-20} second should decay into an electron and a neutrino. The experiment began in September 1982 and ran until December 6, leaving millions of collisions to analyze. Among them they found six possible W particles, five of which were accepted as genuine. The Z particle was subsequently discovered in May 1983.

Rubbia published the discovery of the W particle in January 1983 in a paper listing 130 coauthors. For their part in the discovery of the W and Z particles Rubbia and van der Meer shared the 1984 Nobel Prize for physics.

Rubik, Erno

(1944–   )

HUGARIAN ARCHITECT AND DESIGNER

Rubik (**roo**-bik) was educated at the Technical University and the Academy of Applied Arts in his native city of Budapest; he became director of postgraduate studies at the Academy in 1983.

In order to stimulate the ability of his students to think in three-dimensional terms, he invented in 1975 a $3 \times 3 \times 3$ multicolored cube having 9 squares on each face. The cube could be twisted so as to adopt any one of 43,252,003,274,489,856,000 possible positions. The aim was to restore a scrambled cube to its original state in which each face presents a single color. As some 20 million cubes were sold in the two years of its greatest popularity, few alive in 1980 can have been unaware of the cube. Speed competitions were held at so-called "world championships" with restorations being achieved in less than 23 seconds. Mathematicians sought for algorithms and Morwen Thistlethwaite proved that any cube could be restored in at most 50 moves. The search for "God's algorithm," the minimum number needed for a restoration, led to a figure, without proof, of 22. A rigorous mathematical treatment of the subject, David Singmaster's *Notes on Rubik's Magic Cube* (London, 1980), went through five editions.

The cube first became known to the West when Hungarian scientists began to arrive at international conferences offering to trade cubes for dollars. In 1979 Rubik licensed the Ideal Toy Company to sell the cube. Despite vast sales they found their profits were being threatened by cheap Taiwanese imports. In 1986 Rubik left the Academy to set up the Rubik Studio. While he has produced a number of popular items, including Rubik's snake, Rubik's domino, and Rubik's revenge, he has so far failed to rekindle the mania induced by his cube in the early 1980s. Nonetheless, sales of the cube have made Rubik a very wealthy man.

Rubin, Vera Cooper

(1928–   )

AMERICAN ASTRONOMER

Born in Philadelphia, Pennsylvania, Rubin was educated at Vassar, at Cornell, and at Georgetown University, Washington DC, where she obtained her PhD in 1954. Since 1965 she has worked at the Carnegie Institution, Washington DC, while also being an adjunct staff member of the Mount Wilson and Las Campanas observatories.

Rubin's main work has long been concerned with galactic rotation measurements and it has led to one of the more persistent problems of modern astronomy. She has concentrated on spiral galaxies and has measured the rotational velocities of the arms of the galaxy as their distance from the center increases. The velocities of the spiral arms are measured by determining their doppler shifts. That is light emitted from a body moving away from an observer will show a red shift, and a blue shift when emitted from a body moving toward the observer. The degree of spectral shift is proportional to the velocity of the source.

The initial assumption, based upon Kepler's laws, was that rotational velocity would decrease with distance. Thus the theoretical expectation was that: $v^2 = GM/r^2$ where G is the gravitational constant, M the attracting mass, and r the orbital radius. It is clear from the equation that as r increases, v will decrease. Rubin, however, found that the rotational velocity of spiral galaxies either remains constant with increasing distance from the center or rises slightly. The only possible conclusion, assuming the laws of motion, was that the figure for M was too low. But as all visible matter had been taken into account in assessing the mass of the galaxy, the missing mass must be present in the form of "dark matter." Rubin found similar results as she extended her survey. It seemed to her in 1983 that as much as 90% of the universe is not radiating sufficiently strongly on any wavelength detectable on Earth.

Rubin's work has presented modern astronomy with two major problems. Firstly to calculate the amount of dark matter in the universe and describe its distribution, and secondly to identify particles that make up the dark matter.

Earlier in her career, in collaboration with Kent Ford, Rubin made the extraordinary discovery that the Milky Way had a peculiar velocity of 500 kilometers per second quite independently of the expansion of the universe. When their results were published in 1975 they were met with considerable skepticism and it was assumed they had miscalculated the distances of the measured galaxies. However, later work by John Huchra and others in 1982 seems to have confirmed their measurements.

Rubner, Max

(1854–1932)

GERMAN PHYSIOLOGIST AND HYGIENIST

Rubner (**roob**-ner), who was born at Munich in Germany, was a student of Karl von Voit and became professor of physiology at both Marburg and Berlin universities. He is best known for his work on mammalian heat production and for exposition of the surface law, which indicates that the rate of metabolism is proportional to the surface area of the body, not to weight. This principle appears to be related to mammalian temperature regulation and heat loss via the skin. Rubner also showed that recently fed animals lost heat more readily than fasting ones, indicating some sort of cellular regulatory system. In 1894 Rubner demonstrated the direct analogy between human energy production, accompanied by heat, and actual burning (as in a fire). Since the same amount of energy is released in both cases, given that the quantity of food digested/burned is the same, this clearly indicated that the first law of thermodynamics applies to both animate and inanimate objects, thus refuting the theory of vitalism. Rubner also investigated and compared the energy-producing potential of various foodstuffs, showing that carbohydrates, fats, and proteins were broken down with equal readiness, and proved that an animal's energy consumption for growth purposes is a constant proportion of its total energy output. Rubner's other work included studies of the nutritional requirements of infants and the physiological effects of different climates on man.

Rudbeck, Olof

(1630–1702)

SWEDISH NATURALIST

Rudbeck (**rood**-bek), who was born at Westerås in Sweden, studied at the University of Uppsala, where he taught as professor of anatomy, botany, chemistry, and mathematics at the medical school. He became chancellor of Uppsala University at the age of 31, built a botanic garden, and founded a polytechnic institute, of which he became curator. Rudbeck's scientific investigations are a mixture of fact and fancy. In 1651 he discovered the vertebrate lymphatic system, in particular that of the intestine and its connection with the thoracic duct; but he also believed that Sweden was the site of Plato's Atlantis and the cradle of civilization (described in his *Atlantikan*, 1675–98; Atlantis). The plant genus *Rudbeckia* is named for him.

Ruelle, David

(1935–)

BELGIAN MATHEMATICAL PHYSICIST

Ruelle (roo-**el**) was born in Ghent, Belgium, and educated at the Mons Polytechnic and the Université Libre de Bruxelles. After holding short appointments at the Federal Institute of Technology, Zurich, and at the Institute for Advanced Studies, Princeton, he was appointed in 1964 to the Institut des Hautes Etudes Scientifiques, Bures-sur-Yvette, Paris.

In 1971, in collaboration with the Dutch mathematician Floris Takens, Ruelle published an important paper entitled *On the Nature of Turbulence*. The prevailing theory of turbulence at the time was developed by Lev Landau. He had argued that when a fluid is set into motion a number of modes are excited. A single mode produces a periodic oscillation, and no mode allows a steady flow; an irregular flow is produced by several excited modes, while many modes will set up a turbulent flow.

Ruelle argued that turbulence was not really a superposition of many modes, but resulted from what he termed to be "a strange attractor." The origin of the term derives from the Lorenz attractor used by Edward Lorenz to describe certain chaotic systems. The Lorenz attractor was strange, Ruelle added, because it was fractal in the sense of Benoit Mandelbrot, it had a sensitive dependence on initial conditions, and a continuum of frequencies.

Rumford, Benjamin Thompson, Count

(1753–1814)

AMERICAN–BRITISH PHYSICIST

Benjamin Thompson was the son of a farmer from Woburn, Massachusetts. He started his career apprenticed to a merchant but was injured in a fireworks accident and moved to Boston. In 1772 he married a rich widow and moved to live in Rumford (now Concord, New Hampshire). When the American Revolution broke out, he took the English side and spied for them. By 1775 the hostility of his countrymen toward him had grown to such a pitch that he was forced to sail to England, leaving his wife and daughter behind. Once in England, his opportunist nature quickly raised him to the position of colonial undersecretary of state but, with the end of the American Revolution, he moved to Bavaria.

Here he rose rapidly to high government administrative positions and initiated many social reforms, such as the creation of military workhouses for the poor and the introduction of the potato as a staple food. In 1790 he was made a count in recognition of his service to Bavaria, taking the name of his title from Rumford, New Hampshire.

It was in Bavaria that he first became interested in science, when he was commissioned to oversee the boring of cannon at the Munich Arsenal. Rumford was struck by the amount of heat generated and suggested that it resulted from the mechanical work performed.

According to the old theory of heat, heat produced by friction was caloric "squeezed" from the solid, although it was difficult to explain why the heat should be released indefinitely. Rumford, in his paper to the Royal Society *An Experimental Enquiry concerning the Source of Heat excited by Friction* (1798), suggested the direct conversion of work into heat and made quantitative estimates of the amount of heat generated. It was suggested that the heat came from the lower heat capacity of the metal turnings, although Rumford could discount this by using a blunt borer to show that the turnings produced were not important. Another objection – that the heat came from chemical reaction of air with the fresh surface – was disproved by an experiment of Humphry Davy (1799) in which pieces of ice were rubbed together in a vacuum. The idea that heat was a form of motion replaced Lavoisier's caloric theory over the first half of the 19th century.

Rumford returned to London in 1798 and there began work on a series of inventions, including a kitchen stove. More lastingly, he established the Royal Institution of Great Britain (1800), introducing Davy as director. He went to France in 1804 and settled in Paris, where he married Lavoisier's widow. The marriage was unhappy and ended after four years (Rumford is said to have suggested that Lavoisier was lucky to have been guillotined). Rumford himself appears to have been a disloyal and unappealing character, although at the end of his life he left most of his estate to the United States.

Runcorn, Stanley Keith

(1922–1995)

BRITISH GEOPHYSICIST

Runcorn was born at Southport in Lancashire, England, and was educated at Cambridge University. After working on radar during World War II he held teaching appointments at the University of Manchester (1946–50) and at Cambridge (1950–55), before being appointed in 1956 to the chair of physics at King's College, Newcastle, which became the University of Newcastle upon Tyne in 1963. He became Senior Research Fellow at Imperial College, London, in 1989.

Under the early influence of Patrick Blackett, Runcorn began research on geomagnetism. From detailed field surveys in both Europe and America they were eventually able to reconstruct the movements of the North Magnetic Pole over the past 600 million years. Runcorn found that he obtained different routes for the migration depending on whether he used European or American rocks. Also, the European rocks always pointed to a position to the east of that indicated by the American rocks for the magnetic pole. From this evidence Runcorn argued, in his paper *Paleomagnetic Evidence for Continental Drift* (1962), that if the two continents were brought close to each other they could be so aligned that the magnetic evidence of their rocks pointed to a single path taken by the magnetic pole. This led Runcorn to become an early supporter of the newly emerging theory of continental drift.

Runcorn died in somewhat mysterious circumstances: he was found battered to death in a motel room in Los Angeles, where he had been attending a conference.

Runge, Friedlieb Ferdinand

(1795–1867)

GERMAN CHEMIST

Runge (**ruung**-e), who was born at Hamburg in Germany, was apprenticed to an apothecary in 1810. He studied medicine at Jena, graduating in 1819, and later received his PhD from Berlin. He held the chair of chemistry at Breslau before becoming an industrial chemist in 1830.

His main work was concerned with the chemistry of dyes; he produced a massive three-volume work on the subject, *Farbenchemie* (Part 1, 1834; Part 2, 1842; Part 3, 1850; Color Chemistry). In 1834, using coal tar, he isolated quinoline, a compound that was to have considerable value later in the century. He also pioneered the use of paper chromatography as an analytical tool; he produced a work in 1855 that actually had chromatograms incorporated in the text.

Rush, Benjamin

(1745–1813)

AMERICAN PHYSICIAN, CHEMIST, AND POLITICIAN

Man is said to be a compound of soul and body. However proper this language may be in religion, it is not so in medicine. He is, in the eye of a physician, a single and indivisible being, for so intimately united are his soul and body, that one cannot be moved without the other.

—*Sixteen Introductory Lectures* (1811)

Rush was born in Philadelphia, Pennsylvania. After studying at Jersey College and being apprenticed to the physician Redman (a pupil of Boerhaave), he came to Europe to study medicine at Paris and at Edinburgh, where he received his MD in 1768. He was appointed professor of chemistry at Philadelphia University in 1769; he was also elected to Congress and was one of the signatories of the Declaration of Independence. In 1777 he served for a year as surgeon-general but resigned for political reasons and returned to his chair. In 1799 he became treasurer of the U.S. mint, a post he held until his death.

As a chemist Rush's main role was as a teacher and supporter of others rather than as a basic researcher. In medicine he pioneered more humane therapy for the insane; his *Medical Inquiries and Observations upon Diseases of the Mind* (1812) was one of the earliest modern works on the subject.

Rushton, William Albert Hugh

(1901–1980)

BRITISH PHYSIOLOGIST

Rushton, the son of a London dental surgeon, studied medicine at Cambridge University and University College Hospital, London. He worked in Cambridge from 1931 until 1968, being appointed professor of visual physiology in 1966. In 1968 he moved to the Florida State University, Tallahassee, to serve as research professor of psychobiology until his retirement in 1976.

Rushton studied the theory of nerve excitation until the early 1950s but changed to studying visual pigments following some work with Ragnar Granit in Stockholm. Rushton's novel technique was to shine light into the eye and measure the amount reflected back with a photocell. The effects of rhodopsin, the "visual purple" of Willy Kuhne, could be discounted by working with the fovea, the retinal region of sharpest vision devoid of rods containing rhodopsin. As the fovea is also deficient in blue cones, Rushton argued that by limiting pigment absorption measurements to this small area the properties of the red and green cones alone should be revealed.

By examining color-blind individuals, Rushton showed that red-blind defectives lack the red-sensitive pigment erythrolabe and that people who cannot distinguish between red and green lack the green-sensitive pigment chlorolabe.

Ruska, Ernst August Friedrich

(1906–1988)

GERMAN PHYSICIST

Born in Heidelberg, Germany, Ruska (**ruus**-ka) was educated at the Munich Technical University and at Berlin University, where he obtained his PhD in 1934. He worked in industry until 1955 when he became professor of electron microscopy at the Haber Institute, Berlin, a post he held until his retirement in 1972.

It had long been known that optical microscopes are limited by the wavelength of light to a magnifying power of about 2,000, and the ability to resolve images no closer together than 2–3,000 angstroms (1 angstrom = 10^{-10} meter). In 1927, however, G. P. Thomson first demonstrated that electrons can behave like waves as well as like particles. The wavelength of the electron depends on its momentum according to de Broglie's equation $\lambda = h/p$. The higher the momentum of the electron, the shorter the wavelength. It should be possible to focus short-wavelength electrons and obtain better resolving powers.

In 1928 Ruska attempted to focus an electron beam with an electromagnetic lens. He went on to add a second lens and thus produced the first electron microscope; it had a magnifying power of about seventeen. Improvements, however, came quickly and by 1933 the magnifying power had been increased to 7,000. Soon after he joined the firm of Siemens and began to work on the production of commercial models. The first such model appeared on the market in 1939. It had a resolution of about 250–500 angstroms.

For his work in this field Ruska shared the 1986 Nobel Prize for physics with Binning and Rohrer.

Russell, Bertrand, 3rd Earl Russell

(1872–1970)

BRITISH PHILOSOPHER AND MATHEMATICIAN

> Mathematics may be defined as the subject in which we never know what we are talking about, nor whether what we are saying is true.
>
> —*Mysticism and Logic*

> Even if the open windows of science at first make us shiver after the cosy indoor warmth of traditional humanizing myths, in the end the fresh air brings vigor, and the great spaces have a splendor of their own.
>
> —*What I Believe* (1925)

Russell, who was born at Trelleck, England, was orphaned at an early age and brought up in the home of his grandfather, the politician Lord John Russell. He was educated privately before attending Cambridge University (1890), from which he graduated (1893) in mathematics. In 1895 he became a fellow and lecturer at Cambridge. His work after 1920 was mainly devoted to the development of his philosophical and political opinions. He became well known for his popularization of many areas of philosophy and also, in works such as *The ABC of Atoms* (1923) and *The ABC of Relativity* (1925), of the new trends in scientific thought. For his writings he was awarded the 1950 Nobel Prize for literature. He succeeded his brother to become the 3rd Earl Russell in 1931. Throughout much of his life Russell was an intense advocate of pacifism and during World War I he was imprisoned for expressing these views. Later, in the 1950s and 1960s, he became a central figure in the movements criticizing the use of the atomic bomb, leading demonstrations and mass sitdowns and becoming president of the British Campaign for Nuclear Disarmament in 1958.

At Cambridge Russell became interested in the relatively new discipline of mathematical logic in which he was to be a pioneer. With Guiseppe Peano he was one of the few to recognize the genius of Gottlob Frege and his new system of logic. In 1902 he wrote to Frege, presenting what is now known as *Russell's paradox*, and asking how Frege's system would deal with it. (Unfortunately, as Frege acknowledged, the system could not accommodate it.) The paradox is one of the paradoxes of set theory and rests on the (then ill-defined) notion of a set. Some sets are members of themselves (the set of all sets is an example because it is itself a set; the set of cats is not an example, as it is not itself a cat). Consider the set of all sets that are not members of themselves: is it a member of itself? If it is, it is not and vice versa. To avoid such paradoxes Russell formulated his logical theory of types. In 1903 he began his collaboration with A. N. Whitehead on their ambitious, if not entirely successful, project of placing mathematics on a sound axiomatic footing by deriving it from logic. This culminated in the publication of *Principia Mathematica* (1910, 1912, 1913), containing major advances in logic and the philosophy of mathematics.

Russell, Sir Edward John

(1872–1965)

BRITISH AGRICULTURAL
SCIENTIST

When Russell, who was born at Frampton in England, left school at 14, he had already decided to pursue a career in chemistry. His first job in a chemist's shop disappointed him, but he attended evening classes and gained entrance to Owens College, Manchester, graduating in chemistry in 1896. While doing social work in Manchester, Russell conceived the idea of a rural settlement where the poor could be trained in agriculture and prepared for a healthier life in the country. To learn more about agriculture he applied, in 1901, for a lectureship at Wye College, London, against the advice of his superiors who could see no future for a chemist in agriculture.

Russell soon saw the impracticality of his settlement scheme but nevertheless quickly realized how greatly agriculture could be advanced by planned scientific research. At Wye he met A. D. Hall, with whom he produced *The Soils and Agriculture of Kent, Surrey and Sussex* (1911), which was recognized on publication as a classic example of a regional agricultural survey.

In 1907 Russell followed Hall to Rothamsted Experimental Station, succeeding Hall as director in 1912. In 1912 he also published his most famous book, *Soil Conditions and Plant Growth*, which has expanded over the years through many editions, the later ones being edited by his son E. W. Russell. He did some important research, particularly on soil sterilization, but his major achievement was to extend the staff and facilities at Rothamsted at a time when the British government seemed quite blind to the benefits of agricultural research.

Russell remained active into his old age, finishing his last book, a history of agricultural research, only a few weeks before his death at the age of 92.

Russell, Sir Frederick Stratten

(1897–1984)

BRITISH MARINE BIOLOGIST

Russell was born at Bridport in Dorset, England. Although he had plans to study medicine at Cambridge University, these were delayed by the outbreak of World War I, during which he served with the Royal Naval Air Service. His interest turned from medicine to biology at Cambridge and on graduation he spent a year in Alexandria, Egypt, studying the eggs and larvae of marine fish. He then joined the Marine Biological Association's Laboratory at Plymouth, serving as its director from 1945 to 1965. Russell did extensive research on marine planktonic organisms, their life histories, behavior, and relation to fisheries and water movements. With Sir Maurice Yonge he wrote *The Seas* (first published 1928, and many subsequent editions) as well as monographs on the British medusae (Coelenterata) and the eggs and planktonic stages of British sea fishes. He was knighted in 1965.

Russell, Henry Norris

(1877–1957)

AMERICAN ASTRONOMER

The pursuit of an idea is as exciting as the pursuit of a whale.
—Quoted by A. L. Mackay in *A Dictionary of Scientific Quotations* (1991)

Russell, the son of a Presbyterian minister, was born in Oyster Bay, New York. A brilliant scholar at Princeton, he graduated in 1897 and obtained his PhD in 1899. He spent the period 1902–05 as a research student and assistant at Cambridge University, England, returning then to Princeton where he served as professor of astronomy from 1911 to 1927 and director of the university observatory from 1912 to 1947. He was also a research associate at the Mount Wilson Observatory in California (1922–42) and, after his retirement, at the Harvard and Lick observatories.

Russell's great achievement was his publication in 1913 of a major piece of research contained in what is now called the *Hertzsprung–Russell diagram* (H–R diagram). The same results had in fact been published earlier and independently by Ejnar Hertzsprung with little impact. Russell's work was based upon determinations of absolute magnitudes, i.e., intrinsic brightness, of stars by the measurement of stellar parallax. His measurement technique was developed in collaboration with Arthur Hinks while he was at Cambridge and involved photographic plates, then a fairly recent scientific tool. He found that values of absolute magnitude correlated with the spectral types of the stars. Spectral type was derived from the Harvard system of spectral classification as revised by Annie Cannon and indicated surface temperature.

A graph of absolute magnitude versus spectral type produced the H–R diagram and showed that the majority of stars lie on a diagonal band, now called the "main sequence," in which magnitude increases with increasing surface temperature. A separate group of very bright stars lie above the main sequence. This meant that there could be stars of the same spectral type differing enormously in magnitude. To describe such a difference the now familiar terminology of "giant" and "dwarf" stars was introduced into the literature.

The most obvious feature of the diagram for Russell, however, was that it was not completely occupied by stars. This led him to propose a path of stellar evolution, which he put forward in 1913 at the same time as the diagram. He argued that stars evolve from hot giants, pass down the main sequence and end as cold dwarfs. The mechanism driving the change was that of contraction. The bulky giants of spectral type M contract and with the resulting rise of temperature move leftward in the diagram, gradually becoming B-type dwarfs. But at some stage the contraction and density become too great for the gas laws to apply and the star cools, slipping down the main sequence and evolving finally to an M-type dwarf.

By 1926, however, Arthur Eddington could talk confidently of the overthrow of the "giant and dwarf theory"; it was too simple to fit the growing data on the distribution of mass and luminosity among the different spectral types of stars. Although Russell's evolutionary theory quickly fell from favor the H–R diagram has continued to be of enormous importance and the start for any new theory of stellar evolution.

Eclipsing binary stars, such as Algol, the "winking demon," were also of great interest to Russell. He devised methods by which both orbital and stellar size could be determined and which became widely used. He also analyzed the variations in light output of a large number of eclipsing binaries, which again became invaluable to later researchers.

Another major line of research for Russell was his investigation of the solar spectrum, which began as a result of the publication in 1921 of the ionization equation of Meghnad Saha. The Saha equation was tested and modified by Russell, using the solar spectrum, and was then used by him to calculate the abundance of the chemical elements in the Sun's atmosphere. He realized that the abundances in other stars could also be calculated from their spectra. He showed that the abundance of elements within the Sun itself could be found and in 1929 published the first reliable determination of this, demonstrating surprisingly that 60% of the Sun's volume was hydrogen. Although this was an underestimate, as Donald Menzel was later able to show that a figure of over 80% was more accurate, it did pose the problem as to why the Sun, and presumably other stars too, should contain so much hydrogen. The answer to this question was given in the version of the big-bang theory proposed by George Gamow.

Rutherford, Daniel

(1749–1819)

BRITISH CHEMIST AND BOTANIST

Rutherford, the son of an Edinburgh physician, studied under William Cullen and Joseph Black at Edinburgh University and became a doctor of medicine in 1777. In 1786 he was made professor of botany and keeper of the Royal Botanic Garden at Edinburgh.

Rutherford was the first to distinguish between carbon dioxide and nitrogen. A thesis he wrote in 1772, *De aere fixo dicto aut mephitico* (On Air said to be Fixed or Mephitic), contains some of Joseph Priestley's later discoveries. In his experiment mice were allowed to breathe in a closed container. The fixed air (carbon dioxide) was absorbed by caustic potash. The remaining air, Rutherford pointed out, was not fixed but would not support life or combustion and he called it "mephitic air." He had in fact isolated nitrogen about the same time as Karl Scheele.

Rutherford, Ernest, 1st Baron

(1871–1937)

NEW ZEALAND PHYSICIST

Don't let me catch anyone talking about the Universe in my department.
—Quoted by John Kendrew in "J. D. Bernal and the Origin of Life," BBC radio talk, 26 July 1968

When we have found how the nucleus of atoms is built up we shall have found the greatest secret of all – except life. We shall have found the basis of everything – of the earth we walk on, of the air we breathe, of the sunshine, of our physical body itself, of everything in the world, however great or however small – except life.
—Quoted in *Passing Show*

Rutherford, who was born at Nelson in New Zealand, was certainly the greatest scientist to emerge from that country; he can also fairly be claimed to be one of the greatest experimental physicists of all time. His career almost exactly spans the first great period of nuclear physics, a field he did much to advance and which he dominated for so long. This period stretches from the detection of radioactivity by Henri Becquerel in 1896 to the discovery of nuclear fission by Otto Hahn in 1938, the year after Rutherford's death. He came from a fairly simple background, the fourth of twelve children, the son of a man variously described as a farmer, wheelwright, and miller. He was educated at Canterbury College, Christchurch, and in 1895 won a scholarship to Cambridge University, England.

In New Zealand Rutherford had done some work on high-frequency magnetic fields. At Cambridge, working under J. J. Thomson, he first continued this research, and then in 1896 began to work on the conductivity of air ionized by x-rays. In 1898 he moved to become professor at McGill University in Canada. This was a good appointment for Rutherford in two respects. McGill had one of the best-equipped physics laboratories in the world and, in particular, there was a good supply of the then very costly radium bromide. The other main gain for Rutherford in Montreal was the presence of Frederick Soddy, an Oxford-trained chemist with whom he entered into a most rewarding eighteen-month collaboration, from October 1901 to April 1903, during which time they produced nine major papers laying the foundations for the serious study of radioactivity.

When Rutherford began working on radioactivity at the end of the century little was known about it apart from the result of Pierre and Marie Curie that it was not limited to uranium alone but was also a property of thorium, radium, and polonium. Rutherford's first important advance, in 1899, was his demonstration that there were two quite different kinds of emission, which he referred to as alpha and beta rays. The first kind had little penetrating power but produced considerable ionization while the beta rays (electrons) were as penetrating as x-rays but possessed little ionizing power. To find out exactly what they were took Rutherford the best part of a decade of careful experimentation but, long before he had the final answer, he had used their existence to work out with Soddy a daring theory of atomic transmutation. In 1900 Rutherford showed that a third type of radiation, undeflected by magnetic fields, was high-energy electromagnetic radiation. He called this radiation "gamma rays."

Rutherford also began to investigate the radioactive element thorium, which in addition to alpha, beta, and gamma rays also emits a radioactive gas that he called "emanation." He showed that the emanation decayed in activity at a particular rate, losing half its activity in a fixed period of time (the half-life). Rutherford and Soddy began an intensive investigation of thorium compounds and showed that a more active substance, thorium X, was present. They eventually came to the view that the emanation was produced from the thorium X, which in turn came from the original thorium. In other words, there was a series in which chemical elements were being changed (transmuted) into other elements. Rutherford and Soddy published their theory of a series of transformations in 1905. Rutherford later published a book with the title *The Newer Alchemy* (1937). Soddy went on to continue this work, eventually introducing the idea of isotopes.

Rutherford directed his attention to the alpha radiation emitted in radioactive decay, proving that it consisted of helium atoms that have each lost two electrons. He continued to study alpha radiation, moving to the University of Manchester, England, in 1907. At Manchester Rutherford and Hans Geiger invented the Geiger counter in 1908. Here too Geiger and E. Marsden in 1910, at Rutherford's suggestion, studied the scattering of alpha particles passing through thin metal foils. The particles were detected by a screen coated with zinc sulfide, which gives brief flashes of light (scintillations) when hit by high-energy particles.

Geiger and Marsden found that most of the particles were deflected only slightly on passing through the foil but that a small proportion (about 1 in 8,000) were widely deflected. Rutherford later described this as "quite the most incredible event that has ever happened to me in my life...It was almost as incredible as if you fired a 15-inch shell at a piece of tissue paper and it came back and hit you." To make sense of the results, Rutherford published in 1911 a model of the atom in which he suggested that almost all the mass was concentrated in a very small region and that most of the atom was "empty space." This was the nuclear atom (although Rutherford did not use the term "nucleus" until 1912). He also produced a theoretical formula giving the numbers of particles that would be scattered by a nucleus at different angles. The idea of the nuclear atom was developed further by Niels Bohr.

After the war, which Rutherford spent working for the Admiralty on sonic methods of detecting submarines, he moved in 1919 to take the Cavendish chair of physics and the directorship of the Cavendish Laboratory at Cambridge University, England. It was there that he announced in 1919 his third major discovery, the artificial disintegration of the nucleus. Following some earlier experiments of Marsden he placed an alpha-particle source in a cylinder into which various gases could be introduced. At one end of the cylinder a small hole was covered with a metal disk through which some atoms could escape and register their presence on a zinc sulfide screen. The introduction of nitrogen produced highly energetic particles, which turned out to be hydrogen nuclei (that is, protons). The implications were not lost on Rutherford who concluded that "the nitrogen atom is disintegrated under the intense forces developed in a close collision with the swift alpha particle, and that the hydrogen atom which is liberated formed a constituent part of the nitrogen nucleus." Occasionally, it was later shown, "the alpha particle actually enters the nitrogen nucleus...breaks up...hurling out a proton and leaving behind an oxygen nucleus of mass 17." Rutherford had thus succeeded in bringing about the first transmutation, although when described in nuclear terms it seems a simple enough process. With James Chadwick he went on to show between 1920 and 1924 that most of the lighter elements emitted protons when bombarded with alpha particles.

By his work in 1911 and 1919 Rutherford had shown that not only does the atom have a nucleus but that the nucleus has a structure from which pieces can be knocked out and by which other particles can be absorbed. It was this work which virtually created a whole new discipline, that of nuclear physics. Rutherford received the Nobel Prize for chemistry in 1908.

Ružička, Leopold

(1887–1976)

CROATIAN–SWISS CHEMIST

Ružička (**roo**-zheech-ka or **roo**-zich-ka) was born in Vukovar, Croatia, the son of a cooper. He graduated in chemistry from the Karlsruhe Institute of Technology, in Germany, where he became assistant to Hermann Staudinger, following him to Zurich in 1912. In 1926 he was appointed professor of organic chemistry at the University of Utrecht but in 1929 he returned to the Federal Institute of Technology at Zurich to take up a similar chair.

Beginning in 1916 Ružička worked on the chemistry of natural odorants. While investigating such compounds as musk and civet he discovered a number of ketone compounds containing large rings of carbon atoms.

From the early 1920s Ružička also worked on terpenes. By dehydrogenating the higher terpenes to give aromatic hydrocarbons he was able to determine the structure of pentacyclic triterpenes. He also corrected the formulas of the bile acids and cholesterol proposed by Adolf Windaus and Heinrich Wieland. Ružička's theory that the carbon skeleton of higher terpenes could be seen as consisting of isoprene units proved a useful hypothesis in further work.

In the 1930s Ružička moved into the field of sex hormones. In 1931 Adolf Butenandt, with whom Ružička shared the 1939 Nobel Prize for chemistry, isolated 15 milligrams of the steroid hormone androsterone from 7,000 gallons of urine. Androsterone is a male hormone secreted by the adrenal gland and testis, which when released at puberty causes the development of male sexual characteristics. In 1934 Ružička succeeded in synthesizing it, the first of several such triumphs.

Rydberg, Johannes Robert

(1854–1919)

SWEDISH PHYSICIST AND SPECTROSCOPIST

Johannes Rydberg (**rid**-berg) was born in Halmstad, Sweden, and educated at Lund University, where he received a PhD in 1879. The next year he started teaching mathematics there and stayed at Lund for the rest of his life, taking the chair of physics in 1901.

All of Rydberg's work arose from his interest in the periodic classification of the elements introduced by Dmitri Mendeleev. Rydberg's great intuition was that the periodicity was a result of the structure of the atom. His first research was into the relationship between the spectral lines of elements. In 1890 he found a general formula giving the frequency of the lines in the spectral series as a simple difference between two terms. His formula for a series of lines is:

$$\nu = R(1/m^2 - 1/n^2)$$

where n and m are integers. The constant R is now known as the *Rydberg constant*.

In the early 1900s Rydberg continued to work on the periodic table, reorganizing it, finding new mathematical patterns, and even casting it into spiral form. In the main his theoretical work was confirmed by Henry Moseley's discovery that the positive charge on the nucleus gave a better periodic ordering than the atomic weight.

Ryle, Sir Martin

(1918–1984)

BRITISH RADIO ASTRONOMER

Ryle, the son of a physician, was born at Brighton on the south coast of England and studied at Oxford University. He spent the war with the Telecommunications Research Establishment in Dorset working on radar. After the war he received a fellowship to the Cavendish Laboratory of Cambridge University and in 1948 was appointed lecturer in physics. In 1959 he became the first Cambridge professor of radio astronomy, having been made in 1957 the director of the Mullard Radio Astronomy Observatory in Cambridge. Ryle was appointed Astronomer Royal in 1972 and in 1974 was awarded, jointly with Antony Hewish, the Nobel Prize for physics. He was knighted in 1966.

It was mainly due to Ryle and his colleagues that Cambridge, after the war, became one of the leading centers in the world for astronomical research. He realized that one of the first jobs to be done was simply to map the radio sky. He therefore began in 1950 the important series of Cambridge surveys. The first survey used the principle of interferometry and discovered some 50 radio sources. The second survey in 1955 listed nearly 2,000 sources, many of which turned out to be spurious. The crucial survey was the third one, the results of which were published in 1959 in the *Third Cambridge Catalogue* (3C). This listed the positions and strengths of 500 sources and has since become the definitive catalog used by all radio astronomers. The use of more sensitive receivers in 1965 enabled the 4C survey to detect sources five times fainter than those in the 3C and covered the whole of the northern sky; 5,000 sources were cataloged. Finally, with the opening of two highly sensitive radio telescopes in 1965 and 1971, important areas of the sky are being surveyed in depth: a full survey would take over 2,000 years.

The two new telescopes, the One Mile telescope and then the Five Kilometer telescope, operate by a technique developed by Ryle and called "aperture synthesis." A number of radio dishes are used to give a very large effective aperture, much larger than the aperture of a single dish, and hence produce very considerable resolution of detail in a radio map of an area of the sky. The dishes are mounted along a line, some fixed in position, some movable, and are used in pairs, at different distances apart, to form interferometers.

These telescopes and other equipment were used by Ryle and his colleagues to investigate pulsars, which were discovered at Cambridge by Antony Hewish and Jocelyn Bell, quasars, radio galaxies, and other radio sources. Ryle quickly appreciated that the distribution of radio sources throughout the universe had cosmological implications and that the number of sources found tended to support the evolutionary big-bang theory rather than the steady-state theory.

Sabatier, Paul

(1854–1941)

FRENCH CHEMIST

Sabatier (sa-ba-**tyay**), who was born at Carcassone in southwest France, was a student at the Ecole Normale, Paris, and gained his PhD from the Collège de France in 1880. He became professor of chemistry at the University of Toulouse (1884–1930).

In 1897 Sabatier showed how various organic compounds could undergo hydrogenation, e.g., ethylene will not normally combine with hydrogen but when a mixture of the gases is passed over finely divided nickel, ethane is produced. Benzene can be converted into cyclohexane in the same way. Sabatier discussed the whole problem in his book *Le catalyse en chimie organique* (1912; Catalysis in Organic Chemistry), published the same year in which he was awarded the Nobel Prize for chemistry for his work on catalytic hydrogenations.

Sabin, Albert Bruce

(1906–1993)

POLISH–AMERICAN MICRO-
BIOLOGIST

Sabin (**say**-bin), who was born at Bialystok in Poland, emigrated with his parents to America in 1921; he was educated at New York University, where he gained his MD in 1931. He later joined the staff of the Rockefeller Institute of Medical Research but in 1939 moved to the University of Cincinnati. Following war service with the U.S. Army Medical Corps, he was appointed (1946) research professor of pediatrics at Cincinnati, a post he held until his retirement in 1971.

It was clear to Sabin from the success of John Enders in growing polio virus in tissue culture that a vaccination against the disease was only a matter of time. Sabin already had experience in this field having worked on developing vaccines against dengue fever and Japanese B encephalitis. He therefore began work on the polio vaccine but, unlike Jonas Salk, he was determined to develop a live attenuated vaccine rather than a killed one.

Sabin was not the first to attempt to produce a live vaccine. Herald Cox and Hilary Koprowski working at the Lederle Laboratories of the Cyanamid Company produced such a vaccine, attenuated by repeated passages through mouse brains, in 1952. However they failed to produce convincing tests for their vaccines and, disillusioned, split up in 1956.

This left the field open to Sabin who by then had developed his own live virus, attenuated in monkey kidney tissue. It was impossible to persuade the American public to submit to the testing of another vaccine after the difficulties involved with the Salk campaign of 1954. Sabin therefore hit on the audacious idea of attempting to arouse the interest of the Russians and to persuade them to do his tests for him.

In 1959 Sabin was able to produce the results of 4.5 million vaccinations. They were completely safe, nor was there any reversion to the more virulent form found to develop in the vaccine of Cox and Koprowski. The vaccine also possessed a number of advantages over that of Salk: it gave a stronger longer lasting immunity thus making it unnecessary to give more than a single injection, which was in any case dispensable as the Sabin vaccine could be administered orally. Almost immediately the new vaccine began to take over from that of Salk. Great Britain changed over to the Sabin vaccine as early as 1962 with most other countries following soon afterward.

In 1973 Sabin reported a further major advance, this time in cancer research. With his collaborator G. Tarro he claimed to have evidence linking the herpes virus with a number of cancers. If this were true it would have been the first solid evidence in support of the viral origin of human cancer. In the following year Sabin took the difficult step of completely rejecting his own work when he found that he could no longer repeat his results.

Sabine, Sir Edward

(1788–1883)

BRITISH GEOPHYSICIST

To many men speculations are far more attractive than facts.
—Letter to John Tyndall, 24 April 1855

Sabine, a Dubliner by birth, was educated at the Royal Military Academy, Woolwich, near London, and was commissioned in the Royal Artillery in 1803. He took part in a number of expeditions, sailing as astronomer and meteorologist with John Ross in 1818 and William Parry in 1820 in their search for the Northwest Passage. He made other trips to the tropics and Greenland. Using Henry Katers's pendulum, he made observations at different latitudes to investigate the figure (shape) of the Earth but his results overestimated its ellipticity. He also established magnetic observatories in several British colonies.

Sabine's main scientific achievement was in the field of geomagnetism. In 1851 he announced that he had detected a periodicity of about 10–11 years in the occurrence of magnetic perturbations, in which the magnetic needle deviates abnormally from its average position. This was also discovered by Johann von Lamont at about the same time but Sabine took the further step of correlating the variations in magnetic activity with the sunspot cycle discovered by Heinrich Schwabe in 1843.

Sabine was secretary of the British Association (1838–59) and while in charge of the Royal Observatory at Kew he attempted to organize a number of small observatories throughout the world sending him data to be processed at Kew. He developed a theory in which the Earth's magnetic field was part of the atmosphere, but in 1839 Karl Gauss succeeded in demonstrating that the magnetic field was restricted to the interior and surface of the Earth.

Sabine was knighted in 1869.

Sabine, Wallace Clement Ware

(1868–1919)

AMERICAN PHYSICIST

Born in Richwood, Ohio, Sabine graduated from Ohio State University in 1886 and went on to do graduate work at Harvard. He was employed at Harvard from 1889, being made professor of physics in 1905.

Sabine is recognized as the founder of scientific architectural acoustics. In 1895 Harvard's Fogg Art Museum was opened and its lecture theater found to be "monumental in its acoustic badness." Sabine was asked if he could correct the fault. He found that a normally spoken word would reverberate for as long as 5½ seconds, with the result that a speaker could be completing a long sentence while his first words were still reverberating through the hall. Sabine found that if he covered all the seats, the stage, and most of the floor with ordinary cushions he could reduce the reverberation time to a little more than a second.

Sabine went on to make a systematic study of the acoustics of buildings and eventually formulated a general law relating the reverberation time to the volume, surface area, and absorption coefficient of the room. His *Collected Papers on Acoustics* was published in 1922.

Sachs, Julius von

(1832–1897)

GERMAN BOTANIST

> More and more I find that physiology achieves its most important results when it goes its own way entirely, without concerning itself very much with physics and chemistry.
> —Letter, 15 May 1879

Sachs (zahks), who was born at Breslau (now Wrocław in Poland), started his career as assistant to Johannes Purkinje at the University of Prague, where he gained his PhD in 1856. The following year he qualified as a lecturer in plant physiology and taught at Prague until being appointed assistant in physiology at the Agricultural and Forestry College in Tharandt. (At this time plant physiology encompassed the whole of botany except systematics.) In 1861 Sachs obtained a teaching post at the Agricultural College, Poppelsdorf, and in 1867 succeeded Anton de Bary as professor of botany at Freiburg University. A year later he became professor of botany at Würzburg University, where he remained until his death.

In 1865 Sachs established that the green pigment of plants, chlorophyll, is not distributed throughout the plant but is confined to discrete bodies, later named "chloroplasts." He showed that the starch in chloroplasts is the first visible product of photosynthesis, the process whereby carbon dioxide is taken up by the plant and converted to complex organic compounds. He also demonstrated that plants as well as animals respire, consuming oxygen and producing carbon dioxide.

Sachs was interested in water movement in plants and in 1874 announced his erroneous "inhibition theory," in which he stated that absorbed water does not travel within the cell cavities but moves in tubes in the plant walls. He also studied the formation of annual growth rings in trees and the importance of turgidity in plant tissues for the mechanical support of the plant. He investigated plant growth responses (tropisms) to light and gravity and for these experiments invented the clinostat, which measures the effects of external agents on the movements of plants.

Of his many publications the best known is *Lehrbuch der Botanik* (1868; Textbook of Botany), translated into English in 1875.

Sadron, Charles Louis

(1902–1990)

FRENCH PHYSICAL CHEMIST AND
BIOPHYSICIST

Born at Cluis in France, Sadron (sa-**dron**) was educated at the universities of Poitiers and Strasbourg. After teaching in a number of lycées, he was appointed professor of physics at the University of Strasbourg in 1937 while also serving as director of the Center for Research on Macromolecules from 1947 onward. In 1967 he moved to Orleans where he set up the Center for Molecular Biophysics until his retirement in 1974.

Sadron made substantial contributions to the study of macromolecules, particularly in solution. With his collaborators he developed a wide variety of techniques for investigating the properties of large molecules and for studying polymerization reactions. His group discovered the block copolymers – materials with a regular open matrix of one polymer with filaments or spheres of another polymer dispersed through it. In the early 1960s he turned his attention to studies of nucleic acids, proteins, and other biological macromolecules.

Sagan, Carl Edward

(1934–)

AMERICAN ASTRONOMER

> Our loyalties are to the species and the planet. We speak for Earth. Our obligation to survive is owed not just to ourselves but also to that cosmos, ancient and vast, from which we spring.
>
> —*Cosmos* (1980)

Born in New York City, Sagan studied at the University of Chicago where he obtained his BS in 1955 and his PhD in 1960. He was a research fellow at the University of California, Berkeley, from 1960 to 1962 when he moved to the Smithsonian Astrophysical Observatory in Cambridge, Massachusetts, working at Harvard as lecturer then assistant professor. In 1968 he moved to Cornell where he was appointed director of the Laboratory for Planetary Studies and in 1970 became professor of astronomy and space science. Sagan's main work has been on virtually all aspects of the solar system. One major line of research has been on the physics and chemistry of planetary atmospheres and surfaces, especially of Mars. His other primary interest is the origin of life on Earth and the possibility of extraterrestrial life and he has done much to interest the general public in the new field of exobiology. In laboratory experiments simulating the primitive atmosphere of Earth, he and his colleagues have shown how a variety of organic molecules, such as amino acids, which are the building blocks of proteins, can readily be produced. The energy sources used in these syntheses have included ultraviolet radiation, which would have flooded the Earth's primitive atmosphere, and high-pressure shock waves. It was while working with C. Ponnamperuna and Ruth Mariner at NASA's exobiology division in 1963 that he showed how the fundamental molecule adenosine triphosphate, ATP, could have been produced. ATP is the universal energy intermediary of living organisms and without its presence it is difficult to see how life could have ever originated on Earth.

In 1984 Sagan coauthored, with R. Turco, O. Toon, T. Ackerman and J. Pollock, an influential paper, *Nuclear Winter: Global Consequences of Multiple Nuclear Explosions*, referred to since as the TTAPS paper. The authors argued that even a relatively small-scale nuclear bomb of 5,000 megatons would create enough atmospheric smoke (300 million tons) and dust (15 million tons) to produce a temperature drop of 20–40°C, which would persist for many months. This prolonged nuclear winter would destroy much of the world's agriculture and industry. The impact of the paper on politicians and the public was dramatic.

The nuclear-winter argument itself was heavily criticized by scientists. "These guys don't know what they are talking about," commented Richard Feynman, and Freeman Dyson dismissed the paper as an "absolutely atrocious piece of science." The meteorologist S. Schneider pointed out that the TTAPS model was one-dimensional in that it represented only the vertical structure of the atmosphere and ignored the oceans and seasonal changes. It was, he concluded, "a first generation assessment whose conclusions would have to be modified," and claimed that it threatened more a "nuclear fall" than a nuclear winter.

Sagan has written extensively on the results of planetary science. His *Cosmic Connection* (1973) introduced these results to a wider audience. His later works *The Dragons of Eden* (1977) and *Broca's Brain* (1979) have tried to do the same for recent advances in the theory of evolution and neurophysiology. In a further work, *Cosmos* (1980), based on a major TV series, Sagan charted the history of physics and astronomy. His recent books include *Pale Blue Dot: A Vision of the Human Future in Space* (1994) and *The Demon-Haunted World* (1996).

Saha, Meghnad N.

(1894–1956)

INDIAN ASTROPHYSICIST

Born the son of a small shopkeeper in Dacca (now in Bangladesh), Saha (**sah**-hah) won a scholarship to the Government School there in 1905 but was expelled for participating in the boycott of a visit by the Governor of Bengal. He completed his education in Calcutta, at the Presidency College, where he obtained his MA in applied mathematics in 1915.

After lecturing in mathematics and then physics at Calcutta's University College of Science (1916–19), he visited London and Berlin on a traveling scholarship. He returned to India in 1921 and from 1923 to 1938 taught at the University of Allahabad. In 1938 he moved to the chair of physics at Calcutta where he remained until his death.

Early in his career Saha became interested in both thermodynamics and astrophysics and this led to his work on the thermal ionization that occurs in the very hot atmospheres of stars. In 1920 he published a fundamental paper, *On Ionization in the Solar Chromosphere*, in which he stated his ionization equation. The absorption lines of stellar spectra differ widely, with some stars showing virtually nothing but hydrogen and helium lines while others show vast numbers of lines of different metals. Saha's great insight was to see that all these spectral lines could be represented as the result of ionization. He saw that the degree of ionization, i.e., the number of electrons stripped away from the nucleus, would depend primarily on temperature. As the temperature increases, so does the proportion of ionized atoms. The remaining neutral atoms will thus produce only weak absorption lines that, when the temperature gets high enough, will disappear entirely. But the singly, doubly, and even triply ionized atoms will absorb at different sets of wavelengths, and different sets of lines will appear in stellar spectra, becoming stronger as the proportions of these ions grow.

In later years Saha moved into nuclear physics and worked for the creation of an institute for its study in India, which was later named for him. He also devoted much time to social, economic, and political problems in India.

Sakharov, Andrei Dmitriyevich

(1921–1989)

RUSSIAN PHYSICIST

Every day I saw the huge material, intellectual and nervous resources of thousands of people being poured into the creation of a means of total destruction...I noticed that the control levers were in the hands of people who, though talented in their own ways, were cynical...Beginning in the late fifties, one got an increasingly clearer picture of the collective might of the military-industrial complex and of its vigorous, unprincipled leaders, blind to everything except their "job."

—*Sakharov Speaks* (1974)

Born the son of a physics teacher in Moscow, Sakharov (**sah**-ka-rof) graduated from the university there in 1942 just before the German invasion. He spent the war working as an engineer. In 1945 he joined the Lebedev Physics Institute in Moscow and began to work on cosmic rays. In 1950, in collaboration with Igor Tamm, Sakharov described a process whereby a deuterium plasma could be confined in a magnetic bottle in such a way as to extract energy produced by nuclear fusion. The design became known later in the West as the tokamak.

Soon after, Sakharov was deployed to secret research on the development of nuclear weapons. It is widely assumed that he played a crucial role in the explosion of the first Soviet hydrogen bomb in 1954. He continued this work until 1968, when he published his famous pamphlet, *Progress, Peaceful Coexistence and Intellectual Freedom*, which argued for a global reduction in nuclear weapons and the granting of civil rights in the Soviet Union.

Sakharov was immediately moved to nonclassified work back at the Lebedev Institute, and further agitation led to increased harassment by the authorities. He was awarded the Nobel Peace prize in 1975 and was finally sent into exile to Gorky in 1980. He was eventually released in 1986 and lived just long enough to see the fruition of Gorbachev's reforms, being elected shortly before his death to the Congress of the USSR.

Sakharov also made major contributions to several areas of theoretical physics. In 1966 he offered important evidence in support for the existence of quarks, the particles first proposed in 1964 by Gell-Mann. Also in 1966 he offered an explanation for the apparent dearth of antimatter in the observed universe.

Sakmann, Bert

(1942–   )

GERMAN BIOPHYSICIST

Born in Stuttgart, Germany, Sakmann (**zahk**-man) attended the universities of Tübingen and Munich, and gained his MD from the University of Göttingen. He became a research assistant at the Max Planck Institute of Psychiatry, Munich (1969–70), and subsequently spent two years as a British Council Fellow at the Biophysics Department of University College, London (1971–73). In 1974 he joined the Max Planck Institute for Biophysical Chemistry at the University of Göttingen, becoming head of the membrane physiology unit in 1983 and director in 1985. Two years later he was appointed professor in the department of cell physiology. In 1989 he moved to Heidelberg as director of the cell physiology department of the Max Planck Institute for Medical Research.

While working at Göttingen in the mid-1970s, in collaboration with the biophysicist Erwin Neher, Sakmann developed the so-called "patch-clamp" technique for studying ion channels in cell membranes. This, together with their descriptions of the biophysical properties of the channels, earned them the 1991 Nobel Prize for physiology or medicine.

Salam, Abdus

(1926–)

PAKISTANI PHYSICIST

One-eighth of the Koran is an exhortation to
the believers to study nature and to find the
signs of God in the phenomena of nature. So
Islam has no conflict with science.
—Wolpert and Richards, *A Passion for
Science* (1988)

The whole history of particle physics, or of physics, is one of getting down the
number of concepts to as few as possible.

—As above

Salam (sah-**lahm**), who was born at Jhang in Pakistan, attended Punjab
University and Cambridge University, where he received his PhD in 1952.
From 1951 to 1954 he was a professor of mathematics at the Government
College of Lahore, concurrently with a post as head of the mathematics
department of Punjab University. From 1954 until 1956 he lectured at
Cambridge and from 1957 to 1993 he was a professor of theoretical
physics at the Imperial College of Science and Technology, London. He
was largely responsible for the establishment in 1964 of the International
Center for Theoretical Physics, Trieste, as an institute to assist physicists
from developing countries. He was director of the center from its inception until 1994, dividing his time between there and Imperial College.

Salam's work has been concerned with the theories describing the behavior and properties of elementary particles; for this he received the
1979 Nobel Prize for physics, shared with Sheldon Glashow and Steven
Weinberg. Although the three men did most of their work independently, they each contributed to the development of a theory that could
take account of the "weak" and "electromagnetic" interactions. One of
their predictions was the phenomenon of neutral currents and their
strengths, which was first confirmed in 1973 at the European Organization for Nuclear Research (CERN) and later by other groups. A further
prediction of the theory is that of the existence of "intermediate vector
bosons" with high masses. The discovery of a vector boson was reported
in 1983 by two teams (comprising 180 scientists) working at the European Laboratory for Particle Physics near Geneva.

Salisbury, Sir Edward James

(1886–1978)

BRITISH BOTANIST

Salisbury, who was born at Harpenden in Hertfordshire, England, was educated at University College, London, where he joined the faculty at the end of World War I. He served as professor of botany from 1929 until 1943 when he was appointed director of the Royal Botanic Gardens, Kew, an office he held until his retirement in 1956.

Salisbury's first substantial work was his *Plant Form and Function* (1938) written in collaboration with Felix Fritsch, a widely used textbook. However Salisbury was primarily a plant ecologist and did much work both on the effects of soil conditions and on the seed-producing capacity of British species. This was presented in his *The Reproductive Capacity of Plants* (1942). He also carried out a long-term study of sand-dune ecology, the results of which were published in his *Downs and Dunes* (1952). He also wrote the popular horticultural work *The Living Garden* (1935).

Sources and Further Reading

PASCAL

Nelson, Robert J. *Pascal: Adversary and Advocate*. Cambridge, MA: Harvard University Press, 1982.

PASTEUR

Geison, Gerald L. *The Private Science of Louis Pasteur*. Princeton, NJ: Princeton University Press, 1995.

PAULING

Serafini, Anthony. *Linus Pauling: A Man and his Science*. New York: Paragon House, 1989.

PEIERLS

Peierls, Rudolf. *Bird of Passage: Recollections of a Physicist*. Princeton, NJ: Princeton University Press, 1985.

PENROSE

Peat, F. David. *Superstrings and the Search for the Theory of Everything*. Chicago, IL: Contemporary Books, Inc., 1988.

Penrose, Roger. *The Emperor's New Mind: Concerning Computers, Minds and the Laws of Physics*. New York: Oxford University Press, 1989.

PENZIAS

Bernstein, Jeremy. *Three Degrees Above Zero: Bell Labs in the Information Age*. New York: Scribners, 1984.

PERUTZ

Perutz, Max. *Is Science Necessary? Essays on Science and Scientists*. New York: Oxford University Press, 1991.

PETTENKOFER

Evans, Richard J. *Death in Hamburg: Society and Politics in the Cholera Years 1830–1910*. New York: Oxford University Press, 1987.

PLANCK

Heilbron, J. L. *The Dilemmas of an Upright Man*. Berkeley, CA: University of California Press, 1986.

PLINY

Pliny the Elder. *Natural History: A Selection*. New York: Viking Penguin, 1991.

POINCARÉ

Bell, E. T. *Men of Mathematics*. New York: Simon and Schuster, 1937.

Peterson, Ivars. *Newton's Clock: Chaos in the Solar System*. San Francisco, CA: Freeman, 1993.

POPPER

Popper, Karl. *Unended Quest: An Intellectual Autobiography*. New York: Open Court, 1982.

PRIESTLEY

Gibbs, F. W. *Joseph Priestley*. London: Nelson, 1965.

Schofield, R. E., ed. *A Scientific Autobiography of Joseph Priestley 1733–1804*. Cambridge, MA: MIT Press, 1966.

PRIGOGINE

Coveney, Peter, and Roger Hughfield. *The Arrow of Time*. New York: Fawcett, 1991.

Prigogine, Ilya. *From Being to Becoming*. San Francisco, CA: Freeman, 1980.

PTOLEMY

Gjertsen, Derek. *The Classics of Science*. New York: Lilian Barber Press, 1984.

Pedersen, O., and M. Pihl. *Early Physics and Astronomy*. New York: American Elsevier, 1974.

Stevenson, E. L., ed. *Claudius Ptolemy: The Geography*. New York: Dover Publications, 1991.

RAMANUJAN

Kanigel, Robert. *The Man Who Knew Infinity*. New York: Scribners, 1991.

RAMSAY

Asimov, Isaac. *Building Blocks of the Universe*. New York: Lancer Books, 1966.

RAUP

Raup, David M. *The Nemesis Affair: A Story of the Death of Dinosaurs and the Ways of Science*. New York: W. W. Norton, 1986.

——. *Extinction: Bad Genes or Bad Luck*. New York: W. W. Norton, 1991.

RAY

Raven, C. E. *John Ray, Naturalist: His Life and Work*. New York: Cambridge University Press, 1942.

RAYLEIGH

Strutt, R. J., Baron Rayleigh. *Life of Lord Rayleigh*. Madison, WI: University of Wisconsin Press, 1968.

REBER

Edge, David, and Michael Mulkay. *Astronomy Transformed: The Emergence of Radio Astronomy in Britain*. New York: John Wiley, 1976.

RICHARDSON, Lewis Fry

Ashford, Oliver M. *Prophet or Professor? The Life and Work of Lewis Fry Richardson*. Bristol, England: Adam Hilger, 1985.

Casti, John L. *Searching for Certainty: What Science Can Know About the Future*. New York: William Morrow, 1991.

RIEMANN

Bell, E. T. *Men of Mathematics*. New York: Simon and Schuster, 1937.

Stewart, Ian. *From Here to Infinity*. New York: Oxford University Press, 1996.

ROGET

Emblen, Donald Lewis. *P. M. Roget: The Word and the Man*. New York: Crowell, 1970.

ROSS, Sir Ronald

Desowitz, Robert S. *The Malaria Capers*. New York: W. W. Norton, 1991.

Harrison, Gordon. *Mosquitoes, Malaria and Man*. London: John Murray, 1978.

ROWLAND, Frank Sherwood

Roan, Sharon L. *The Ozone Crisis*. New York: John Wiley, 1989.

RUBBIA

Taubes, Gary. *Nobel Dreams*. New York: Random House, 1986.

Watkins, Peter Maitland. *The Story of the W and Z*. New York: Cambridge University Press, 1986.

RUMFORD

Brown, Sanborn C. *Count Rumford: Physicist Extraordinary*. New York: Doubleday, 1962.

Sparrow, W. J. *Knight of the White Eagle: A Biography of Count Rumford*. London: Hutchinson, 1964.

RUSSELL, Bertrand

Russell, Bertrand. *Autobiography*. London: Allen and Unwin, 3 vols., 1967–69.

RUSSELL, Henry Norris

Gingerich, O., ed. *The General History of Astronomy. 4A: Astrophysics and 20th Century Astronomy to 1950*. New York: Cambridge University Press, 1984.

RUTHERFORD, Ernest

Andrade, E. N. da C. *Rutherford and the Nature of the Atom*. New York: Doubleday, 1964.

Wilson, David. *Rutherford: Simple Genius*. London: Hodder and Stoughton, 1983.

SAGAN

Sagan, Carl. *The Cosmic Connection*. New York: Doubleday, 1973.

Sagan, Carl, and R. Turco. *A Path Where No Man Thought: Nuclear Winter and the End of the Arms Race*. New York: Random House, 1990.

SAKHAROV

Sakharov, Andrei. *Memoirs*. New York: Alfred A. Knopf, 1990.

Glossary

absolute zero The zero value of thermodynamic temperature, equal to 0 kelvin or −273.15°C.

acceleration of free fall The acceleration of a body falling freely, at a specified point on the Earth's surface, as a result of the gravitational attraction of the Earth. The standard value is 9.80665 m s^{-2} (32.174 ft s^{-2}).

acetylcholine A chemical compound that is secreted at the endings of some nerve cells and transmits a nerve impulse from one nerve cell to the next or to a muscle, gland, etc.

acquired characteristics Characteristics developed during the life of an organism, but not inherited, as a result of use and disuse of organs.

adrenaline (epinephrine) A hormone, secreted by the adrenal gland, that increases metabolic activity in conditions of stress.

aldehyde Any of a class of organic compounds containing the group –CHO.

aliphatic Denoting an organic compound that is not aromatic, including the alkanes, alkenes, alkynes, cycloalkanes, and their derivatives.

alkane Any of the saturated hydrocarbons with the general formula C_nH_{2n+2}.

alkene Any one of a class of hydrocarbons characterized by the presence of double bonds between carbon atoms and having the general formula C_nH_{2n}. The simplest example is ethylene (ethene).

alkyne Any one of a class of hydrocarbons characterized by the presence of triple bonds between carbon atoms. The simplest example is ethyne (acetylene).

allele One of two or more alternative forms of a particular gene.

amino acid Any one of a class of organic compounds that contain both an amino group (–NH$_2$) and a carboxyl group (–COOH) in their molecules. Amino acids are the units present in peptides and proteins.

amount of substance A measure of quantity proportional to the number of particles of substance present.

anabolism The sum of the processes involved in the synthesis of the constituents of living cells.

androgen Any of a group of steroid hormones with masculinizing properties, produced by the testes in all vertebrate animals.

antibody A protein produced by certain white blood cells (lymphocytes) in response to the presence of an antigen. An antibody forms a complex with an antigen, which is thereby inactivated.

antigen A foreign or potentially harmful substance that, when introduced into the body, stimulates the production of a specific antibody.

aromatic Denoting a chemical compound that has the property of aromaticity, as characterized by benzene.

asteroid Any of a large number of small celestial bodies orbiting the Sun, mainly between Mars and Jupiter.

atomic orbital A region around the nucleus of an atom in which an electron moves. According to wave mechanics, the electron's location is described by a probability distribution in space, given by the wave function.

ATP Adenosine triphosphate: a compound, found in all living organisms, that functions as a carrier of chemical energy, which is released when required for metabolic reactions.

bacteriophage A virus that lives and reproduces as a parasite within a bacterium.

bacterium (*pl.* **bacteria**) Any one of a large group of microorganisms that all lack a membrane around the nucleus and have a cell wall of unique composition.

band theory The application of quantum mechanics to the energies of electrons in crystalline solids.

baryon Any of a class of elementary particles that have half-integral spin and take part in strong interactions. They consist of three quarks each.

beta decay A type of radioactive decay in which an unstable nucleus ejects either an electron and an antineutrino or a positron and a neutrino.

black body A hypothetical body that absorbs all the radiation falling on it.

bremsstrahlung Electromagnetic radiation produced by the deceleration of charged particles.

carbohydrate Any of a class of compounds with the formula $C_nH_{2m}O_m$. The carbohydrates include the sugars, starch, and cellulose.

carcinogen Any agent, such as a chemical or type of radiation, that causes cancer.

catabolism The sum of the processes involved in the breakdown of molecules in living cells in order to provide chemical energy for metabolic processes.

catalysis The process by which the rate of a chemical reaction is increased by the presence of another substance (the catalyst) that does not appear in the stoichiometric equation for the reaction.

cathode-ray oscilloscope An instrument for displaying changing electrical signals on a cathode-ray tube.

cellulose A white solid carbohydrate, $(C_6H_{10}O_5)_n$, found in all plants as the main constituent of the cell wall.

chelate An inorganic metal complex in which there is a closed ring of atoms, caused by attachment of a ligand to a metal atom at two points.

chlorophyll Any one of a group of green pigments, found in all plants, that absorb light for photosynthesis.

cholesterol A steroid alcohol occurring widely in animal cell membranes and tissues. Excess amounts in the blood are associated with atherosclerosis (obstruction of the arteries).

chromatography Any of several related techniques for separating and analyzing mixtures by selective adsorption or absorption in a flow system.

chromosome One of a number of threadlike structures, consisting mainly of DNA and protein, found in the nucleus of cells and constituting the genetic material of the cell.

codon The basic coding unit of DNA and RNA, consisting of a sequence of three nucleotides that specifies a particular amino acid in the synthesis of proteins in a cell.

collagen A fibrous protein that is a major constituent of the connective tissue in skin, tendons, and bone.

colligative property A property that depends on the number of particles of substance present in a substance, rather than on the nature of the particles.

continental drift The theory that the Earth's continents once formed a single mass, parts of which have drifted apart to their present positions.

cortisone A steroid hormone, produced by the cortex (outer part) of the adrenal gland, that regulates the metabolism of carbohydrate, fat, and protein and reduces inflammation.

critical mass The minimum mass of fissile material for which a chain reaction is self-sustaining.

cryogenics The branch of physics concerned with the production of very low temperatures and the study of phenomena occurring at these temperatures.

cyclotron A type of particle accelerator in which the particles move in spiral paths under the influence of a uniform vertical magnetic field and are accelerated by an electric field of fixed frequency.

cytoplasm The jellylike material that surrounds the nucleus of a living cell.

dendrochronology A method of dating wooden specimens based on the growth rings of trees. It depends on the assumption that trees grown in the same climatic conditions have a characteristic pattern of rings.

dialysis The separation of mixtures by selective diffusion through a semipermeable membrane.

diffraction The formation of light and dark bands (diffraction patterns) around the boundary of a shadow cast by an object or aperture.

diploid Describing a nucleus, cell, or organism with two sets of chromosomes, one set deriving from the male parent and the other from the female parent.

DNA Deoxyribonucleic acid: a nucleic acid that is a major constituent of the chromosomes and is the hereditary material of most organisms.

dissociation The breakdown of a molecule into radicals, ions, atoms, or simpler molecules.

distillation A process used to purify or separate liquids by evaporating them and recondensing the vapor.

ecology The study of living organisms in relation to their environment.

eigenfunction One of a set of allowed wave functions of a particle in a given system as determined by wave mechanics.

electrolysis Chemical change produced by passing an electric current through a conducting solution or fused ionic substance.

electromagnetic radiation Waves of energy (electromagnetic waves) consisting of electric and magnetic fields vibrating at right angles to the direction of propagation of the waves.

electromotive force The energy supplied by a source of current in driving unit charge around an electrical circuit. It is measured in volts.

electromotive series A series of the metals arranged in decreasing order of their tendency to form positive ions by a reaction of the type $M = M^+ + e$.

electron An elementary particle with a negative charge equal to that of the proton and a rest mass of 9.1095×10^{-31} kilograms (about 1/1836 that of the proton).

electron microscope A device in which a magnified image of a sample is produced by illuminating it with a beam of high-energy electrons rather than light.

electroweak theory A unified theory of the electromagnetic interaction and the weak interaction.

enthalpy A thermodynamic property of a system equal to the sum of its internal energy and the product of its pressure and its volume.

entomology The branch of zoology concerned with the study of insects.

entropy A measure of the disorder of a system. In any system undergoing a reversible change the change of entropy is defined as the energy absorbed divided by the thermodynamic temperature. The entropy of the system is thus a measure of the availability of its energy for performing useful work.

escape velocity The minimum velocity that would have to be given to an object for it to escape from a specified gravitational field. The escape velocity from the Earth is 25,054 mph (7 miles per second).

ester A compound formed by a reaction between an alcohol and a fatty acid.

estrogen Any one of a group of steroid hormones, produced mainly by the ovaries in all vertebrates, that stimulate the growth and maintenance of the female reproductive organs.

ethology The study of the behavior of animals in their natural surroundings.

excitation A change in the energy of an atom, ion, molecule, etc., from one energy level (usually the ground state) to a higher energy level.

fatty acid Any of a class of organic acids with the general formula R.CO.OH, where R is a hydrocarbon group.

fermentation A reaction in which compounds, such as sugar, are broken down by the action of microorganisms that form the enzymes required to catalyze the reaction.

flash photolysis A technique for investigating the spectra and reactions of free radicals.

free energy A thermodynamic function used to measure the ability of a system to perform work. A change in free energy is equal to the work done.

free radical An atom or group of atoms that has an independent existence without all its valences being satisfied.

fuel cell A type of electric cell in which electrical energy is produced directly by electrochemical reactions involving substances that are continuously added to the cell.

fungus Any one of a group of spore-producing organisms formerly classified as plants but now placed in a separate kingdom (Fungi). They include the mushrooms, molds, and yeasts.

galaxy Any of the innumerable aggregations of stars that, together with gas, dust, and other material, make up the universe.

gene The functional unit of heredity. A single gene contains the information required for the manufacture, by a living cell, of one particular polypeptide, protein, or type of RNA and is the vehicle by which such information is transmitted to subsequent generations. Genes correspond to discrete regions of the DNA (or RNA) making up the genome.

genetic code The system by which genetic material carries the information that directs the activities of a living cell. The code is contained in the sequence of nucleotides of DNA and/or RNA (*see* codon).

genome The sum total of an organism's genetic material, including all the genes carried by its chromosomes.

global warming *See* greenhouse effect.

glycolysis The series of reactions in which glucose is broken down with the release of energy in the form of ATP.

greenhouse effect An effect in the Earth's atmosphere resulting from the presence of such gases as CO_2, which absorb the infrared radiation produced by the reradiation of solar ultraviolet radiation at the Earth's surface. This causes a rise in the Earth's average temperature, known as "global warming."

half-life A measure of the stability of a radioactive substance, equal to the time taken for its activity to fall to one half of its original value.

halogens The nonmetallic elements fluorine, chlorine, bromine, iodine, and astatine.

haploid Describing a nucleus or cell that contains only a single set of chromosomes; haploid organisms consist exclusively of haploid cells. During sexual reproduction, two haploid sex cells fuse to form a single diploid cell.

heat death The state of a closed system when its total entropy has increased to its maximum value. Under these conditions there is no available energy.

histamine A substance released by various tissues of the body in response to invasion by microorganisms or other stimuli. It triggers inflammation and is responsible for some of the symptoms (e.g., sneezing) occurring in such allergies as hay fever.

histology The study of the tissues of living organisms.

hormone Any of various substances that are produced in small amounts by certain glands within the body (the endocrine glands) and released into the bloodstream to regulate the growth or activities of organs and tissues elsewhere in the body.

hydrocarbon Any organic compound composed only of carbon and hydrogen.

hydrogen bond A weak attraction between an electronegative atom, such as oxygen, nitrogen, or fluorine, and a hydrogen atom that is covalently linked to another electronegative atom.

hysteresis An apparent lag of an effect with respect to the magnitude of the agency producing the effect.

ideal gas An idealized gas composed of atoms that have a negligible volume and undergo perfectly elastic collisions. Such a gas would obey the gas laws under all conditions.

immunology The study of the body's mechanisms for defense against disease and the various ways in which these can be manipulated or enhanced.

insulin A hormone that is responsible for regulating the level of glucose in the blood, i.e., "blood sugar." It is produced by certain cells in the pancreas; deficiency causes the disease diabetes mellitus.

integrated circuit An electronic circuit made in a single small unit.

interferon Any one of a group of proteins, produced by various cells and tissues in the body, that increase resistance to invading viruses. Some types are synthesized for use in medicine as antiviral drugs.

internal energy The total energy possessed by a system on account of the kinetic and potential energies of its component molecules.

ion An atom or group of atoms with a net positive or negative charge. Positive ions (cations) have a deficiency of electrons and negative ions (anions) have an excess.

ionizing radiation Electromagnetic radiation or particles that cause ionization.

ionosphere A region of ionized air and free electrons around the Earth in the Earth's upper atmosphere, extending from a height of about 31 miles to 621 miles.

isomerism The existence of two or more chemical compounds with the same molecular formula but different arrangements of atoms in their molecules.

isotope Any of a number of forms of an element, all of which differ only in the number of neutrons in their atomic nuclei.

ketone Any of a class of organic compounds with the general formula RCOR', where R and R' are usually hydrocarbon groups.

kinetic energy The energy that a system has by

virtue of its motion, determined by the work necessary to bring it to rest.

kinetic theory Any theory for describing the physical properties of a system with reference to the motion of its constituent atoms or molecules.

laser A device for producing intense light or infrared or ultraviolet radiation by stimulated emission.

latent heat The total heat absorbed or produced during a change of phase (fusion, vaporization, etc.) at a constant temperature.

lepton Any of a class of elementary particles that have half-integral spin and take part in weak interactions; they include the electron, the muon, the neutrino, and their antiparticles.

lipid An ester of a fatty acid. Simple lipids include fats and oils; compound lipids include phospholipids and glycolipids; derived lipids include the steroids.

liquid crystal A state of certain molecules that flow like liquids but have an ordered arrangement of molecules.

macromolecule A very large molecule, as found in polymers or in such compounds as proteins.

magnetohydrodynamics The study of the motion of electrically conducting fluids and their behavior in magnetic fields.

meiosis A type of nuclear division, occurring only in certain cells of the reproductive organs, in which a diploid cell produces four haploid sex cells, or gametes.

meson Any member of a class of elementary particles characterized by a mass intermediate between those of the electron and the proton, an integral spin, and participation in strong interactions. They consist of two quarks each.

metabolism The totality of the chemical reactions taking place in a living cell or organism.

mitosis The type of nuclear division occurring in the body cells of most organisms, in which a diploid cell produces two diploid daughter cells.

moderator A substance used in fission reactors to slow down fast neutrons.

monoclonal antibody Any antibody produced by members of a group of genetically identical cells (which thus constitute a "clone"). Such antibodies have identical structures and each combines with the same antigen in precisely the same manner.

morphology The study of the form of organisms, especially their external shape and structure.

muon An elementary particle having a positive or negative charge and a mass equal to 206.77 times the mass of the electron.

mutation Any change in the structure of a gene, which can arise spontaneously or as a result of such agents as x-rays or certain chemicals. It may have a beneficial effect on the organism but most mutations are neutral, harmful, or even lethal. Mutations affecting the germ cells can be passed on to the organism's offspring.

natural selection The process by which the individuals of a population that are best adapted to life in a particular environment tend to enjoy greater reproductive success than members which are less well adapted. Hence, over successive generations, the descendants of the former constitute an increasing proportion of the population.

neutrino An elementary particle with zero rest mass, a velocity equal to that of light, and a spin of one half.

nuclear fission The process in which an atomic nucleus splits into fragment nuclei and one or more neutrons with the emission of energy.

nuclear fusion A nuclear reaction in which two light nuclei join together to form a heavier nucleus with the emission of energy.

nuclear winter The period of darkness and low temperature, predicted to follow a nuclear war, as a result of the obscuring of sunlight by dust and other debris.

nucleic acid Any of a class of large biologically important molecules consisting of one or more chains of nucleotides. There are two types: deoxyribonucleic acid (DNA) and ribonucleic acid (RNA).

nucleotide Any of a class of compounds consisting of a nitrogen-containing base (a purine or pyrimidine) combined with a sugar group (ribose or deoxyribose) bearing a phosphate group. Long chains of nucleotides form the nucleic acids, DNA and RNA.

nucleon A particle that is a constituent of an atomic nucleus; either a proton or a neutron.

nucleus 1. The positively charged part of the atom about which the electrons orbit. The nucleus is composed of neutrons and protons held together by strong interactions. 2. A prominent body found in the cells of animals, plants, and other organisms (but not bacteria) that contains the chromosomes and is bounded by a double membrane.

oncogene A gene, introduced into a living cell by certain viruses, that disrupts normal metabolism and transforms the cell into a cancer cell.

optical activity The property of certain substances of rotating the plane of polarization of plane-polarized light.

osmosis Preferential flow of certain substances in solution through a semipermeable membrane. If the membrane separates a solution from a pure solvent, the solvent will flow through the membrane into the solution.

oxidation A process in which oxygen is combined with a substance or hydrogen is removed from a compound.

ozone layer A layer containing ozone in the Earth's atmosphere. It lies between heights of 9 and 19 miles and absorbs the Sun's higher-energy ultraviolet radiation.

parity A property of elementary particles depending on the symmetry of their wave function with respect to changes in sign of the coordinates.

parthenogenesis A form of reproduction in which a sex cell, usually an egg cell, develops into an embryo without fertilization. It occurs in certain plants and invertebrates and results in offspring that are genetically identical to the parent.

pathology The study of the nature and causes of disease.

peptide A compound formed by two or more amino acids linked together. The amino group ($-NH_2$) of one acid reacts with the carboxyl group ($-COOH$) of another to give the group $-NH-CO-$, known as the "peptide linkage."

periodic table A tabular arrangement of the elements in order of increasing atomic number such that similarities are displayed between groups of elements.

pH A measure of the acidity or alkalinity of a solution, equal to the logarithm to base 10 of the reciprocal of the concentration of hydrogen ions.

photocell Any device for converting light or other electromagnetic radiation directly into an electric current.

photoelectric effect The ejection of electrons from a solid as a result of irradiation by light or other electromagnetic radiation. The number of electrons emitted depends on the intensity of the light and not on its frequency.

photolysis The dissociation of a chemical compound into other compounds, atoms, and free radicals by irradiation with electromagnetic radiation.

photon A quantum of electromagnetic radiation.

photosynthesis The process by which plants, algae, and certain bacteria "fix" inorganic carbon, from carbon dioxide, as organic carbon in the form of carbohydrate using light as a source of energy and, in green plants and algae, water as a source of hydrogen. The light energy is trapped by special pigments, e.g., chlorophyll.

piezoelectric effect An effect observed in certain crystals in which they develop a potential difference across a pair of opposite faces when subjected to a stress.

pion A type of meson having either zero, positive, or negative charge and a mass 264.2 times that of the electron.

plankton The mass of microscopic plants and animals that drift passively at or near the surface of oceans and lakes.

plasma 1. An ionized gas consisting of free electrons and an approximately equal number of ions. **2.** Blood plasma: the liquid component of blood, excluding the blood cells.

plate tectonics The theory that the Earth's surface consists of lithospheric plates, which have moved throughout geological time to their present positions.

polypeptide A chain of amino acids held together by peptide linkages. Polypeptides are found in proteins.

potential energy The energy that a system has by virtue of its position or state, determined by the work necessary to change the system from a reference position to its present state.

probability The likelihood that an event will occur. If an event is certain to occur its probability is 1; if it is certain not to occur the probability is 0. In any other circumstances the probability lies between 0 and 1.

protein Any of a large number of naturally occurring organic compounds found in all living matter. Proteins consist of chains of amino acids joined by peptide linkages.

proton A stable elementary particle with a positive electric charge equal to that of the electron. It is the nucleus of a hydrogen atom and weighs 1,836 times the mass of the electron.

protozoa A large group of minute single-celled organisms found widely in freshwater, marine, and damp terrestrial habitats. Unlike bacteria they possess a definite nucleus and are distinguished from plants in lacking cellulose.

pulsar A star that acts as a source of regularly fluctuating electromagnetic radiation, the period of the pulses usually being very rapid.

quantum electrodynamics The quantum theory of electromagnetic interactions between particles and between particles and electromagnetic radiation.

quantum theory A mathematical theory involving the idea that the energy of a system can change only in discrete amounts (quanta), rather than continuously.

quark Any of six elementary particles and their corresponding antiparticles with fractional charges that are the building blocks of baryons and mesons. Together with leptons they are the basis of all matter.

quasar A class of starlike astronomical objects with large redshifts, many of which emanate strong radio waves.

radioactive labeling The use of radioactive atoms in a compound to trace the path of the compound through a biological or mechanical system.

radioactivity The spontaneous disintegration of the nuclei of certain isotopes with emission of beta rays (electrons), alpha rays (helium nuclei), or gamma rays.

radio astronomy The branch of astronomy involving the use of radio telescopes.

radiocarbon dating A method of dating archeological specimens of wood, cotton, etc., based on the small amount of radioactive carbon (carbon–14) incorporated into the specimen when it was living and the extent to which this isotope has decayed since its death.

radioisotope A radioactive isotope of an element.

recombination The reassortment of maternally derived and paternally derived genes that occurs during meiosis preceding the formation of sex cells. Recombination is an important source of genetic variation.

redox reaction A reaction in which one reactant is oxidized and the other is reduced.

redshift The displacement of the spectral lines emitted by a moving body towards the red end of the visual spectrum. It is caused by the Doppler effect and, when observed in the spectrum of distant stars and galaxies, it indicates that the body is receding from the earth.

reduction A process in which oxygen is removed from or hydrogen is combined with a compound.

reflex An automatic response of an organism or body part to a stimulus, i.e., one that occurs without conscious control.

refractory A solid that has a high melting point and can withstand high temperatures.

relativistic mass The mass of a body as predicted by the theory of relativity. The relativistic mass of a particle moving at velocity v is $m_0(1 - v^2/c^2)^{-1/2}$, where m_0 is the rest mass.

rest mass The mass of a body when it is at rest relative to its observer, as distinguished from its relativistic mass.

retrovirus A type of virus whose genome, consisting of RNA, is transcribed into a DNA version and then inserted into the DNA of its host. The flow of genetic information, from RNA to DNA, is thus the reverse of that found in organisms generally.

RNA Ribonucleic acid: any one of several types of nucleic acid, including messenger RNA, that process the information carried by the genes and use it to direct the assembly of proteins in cells. In certain viruses RNA is the genetic material.

semiconductor A solid with an electrical conductivity that is intermediate between those of insulators and metals and that increases with increasing temperature. Examples are germanium, silicon, and lead telluride.

semipermeable membrane A barrier that permits the passage of some substances but is impermeable to others.

serum The fraction of blood plasma excluding the components of the blood-clotting system.

sex chromosome A chromosome that participates in determining the sex of individuals. Humans have two sex chromosomes, X and Y; females have two X chromosomes (XX) and males have one of each (XY).

sex hormone Any hormone that controls the development of sexual characteristics and regulates reproductive activity. The principal human sex hormones are progesterone and estrogens in females, testosterone and androsterone in males.

simple harmonic motion Motion of a point moving along a path so that its acceleration is directed towards a fixed point on the path and is directly proportional to the displacement from this fixed point.

SI units A system of units used, by international agreement, for all scientific purposes. It is based on the meter-kilogram-second (MKS) system and consists of seven base units and two supplementary units.

soap A salt of a fatty acid.

solar cell Any electrical device for converting solar energy directly into electrical energy.

solar constant The energy per unit area per unit time received from the Sun at a point that is the Earth's mean distance from the Sun away. It has the value 1,400 joules per square meter per second.

solar wind Streams of electrons and protons emitted by the Sun. The solar wind is responsible for the formation of the Van Allen belts and the aurora.

solid-state physics The experimental and theoretical study of the properties of the solid state, in particular the study of energy levels and the electrical and magnetic properties of metals and semiconductors.

speciation The process in which new species evolve from existing populations of organisms.

specific heat capacity The amount of heat required to raise the temperature of unit mass of a substance by unit temperature; it is usually measured in joules per kilogram per kelvin.

spectrometer Any of various instruments used for producing a spectrum (distribution of wavelengths of increasing magnitude) and measuring the wavelengths, energies, etc.

speed of light The speed at which all electromagnetic radiation travels; it is the highest speed attainable in the universe and has the value 2.998×10^8 meters per second in a vacuum.

standing wave A wave in which the wave profile remains stationary in the medium through which it is passing.

state of matter One of the three physical states – solid, liquid, or gas – in which matter may exist.

stereochemistry The arrangement in space of the groups in a molecule and the effect this has on the compound's properties and chemical behavior.

steroid Any of a group of complex lipids that occur widely in plants and animals and include various hormones, such as cortisone and the sex hormones.

stimulated emission The process in which a photon colliding with an excited atom causes emission of a second photon with the same energy as the first. It is the basis of lasers.

stoichiometric Involving chemical combination in exact ratios.

strangeness A property of certain hadrons that causes them to decay more slowly than expected from the energy released.

strong interaction A type of interaction between elementary particles occurring at short range (about 10^{-15} meter) and having a magnitude about 100 times greater than that of the electromagnetic interaction.

sublimation The passage of certain substances from the solid state into the gaseous state and then back into the solid state, without any intermediate liquid state being formed.

substrate A substance that is acted upon in some way, especially the compound acted on by a catalyst or the solid on which a compound is adsorbed.

sugar Any of a group of water-soluble simple carbohydrates, usually having a sweet taste.

sunspot A region of the Sun's surface that is much cooler and therefore darker than the surrounding area, having a temperature of about 4,000°C as opposed to 6,000°C for the rest of the photosphere.

superconductivity A phenomenon occurring

in certain metals and alloys at temperatures close to absolute zero, in which the electrical resistance of the solid vanishes below a certain temperature.

superfluid A fluid that flows without friction and has extremely high thermal conductivity.

supernova A star that suffers an explosion, becoming up to 10^8 times brighter in the process and forming a large cloud of expanding debris (the supernova remnant).

surfactant A substance used to increase the spreading or wetting properties of a liquid. Surfactants are often detergents, which act by lowering the surface tension.

symbiosis A long-term association between members of different species, especially where mutual benefit is derived by the participants.

taxonomy The science of classifying organisms into groups.

tensile strength The applied stress necessary to break a material under tension.

thermal conductivity A measure of the ability of a substance to conduct heat, equal to the rate of flow of heat per unit area resulting from unit temperature gradient.

thermal neutron A neutron with a low kinetic energy, of the same order of magnitude as the kinetic energies of atoms and molecules.

thermionic emission Emission of electrons from a hot solid. The effect occurs when significant numbers of electrons have enough kinetic energy to overcome the solid's work function.

thermodynamics The branch of science concerned with the relationship between heat, work, and other forms of energy.

thermodynamic temperature Temperature measured in kelvins that is a function of the internal energy possessed by a body, having a value of zero at absolute zero.

thixotropy A phenomenon shown by some fluids in which the viscosity decreases as the rate of shear increases, i.e., the fluid becomes less viscous the faster it moves.

transducer A device that is supplied with the energy of one system and converts it into the energy of a different system, so that the output signal is proportional to the input signal but is carried in a different form.

transistor A device made of semiconducting material in which a flow of current between two electrodes can be controlled by a potential applied to a third electrode.

tribology The study of friction between solid surfaces, including the origin of frictional forces and the lubrication of moving parts.

triple point The point at which the solid, liquid, and gas phases of a pure substance can all coexist in equilibrium.

tritiated Denoting a chemical compound containing tritium (^{3}H) atoms in place of hydrogen atoms.

ultracentrifuge A centrifuge designed to work at very high speeds, so that the force produced is large enough to cause sedimentation of colloids.

unified-field theory A theory that seeks to explain gravitational and electromagnetic interactions and the strong and weak nuclear interactions in terms of a single set of equations.

vaccine An antigenic preparation that is administered to a human or other animal to produce immunity against a specific disease-causing agent.

valence The combining power of an element, atom, ion, or radical, equal to the number of hydrogen atoms that the atom, ion, etc., could combine with or displace in forming a compound.

valence band The energy band of a solid that is occupied by the valence electrons of the atoms forming the solid.

valence electron An electron in the outer shell of an atom that participates in the chemical bonding when the atom forms compounds.

vector 1. A quantity that is specified both by its magnitude and its direction. **2.** An agent, such as an insect, that harbors disease-causing microorganisms and transmits them to humans, other animals, or plants.

virtual particle A particle thought of as existing for a very brief period in an interaction between two other particles.

virus A noncellular agent that can infect a living animal, plant, or bacterial cell and use the apparatus of the host cell to manufacture new virus particles. In some cases this causes disease in the host organism. Outside the host cell, viruses are totally inert.

viscosity The property of liquids and gases of resisting flow. It is caused by forces between the molecules of the fluid.

water of crystallization Water combined in the form of molecules in definite proportions in the crystals of many substances.

wave equation A partial differential equation relating the displacement of a wave to the time and the three spatial dimensions.

wave function A mathematical expression giving the probability of finding the particle associated with a wave at a specified point according to wave mechanics.

wave mechanics A form of quantum mechanics in which particles (electrons, protons, etc.) are regarded as waves, so that any system of particles can be described by a wave equation.

weak interaction A type of interaction between elementary particles, occurring at short range and having a magnitude about 10^{10} times weaker than the electromagnetic force.

work function The minimum energy necessary to remove an electron from a metal at absolute zero.

x-ray crystallography The determination of the structure of crystals and molecules by use of x-ray diffraction.

zero point energy The energy of vibration of atoms at the absolute zero of temperature.

zwitterion An ion that has both a positive and negative charge.

INDEX

183, 203, 205, 213, 219; **2**: 41, 42, 44, 50, 130, 153, 164, 171, 180, 206; **3**: 28, 38, 41, 43, 46, 55, 68, 95, 107, 112, 121, 131, 170, 180, 192, 200, 214; **4**: 23, 29, 43, 44, 75, 96, 104, 106, 108, 115, 116, 121, 125, 131, 148, 173, 194, 220; **5**: 20, 27, 40, 55, 77, 106, 179, 193, 198, 215; **6**: 8, 37, 49, 74, 75, 90, 91, 155, 185, 201; **7**: 8, 30, 64, 69, 73, 105, 114, 121, 122, 176, 197, 210; **8**: 29, 99, 104, 105, 111, 130, 147, 175, 183, 211; **9**: 10, 14, 25, 26, 33, 34, 37, 44, 62, 63, 124, 128, 159, 173, 176, 195, 200, 211, 212; **10**: 11, 18, 19, 29, 53, 84, 90, 109, 128, 148, 154, 163, 175, 179, 182, 183, 196, 201, 202

American physiologists: 2: 56, 99, 150; **3**: 157; **4**: 81, 170, 215; **5**: 8, 102, 109, 200; **6**: 30, 117, 151, 152, 182; **7**: 207, 213; **8**: 48; **9**: 11, 95, 150, 171; **10**: 112
American psychologist: 5: 171
American rocket engineer: 10: 47
American sociologist: 7: 50
American zoologists: 3: 12, 26; **4**: 163; **5**: 130, 208; **7**: 23
Amici, Giovanni Battista **1**: 42
Amino acids: 3: 210; **5**: 89; **6**: 26; **8**: 171; **9**: 7; **10**: 32
Amontons, Guillaume **1**: 43
Ampère, André Marie **1**: 43
Anatomists: 1: 23, 72, 101, 126; **2**: 58, 170, 181, 219; **3**: 17, 154, 169, 178, 182; **4**: 10, 50, 67, 74, 91, 151; **5**: 19, 25, 61, 117, 185; **6**: 95; **7**: 93, 96, 97, 205; **8**: 14, 30, 132, 134; **9**: 125; **10**: 31, 36, 64, 121, 141, 160
Anaxagoras of Clazomenae 1: 45
Anaximander of Miletus 1: 46
Anaximenes of Miletus 1: 46
Anderson, Carl David **1**: 47
Anderson, Philip Warren **1**: 48
Anderson, Thomas **1**: 49
Andrade, Edward **1**: 50
Andrews, Roy Chapman **1**: 51
Andrews, Thomas **1**: 52
Anfinsen, Christian Boehmer **1**: 53
Ångström, Anders Jonas **1**: 54
Anthropologists: 1: 207; **2**: 52; **4**: 72; **5**: 155; **6**: 77, 78, 79, 95; **7**: 179; **8**: 46
Antibiotics: 3: 85, 98, 100; **4**: 3
Antibodies: 3: 119; **5**: 152; **8**: 77; **9**: 207
Antimatter: 3: 75; **8**: 218
Antoniadi, Eugène Michael **1**: 55
Apker, Leroy **1**: 56
Apollonius of Perga 1: 56
Apothecary: 9: 48
Appel, Kenneth **1**: 57
Appert, Nicolas-François **1**: 58
Appleton, Sir Edward **1**: 59
Arab astronomers: 1: 22, 29
Arab geographer: 1: 29
Arabian alchemist: 4: 89
Arab mathematician: 1: 29

Arago, Dominique François Jean **1**: 60
Arber, Werner **1**: 61
Archeologists: 2: 18; **6**: 77; **9**: 188; **10**: 169
Archimedes 1: 62
Architects: 8: 30, 185; **9**: 172
Argelander, Friedrich Wilhelm August **1**: 64
Argentinian biochemist: 6: 101
Argentinian inventor: 1: 191
Argentinian physiologist: 5: 94
Aristarchus of Samos 1: 65
Aristotle 1: 65
Arithmetic: 3: 40; **4**: 37, 122; **8**: 12
Arkwright, Sir Richard **1**: 68
Armenian astronomer: 1: 40
Armstrong, Henry Edward **1**: 69
Arnald of Villanova 1: 69
Arrhenius, Svante August **1**: 70
Artificial intelligence: 6: 106; **7**: 24, 82; **8**: 24
Aschoff, Karl **1**: 72
Aselli, Gaspare **1**: 72
Astbury, William Thomas **1**: 73
Aston, Francis William **1**: 74
Astrologers: 2: 103, 211
Astronomers: 1: 8, 10, 19, 20, 22, 29, 40, 42, 54, 55, 64, 65, 88, 92, 105, 124, 137, 146, 155, 179, 186, 202, 208, 218; **2**: 3, 4, 9, 16, 25, 32, 35, 37, 59, 64, 79, 80, 93, 98, 115, 126, 135, 136, 138, 152, 157, 162, 174, 182, 217; **3**: 22, 31, 45, 61, 82, 86, 90, 91, 92, 94, 111, 117, 147, 155, 165, 178, 218, 219; **4**: 5, 22, 43, 45, 64, 68, 95, 96, 112, 128, 144, 149, 160, 161, 189, 192, 198, 211, 215; **5**: 18, 23, 29, 30, 31, 36, 43, 45, 57, 92, 95, 99, 104, 108, 110, 111, 128, 132, 145, 146, 148, 177, 182, 183, 195, 202, 206, 211; **6**: 21, 22, 23, 34, 39, 45, 50, 51, 59, 62, 67, 80, 102, 111, 132, 148, 170, 173, 181, 187; **7**: 1, 6, 12, 13, 15, 44, 48, 55, 57, 63, 74, 76, 80, 83, 84, 104, 113, 150, 161, 186, 189, 193, 194; **8**: 16, 24, 41, 42, 43, 44, 54, 61, 67, 69, 78, 90, 92, 96, 98, 102, 103, 122, 125, 131, 137, 138, 139, 140, 145, 154, 167, 174, 186, 198, 206, 214, 215; **9**: 5, 16, 22, 35, 40, 45, 50, 52, 60, 61, 77, 86, 87, 97, 103, 109, 113, 114, 141, 142, 143, 169, 177, 183, 205, 210, 217; **10**: 7, 13, 21, 22, 26, 44, 99, 111, 130, 131, 149, 158, 159, 168, 201
Atanasoff, John Vincent **1**: 76
Atom bomb: 1: 218; **2**: 172; **3**: 194; **4**: 49; **7**: 198; **9**: 40, 160, 173; **10**: 16
Atomic structure: 1: 216; **4**: 12; **5**: 38; **7**: 134; **8**: 203; **9**: 27, 99
Atomic weight: 1: 178; **2**: 97; **8**: 95, 142; **9**: 120
Audubon, John James **1**: 77
Auenbrugger von Auenbrugg,

Joseph Leopold **1**: 78
Auer, Karl, Baron von Welsbach **1**: 79
Auger, Pierre Victor **1**: 80
Australian anatomist: 3: 17
Australian astronomers: 7: 74; **10**: 130
Australian chemists: 2: 190; **3**: 205
Australian earth scientist: 2: 76
Australian immunologist: 7: 71
Australian mathematician: 2: 76
Australian pathologists: 2: 83, 95; **4**: 8
Australian physicists: 7: 74, 191
Australian physiologist: 3: 115
Austrian astronomers: 1: 186; **2**: 4; **8**: 98, 137
Austrian biologist: 10: 198
Austrian botanist: 7: 40
Austrian chemists: 1: 79; **6**: 167; **7**: 209; **8**: 83; **9**: 29, 77; **10**: 197
Austrian earth scientists: 7: 116; **9**: 146
Austrian entomologist: 4: 47
Austrian ethologists: 4: 47; **6**: 165
Austrian mathematicians: 2: 4; **8**: 98, 137
Austrian pathologist: 8: 165
Austrian philosopher: 3: 199
Austrian physicians: 1: 78, 187; **7**: 53; **9**: 75
Austrian physicists: 2: 1; **3**: 88; **6**: 192; **9**: 27, 123
Austrian psychoanalyst: 4: 39
Austrian psychologist: 1: 14
Austrian zoologists: 4: 47; **5**: 172
Austro-Hungarian physician: 1: 117
Averroës 1: 81
Avery, Oswald Theodore **1**: 81
Avicenna 1: 82
Avogadro, Amedeo **1**: 84
Axelrod, Julius **1**: 85
Ayala, Francisco José **1**: 86
Ayrton, William Edward **1**: 87
Azerbaijani physicist: 6: 53

Baade, Wilhelm Heinrich Walter **1**: 88
Babbage, Charles **1**: 90
Babcock, Harold Delos **1**: 92
Babcock, Horace Welcome **1**: 92
Babcock, Stephen Moulton **1**: 94
Babinet, Jacques **1**: 94
Babo, Lambert Heinrich Clemens von **1**: 95
Babylonian astronomers: 5: 202; **9**: 45
Bache, Alexander Dallas **1**: 96
Backus, John **1**: 96
Bacon, Francis **1**: 97
Bacon, Roger **1**: 99
Bacteria: 1: 82; **2**: 169; **3**: 47, 150; **4**: 154, 164; **5**: 142; **6**: 89, 89, 182; **8**: 180; **10**: 185, 195
Bacteriologists: 1: 81; **2**: 66, 71, 168; **3**: 66, 127; **4**: 3, 60, 154, 205; **5**: 214; **6**: 3, 100, 153; **7**: 148, 164, 171; **8**: 36, 38; **9**: 83, 134; **10**: 8, 76, 95, 185
Bacteriophage: 3: 47, 67; **5**: 33; **7**:

Chinese pharmacologist: **6**: 121
Chittenden, Russell Henry **2**: 150
Chladni, Ernst Florens **2**: 151
Chlorophyll: **3**: 212; **8**: 19, 212; **10**: 142, 167
Cholera: **6**: 4; **9**: 90
Cholesterol: **1**: 204; **2**: 62, 87, 190; **4**: 134; **8**: 204; **10**: 150, 167
Chou Kung **2**: 152
Christie, Sir William Henry Mahoney **2**: 152
Chromatography: **10**: 1
Chromosomes: **4**: 6; **7**: 103; **9**: 127, 145
Chu, Paul Ching-Wu **2**: 153
Chu Shih-Chieh **2**: 154
Civil Engineer: **3**: 140
Clairaut, Alexis Claude **2**: 155
Claisen, Ludwig **2**: 156
Clark, Alvan Graham **2**: 157
Clarke, Sir Cyril Astley **2**: 158
Claude, Albert **2**: 159
Claude, Georges **2**: 160
Clausius, Rudolf **2**: 161
Clemence, Gerald Maurice **2**: 162
Cleve, Per Teodor **2**: 163
Climate: **3**: 14; **6**: 48
Cloud chamber: **1**: 198; **10**: 145
Cloud formation: **1**: 164
Coblentz, William Weber **2**: 164
Cockcroft, Sir John **2**: 164
Cocker, Edward **2**: 165
Coenzymes: **3**: 168; **4**: 207; **9**: 181, 205; **10**: 74
Cohen, Paul Joseph **2**: 166
Cohen, Seymour Stanley **2**: 166
Cohen, Stanley **2**: 167
Cohn, Ferdinand Julius **2**: 168
Cohnheim, Julius **2**: 169
Colloids: **4**: 153; **10**: 198
Colombo, Matteo Realdo **2**: 170
Comets: **7**: 195; **10**: 112
Compton, Arthur Holly **2**: 171
Computer Scientists: **1**: 18, 41, 76, 96; **2**: 49, 90; **3**: 116, 190; **4**: 15; **5**: 71, 76, 90, 153, 176, 204; **6**: 2, 106; **7**: 10, 24, 81, 151, 192; **9**: 12, 131, 138; **10**: 133, 151, 200
Comte, Auguste Isidore **2**: 172
Conant, James Bryant **2**: 174
Conon of Samos **2**: 174
Continental drift: **1**: 198; **2**: 76; **3**: 109; **5**: 80, 148; **8**: 191; **10**: 88
Contraceptive pill: **8**: 48; **9**: 100
Conway, John Horton **2**: 175
Conybeare, William **2**: 177
Cook, James **2**: 178
Cooke, Sir William **2**: 179
Cooper, Leon Neil **2**: 180
Cope, Edward Drinker **2**: 181
Copernicus, Nicolaus **2**: 182
Corey, Elias James **2**: 184
Cori, Carl Ferdinand **2**: 185
Cori, Gerty Theresa **2**: 186
Coriolis, Gustave-Gaspard **2**: 187
Cormack, Allan Macleod **2**: 188
Corner, Edred **2**: 189
Cornforth, Sir John **2**: 190
Correns, Karl Erich **2**: 190

Cort, Henry **2**: 191
Corvisart, Jean-Nicolas **2**: 192
Cosmic background radiation: **3**: 69; **8**: 25
Cosmic rays: **1**: 198; **2**: 17, 171; **5**: 41; **7**: 73; **8**: 80
Cosmologists: **2**: 4; **3**: 3; **4**: 173; **5**: 2, 99; **6**: 102
Coster, Dirk **2**: 193
Cottrell, Sir Alan **2**: 193
Coulomb, Charles Augustin de **2**: 194
Coulson, Charles Alfred **2**: 196
Couper, Archibald Scott **2**: 197
Cournand, André **2**: 198
Courtois, Bernard **2**: 199
Cousteau, Jacques Yves **2**: 200
Crafts, James Mason **2**: 201
Craig, Lyman Creighton **2**: 201
Cram, Donald James **2**: 202
Crick, Francis **2**: 203
Croll, James **2**: 205
Cronin, James Watson **2**: 206
Cronstedt, Axel Frederic **2**: 207
Crookes, Sir William **2**: 207
Cross, Charles Frederick **2**: 208
Crum Brown, Alexander **2**: 209
Crutzen, Paul **2**: 210
Crystallographers: **1**: 168; **5**: 178; **6**: 159; **10**: 179
Crystallography: **9**: 125
Cuban physician: **3**: 206
Cugnot, Nicolas-Joseph **2**: 211
Culpeper, Nicholas **2**: 211
Curie, Marie Skłodowska **2**: 212
Curie, Pierre **2**: 215
Curtis, Heber Doust **2**: 217
Curtius, Theodor **2**: 218
Cushing, Harvey **2**: 218
Cuvier, Baron Georges **2**: 219
Cybernetics: **10**: 125
Cytologists: **1**: 159; **2**: 114; **3**: 103; **4**: 6, 136; **7**: 56
Czech chemist: **5**: 47
Czech physiologist: **8**: 100

d'Abano, Pietro **3**: 1
Daguerre, Louis-Jacques-Mandé **3**: 2
d'Ailly, Pierre **3**: 3
Daimler, Gottlieb Wilhelm **3**: 4
Dainton, Frederick Sydney **3**: 5
Dale, Sir Henry Hallett **3**: 6
d'Alembert, Jean Le Rond **3**: 7
Dalén, Nils Gustaf **3**: 8
Dalton, John **3**: 9
Dam, Carl Peter Henrik **3**: 11
Dana, James Dwight **3**: 12
Daniell, John Frederic **3**: 13
Daniels, Farrington **3**: 14
Danish anatomist: **9**: 125
Danish archeologists: **9**: 188; **10**: 169
Danish astronomers: **2**: 35; **3**: 94; **5**: 36; **8**: 167; **9**: 141
Danish bacteriologist: **4**: 154
Danish biochemist: **3**: 11
Danish biologist: **9**: 22
Danish botanist: **5**: 154
Danish chemists: **1**: 195; **2**: 57; **5**: 216; **9**: 103, 189

Danish earth scientists: **6**: 96; **7**: 173; **9**: 125
Danish geneticist: **5**: 154
Danish immunologist: **5**: 152
Danish mathematicians: **1**: 129; **7**: 173
Danish meteorologist: **3**: 14
Danish physicians: **3**: 203, 207
Danish physicists: **1**: 215, 216; **7**: 112, 120, 184
Danish physiologist: **6**: 27
Danish zoologist: **9**: 122
Dansgaard, Willi **3**: 14
Darby, Abraham **3**: 15
Dark matter: **8**: 187
Darlington, Cyril Dean **3**: 16
Dart, Raymond Arthur **3**: 17
Darwin, Charles Robert **3**: 18
Darwin, Erasmus **3**: 21
Darwin, Sir George **3**: 22
Daubrée, Gabriel Auguste **3**: 23
Dausset, Jean **3**: 24
Davaine, Casimir Joseph **3**: 25
Davenport, Charles **3**: 26
Davis, Raymond **3**: 26
Davis, William Morris **3**: 27
Davisson, Clinton Joseph **3**: 28
Davy, Sir Humphry **3**: 29
Dawes, William Rutter **3**: 31
Dawkins, Richard **3**: 32
Day, David Talbot **3**: 33
Deacon, Henry **3**: 34
de Bary, Heinrich Anton **3**: 34
De Beer, Sir Gavin **3**: 35
Debierne, André Louis **3**: 36
de Broglie, Prince Louis Victor Pierre Raymond **3**: 37
Debye, Peter **3**: 38
Dedekind, (Julius Wilhelm) Richard **3**: 39
de Duve, Christian René **3**: 40
Deficiency diseases: **3**: 130; **4**: 56, 130; **6**: 131
De Forest, Lee **3**: 41
De Geer, Charles **3**: 42
Dehmelt, Hans Georg **3**: 43
De la Beche, Sir Henry **3**: 44
Delambre, Jean Baptiste **3**: 45
De la Rue, Warren **3**: 45
Delbrück, Max **3**: 46
D'Elhuyar, Don Fausto **3**: 48
DeLisi, Charles **3**: 49
Del Rio, Andrès Manuel **3**: 50
De Luc, Jean André **3**: 50
Demarçay, Eugene Anatole **3**: 52
Demerec, Milislav **3**: 52
Democritus of Abdera **3**: 53
De Moivre, Abraham **3**: 54
Dempster, Arthur Jeffrey **3**: 55
Dendrochronologist: **3**: 90
Dentists: **7**: 107; **10**: 98
Derham, William **3**: 56
Desaguliers, John **3**: 57
Desargues, Girard **3**: 57
Descartes, René du Perron **3**: 58
Desch, Cyril Henry **3**: 60
de Sitter, Willem **3**: 61
Desmarest, Nicolas **3**: 61
Désormes, Charles Bernard **3**: 62
Deville, Henri **3**: 63
de Vries, Hugo **3**: 64
Dewar, Sir James **3**: 65

Metchnikoff, Elie 7: 56
Meteorologists: 1: 1, 164, 193, 194; 2: 88, 210; 3: 13, 14, 50, 162, 196, 216; 4: 180; 6: 14, 48, 160, 163; 7: 209; 8: 122, 143, 173; 9: 56, 72; 10: 86
Metius, Jacobus 7: 57
Meton 7: 57
Mexican chemist: 7: 90
Meyer, Julius Lothar 7: 58
Meyer, Karl 7: 59
Meyer, Viktor 7: 60
Meyerhof, Otto Fritz 7: 61
Michaelis, Leonor 7: 61
Michel, Hartmut 7: 62
Michell, John 7: 63
Michelson, Albert Abraham 7: 64
Microscope: 6: 145; 7: 51; 10: 193
Midgley, Thomas Jr. 7: 66
Miescher, Johann Friedrich 7: 67
Milankovich, Milutin 7: 68
Military Scientists: 6: 206; 9: 163
Miller, Dayton Clarence 7: 69
Miller, Hugh 7: 70
Miller, Jacques Francis Albert Pierre 7: 71
Miller, Stanley Lloyd 7: 72
Millikan, Robert Andrews 7: 73
Mills, Bernard Yarnton 7: 74
Mills, William Hobson 7: 75
Milne, Edward Arthur 7: 76
Milne, John 7: 77
Milstein, César 7: 78
Mineralogists: 1: 147; 2: 207; 3: 12, 48, 50; 4: 60, 160; 5: 1, 62, 212; 7: 89; 8: 127; 10: 100
Mining Engineer: 1: 127
Minkowski, Hermann 7: 79
Minkowski, Rudolph Leo 7: 80
Minot, George Richards 7: 81
Minsky, Marvin Lee 7: 81
Misner, Charles William 7: 83
Mitchell, Maria 7: 84
Mitchell, Peter Dennis 7: 85
Mitscherlich, Eilhardt 7: 86
Möbius, August Ferdinand 7: 87
Mohl, Hugo von 7: 87
Mohorovičić, Andrija 7: 88
Mohs, Friedrich 7: 89
Moissan, Ferdinand Frédéric Henri 7: 89
Molina, Mario José 7: 90
Mond, Ludwig 7: 91
Mondino de Luzzi 7: 93
Monge, Gaspard 7: 94
Monod, Jacques Lucien 7: 95
Monro, Alexander (Primus) 7: 96
Monro, Alexander (Secundus) 7: 97
Montagnier, Luc 7: 98
Montgolfier, Etienne Jacques de 7: 99
Montgolfier, Michel Joseph de 7: 99
Moore, Stanford 7: 100
Mordell, Louis Joel 7: 101
Morgagni, Giovanni Batista 7: 102
Morgan, Thomas Hunt 7: 103

Morgan, William Wilson 7: 104
Morley, Edward Williams 7: 105
Morse, Samuel 7: 106
Morton, William 7: 107
Mosander, Carl Gustav 7: 108
Moseley, Henry Gwyn Jeffreys 7: 109
Mössbauer, Rudolph Ludwig 7: 110
Mott, Sir Nevill Francis 7: 111
Mottelson, Benjamin Roy 7: 112
Moulton, Forest Ray 7: 113
Mueller, Erwin Wilhelm 7: 114
Muller, Alex 7: 115
Müller, Franz Joseph, Baron von Reichenstein 7: 116
Muller, Hermann Joseph 7: 117
Müller, Johannes Peter 7: 118
Müller, Otto Friedrich 7: 120
Müller, Paul Hermann 7: 120
Muller, Richard August 7: 121
Mulliken, Robert Sanderson 7: 122
Mullis, Kary Banks 7: 123
Munk, Walter Heinrich 7: 124
Murchison, Sir Roderick Impey 7: 125
Murphy, William Parry 7: 126
Murray, Sir John 7: 127
Murray, Joseph Edward 7: 127
Muscle contraction: 5: 54, 90, 124; 9: 163
Muspratt, James 7: 129
Musschenbroek, Pieter van 7: 130
Muybridge, Eadweard James 7: 131

Naegeli, Karl Wilhelm von 7: 133
Nagaoka, Hantaro 7: 134
Nambu, Yoichipo 7: 135
Nansen, Fridtjof 7: 136
Napier, John 7: 137
Nasmyth, James 7: 138
Nathans, Daniel 7: 139
Natta, Giulio 7: 140
Naturalists: 1: 26, 51, 77, 133, 146, 156; 2: 6, 32, 72, 74, 133; 3: 18; 4: 13, 105; 7: 142; 8: 118, 188; 9: 152; 10: 66, 114
Naudin, Charles 7: 141
Nebulae: 1: 124; 5: 108; 7: 55; 10: 159
Nebular hypothesis: 5: 147, 174; 6: 63; 10: 95
Needham, Dorothy Mary Moyle 7: 142
Needham, John Turberville 7: 142
Needham, Joseph 7: 143
Néel, Louis Eugène Félix 7: 144
Ne'eman, Yuval 7: 145
Nef, John Ulric 7: 146
Neher, Erwin 7: 147
Neisser, Albert Ludwig Siegmund 7: 148
Nernst, Walther Hermann 7: 148
Nerve action: 1: 15; 3: 97, 157; 4: 81; 5: 68, 182; 6: 178
Nerve cells: 3: 115; 7: 119; 8: 114, 132

Nervous system: 1: 152; 4: 10, 79, 136; 6: 200; 9: 60
Newcomb, Simon 7: 150
Newcomen, Thomas 7: 151
Newell, Allan 7: 151
Newlands, John Alexander Reina 7: 152
Newton, Alfred 7: 153
Newton, Sir Isaac 7: 154
New Zealand biochemist: 10: 143
New Zealand physicist: 8: 201
Nicholas of Cusa 7: 160
Nicholson, Seth Barnes 7: 161
Nicholson, William 7: 162
Nicol, William 7: 163
Nicolle, Charles Jules Henri 7: 164
Niepce, Joseph-Nicéphore 7: 165
Nieuwland, Julius Arthur 7: 166
Nilson, Lars Fredrick 7: 166
Nirenberg, Marshall Warren 7: 167
Nitrogen fixation: 1: 190; 4: 177
Nobel, Alfred Bernhard 7: 168
Nobili, Leopoldo 7: 169
Noddack, Ida Eva Tacke 7: 170
Noddack, Walter 7: 170
Noguchi, (Seisako) Hideyo 7: 171
Nollet, Abbé Jean Antoine 7: 172
Nordenskiöld, Nils Adolf Eric 7: 173
Norlund, Niels Erik 7: 173
Norman, Robert 7: 174
Norrish, Ronald 7: 174
Northrop, John Howard 7: 175
Norton, Thomas 7: 176
Norwegian bacteriologist: 4: 205
Norwegian biologist: 7: 136
Norwegian chemists: 1: 190; 4: 132, 171, 218; 10: 57
Norwegian engineer: 3: 174
Norwegian explorer: 7: 136
Norwegian industrialist: 3: 174
Norwegian mathematicians: 1: 6; 6: 124; 9: 76
Norwegian meteorologists: 1: 193, 194
Norwegian physicist: 1: 190
Noyce, Robert Norton 7: 176
Noyes, William Albert 7: 177
Nuclear fission: 4: 49, 184; 7: 35, 170; 9: 173; 10: 12
Nuclear magnetic resonance: 1: 203; 6: 209; 8: 99
Nucleic acids: 2: 31; 6: 17; 7: 67
Nucleotide bases: 3: 210; 6: 110; 9: 205
Nucleus: 1: 215; 4: 125; 5: 151; 7: 112; 8: 105
Nüsslein-Volhard, Christiane 7: 178

Oakley, Kenneth Page 7: 179
Oberth, Hermann Julius 7: 180
Occhialini, Giuseppe Paolo Stanislao 7: 181
Ocean currents: 3: 140; 5: 9, 113; 7: 17
Oceanography: 2: 200
Ochoa, Severo 7: 182

Walker, Sir James **10**: 65
Wallace, Alfred Russel **10**: 66
Wallach, Otto **10**: 69
Wallis, John **10**: 70
Walton, Ernest **10**: 71
Wankel, Felix **10**: 72
Warburg, Otto Heinrich **10**: 73
Ward, Joshua **10**: 75
Wassermann, August von **10**: 76
Waterston, John James **10**: 76
Watson, David Meredith Seares **10**: 77
Watson, James Dewey **10**: 78
Watson, Sir William **10**: 79
Watson-Watt, Sir Robert **10**: 80
Watt, James **10**: 82
Weather forecasting: **1**: 1; **2**: 145; **8**: 143
Weber, Ernst Heinrich **10**: 83
Weber, Joseph **10**: 84
Weber, Wilhelm Eduard **10**: 85
Wegener, Alfred Lothar **10**: 86
Weierstrass, Karl Wilhelm Theodor **10**: 88
Weil, André **10**: 89
Weinberg, Steven **10**: 90
Weismann, August Friedrich Leopold **10**: 92
Weizmann, Chaim Azriel **10**: 93
Weizsäcker, Baron Carl Friedrich von **10**: 94
Welch, William Henry **10**: 95
Weldon, Walter **10**: 96
Weller, Thomas Huckle **10**: 97
Wells, Horace **10**: 98
Wendelin, Gottfried **10**: 99
Wenzel, Carl Friedrich **10**: 99
Werner, Abraham Gottlob **10**: 100
Werner, Alfred **10**: 101
Wernicke, Carl **10**: 102
West, Harold Dadford **10**: 103
Westinghouse, George **10**: 104
Wexler, Nancy **10**: 105
Weyl, Hermann **10**: 106
Wharton, Thomas **10**: 107
Wheatstone, Sir Charles **10**: 108
Wheeler, John Archibald **10**: 109
Whewell, William **10**: 110
Whipple, Fred Lawrence **10**: 111
Whipple, George Hoyt **10**: 112
Whiston, William **10**: 113
White, Gilbert **10**: 114
White, Ray **10**: 114
Whitehead, Alfred North **10**: 116
Whittaker, Sir Edmund **10**: 117
Whittington, Harry Blackmore **10**: 118
Whittle, Sir Frank **10**: 119
Whitworth, Sir Joseph **10**: 120
Whytt, Robert **10**: 121
Wieland, Heinrich Otto **10**: 122
Wien, Wilhelm Carl Werner Otto Fritz Franz **10**: 123
Wiener, Norbert **10**: 124
Wieschaus, Eric **10**: 125

Wiesel, Torsten Nils **10**: 126
Wigglesworth, Sir Vincent Brian **10**: 127
Wigner, Eugene Paul **10**: 128
Wilcke, Johan Carl **10**: 129
Wild, John Paul **10**: 130
Wildt, Rupert **10**: 131
Wiles, Andrew John **10**: 131
Wilkes, Maurice Vincent **10**: 133
Wilkins, John **10**: 134
Wilkins, Maurice Hugh Frederick **10**: 135
Wilkins, Robert Wallace **10**: 136
Wilkinson, Sir Denys Haigh **10**: 136
Wilkinson, Sir Geoffrey **10**: 137
Williams, Robert R. **10**: 138
Williams, Robley Cook **10**: 138
Williamson, Alexander William **10**: 139
Williamson, William Crawford **10**: 140
Willis, Thomas **10**: 141
Willstätter, Richard **10**: 142
Wilson, Alexander **10**: 143
Wilson, Allan Charles **10**: 143
Wilson, Charles Thomson Rees **10**: 145
Wilson, Edward Osborne **10**: 146
Wilson, John Tuzo **10**: 147
Wilson, Kenneth G. **10**: 148
Wilson, Robert Woodrow **10**: 149
Windaus, Adolf Otto Reinhold **10**: 150
Winkler, Clemens Alexander **10**: 151
Winograd, Terry Allen **10**: 151
Wislicenus, Johannes **10**: 152
Withering, William **10**: 153
Witten, Ed(ward) **10**: 154
Wittig, Georg **10**: 155
Wöhler, Friedrich **10**: 156
Wolf, Johann Rudolf **10**: 158
Wolf, Maximilian Franz Joseph Cornelius **10**: 159
Wolff, Kaspar Friedrich **10**: 160
Wolfram, Stephen **10**: 160
Wollaston, William Hyde **10**: 161
Wolpert, Lewis **10**: 162
Women Scientists: **1**: 155; **2**: 79, 90, 98, 121, 147, 186, 212; **4**: 5, 33, 95, 103, 125, 139; **5**: 29, 69, 90, 130, 131, 158, 178, 205; **6**: 20, 71, 78, 80, 96, 112, 159, 212, 218; **7**: 15, 25, 34, 84, 142, 170, 178; **8**: 26, 186; **9**: 97; **10**: 105, 174, 175, 182
Wood, Robert Williams **10**: 163
Woodward, Sir Arthur Smith **10**: 164
Woodward, John **10**: 166
Woodward, Robert Burns **10**: 167

Woolley, Sir Richard van der Riet **10**: 168
Worsaae, Jens Jacob Asmussen **10**: 169
Wright, Sir Almroth Edward **10**: 170
Wright, Sewall **10**: 171
Wright, Wilbur **10**: 172
Wright, Orville **10**: 172
Wrinch, Dorothy **10**: 174
Wróblewski, Zygmunt Florenty von **10**: 175
Wu, Chien-Shiung **10**: 175
Wu, Hsien **10**: 176
Wunderlich, Carl Reinhold August **10**: 177
Wurtz, Charles Adolphe **10**: 178
Wyckoff, Ralph Walter Graystone **10**: 179
Wynne-Edwards, Vero Copner **10**: 180

Xenophanes of Colophon **10**: 181
X-ray crystallography: **1**: 73, 169; **4**: 33; **5**: 194; **8**: 32; **10**: 135
X-ray diffraction: **2**: 34, 34; **3**: 39; **10**: 53
X-rays: **1**: 122; **7**: 117; **8**: 168
X-ray spectrum: **2**: 34; **7**: 109; **9**: 66
X-ray tomography: **2**: 188; **5**: 94;

Yalow, Rosalyn Sussman **10**: 182
Yang, Chen Ning **10**: 183
Yanofsky, Charles **10**: 184
Yersin, Alexandre Emile John **10**: 185
Yoshimasu, Todu **10**: 185
Young, James **10**: 186
Young, Thomas **10**: 187
Yukawa, Hideki **10**: 189

Zeeman, Pieter **10**: 191
Zeno of Eelea **10**: 192
Zernike, Frits **10**: 193
Ziegler, Karl **10**: 194
Zinder, Norton David **10**: 195
Zinn, Walter Henry **10**: 196
Zoologists: **1**: 110; **2**: 22, 39; **3**: 12, 26, 35; **4**: 24, 47, 139, 143, 156, 163; **5**: 130, 172, 208; **6**: 19, 61, 109, 212; **7**: 23, 56, 127; **8**: 79; **9**: 13, 30, 65, 106, 122, 198, 215; **10**: 180, 199,
Zozimus of Panopolis **10**: 197
Zsigmondy, Richard Adolf **10**: 197
Zuckerandl, Emile **10**: 198
Zuckerman, Solly, Baron Zuckerman **10**: 199
Zuse, Konrad **10**: 200
Zwicky, Fritz **10**: 201
Zworykin, Vladimir Kosma **10**: 202